PB 41

BUREAUCRATIC SYSTEM AND PUBLIC POLICY

BUREAUCRATIC SYSTEM AND PUBLIC POLICY

M.G. Ramakant Rao
Prashant K. Mathur

KANISHKA PUBLISHERS, DISTRIBUTORS
NEW DELHI-110 002

KANISHKA PUBLISHERS, DISTRIBUTORS
4697/5-21 A, Ansari Road, Daryaganj
New Delhi-110 002
Phones : 2327 0497, 2328 8285
Fax : 011-2328 8285
E-mail: kanishka_publishing@yahoo.co.in

First Published 1999
Second Edition 2001
Third Edition 2010

ISBN 978-81-7391-274-2

PRINTED IN INDIA

Published by Madan Sachdeva for Kanishka Publishers, Distributors, 4697/5-21A, Ansari Road, Daryaganj, New Delhi-110 002, Typeset by Sunshine Graphics, Delhi, and Printed at Rajdhani Printers, Delhi.

Preface

Fundamentals for the study of behaviour in any bureaucracy are the inter-related issues of motivation and control. Motivation has to do with the factors that lead individuals to act in a given setting. Types of motivating factors are commonly perceived as being significant in the actions of bureaucrats: a desire for material gain, a desire for ego satisfaction, a desire to avoid mental stress or anxiety, a desire for status recognition, a desire to avoid physical stress or discomfort, and a desire to fulfil internalized social, cultural, or religious norms.

The character of a bureaucracy is greatly shaped by the dominant patterns of motivations and control mechanism that it uses. Control is the observe of motivation. Whereas motivation deals with the forces that lead individuals to act or avoid action in a given situation, control deals with the stimuli that mobilize those forces.

Executive work at all levels of organisation has common needs and requirements. Every aspect of administration is important to the total result and must be meshed with every other aspect of it. Especially important, however, are policy determination, programme planning, supervision, co-ordination, motivation and communication. Leadership runs throughout this composite process, supplying incentives and motivation, and providing the basis for delegation and its counterpoise co-ordination.

This book has been designed to provide the upto-date information regarding bureaucratic system and public policy. An attempt has been made to make this book useful for the students as well as the general readers. It will also be useful for all who are interested in this field.

EDITORS

Contents

1

Individuals and Organisations : Some Bureaucratic Perspectives

A system of government comprises several types of organisations. One of the main types of organisation consists of public corporations and what is sometimes called authorities. These many legal and administrative entities, modelled after the private corporation and enjoying various degrees of financial autonomy and administrative flexibility, exist at all levels of government. There are over two hundred in the Indian government alone, including such large ones as the Airports Authority and the Industrial Credit Corporation as well as smaller ones for agricultural and co-operative banking, home loan operations, and the like. This type of corporate organisation is becoming especially popular among state and local governments, for as appropriated funds become harder to secure, the tendency is to create bodies similar to the Port of New York Authority and toll road and bridge authorities to administer a service that produces revenue. The administration of these agencies offers many lucrative employment opportunities to people trained in the right substantive skills.

The next important classification is by particular human groups within the population. Certain bureaus and agencies at one or more levels of government deal with certain groups such as women, children, veterans, the aged, prisoners, the handicapped, merchant seamen, railway labour and many more. Here again is the opportunity for the employment of substantive specialists. In such a career, administrators are clientele as well as functional specialists.

Another classification is by classes in the economy. In the federal and many state and local governments, the three main classes—business, labour and agriculture—have their own executive departments to represent and foster their interests. In addition, government puts its arm around the professions, setting standards, administering qualifying examinations, and issuing licenses. Lawyers, doctors, psychiatrists, osteopaths, veterinarians, beauticians, morticians, family counsellors, barbers, and real estate brokers are among the groups subject to this kind of control in order to protect the standards of the profession. Most of this activity occurs at the state level and to a lesser degree at the local level of government.

Finally, the fields of public administration may be classified according to the needs of the national economy. This is the largest and most important category of all because it covers the whole productive, distributive, and consuming network of relationships in the economic life of the nation. Economists recognise that in an affluent society such as ours, it is nearly impossible to set forth all the intricacies of process and organisation in sufficient detail to convey a true impression of what takes place. Nevertheless, we shall give it a try, sacrificing detail for the sake of the overall picture.

American System

According to the main areas in the national economy, public administration is concerned with the following activities and subject matter :

(a) Certain government agencies at all levels, but primarily at the national, are especially concerned with the resources of the nation. This is a wide category, for even human beings may be so classified. Agencies to protect material resources are, among others, the U.S. Forest Service, the Bureau of Reclamation, the Fish and Wildlife Service, the Atomic Energy Commission, and the Soil Conservation Service. Counterparts of some of these federal units are also found among state and the larger municipal governments.

(b) In the area of production, certain federal and state agencies regulate electric power, gas, oil, communications, and the like. In addition, many bureaus in the U.S. Department of Agriculture

foster and regulate the production of food and fibre. This department is one of the oldest and largest of the federal executive departments whose frame of reference is chiefly economic.

(c) With regard to distribution, there are agencies at all levels of government that try to police the competitive system to keep it from becoming monopolistic, and to prevent false and misleading advertising and other undesirable business practices. Most recently, new and tighter laws attempt to control the labelling of food, fibre and other products so as to inform the consumer as to the content of his purchase.

For the Department of Agriculture, the major problem of control is not in the matter of production so much as it is the management of farm surpluses and securing for the farmer a larger share of the consumer dollar. For the Federal Communications Commission the problem of distribution relates to the use of the airwaves: what share of time shall go to advertisers, educational programmes, and public service features? In the matter of oil and natural gas, there is the problem not only of distribution but also of conservation, for these are prime natural resources.

(d) Then there are programmes for the protection of consumers. As technology tends to concentrate social and economic power, consumers are presented with increasingly less choice in what they may buy and hence lose their bargaining power as to quality and price. Consequently government must provide the protections that once inhered in the free operation of the competitive market. In Britain, which has extensive public ownership, consumer councils have become a standard feature of the administrative services. In the United States, New Deal experiments in this area died out during Second World War. Since then, however, consumers have become more conscious of their vulnerability, and there are now attempts at all levels of government to revive and extend special agencies for their protection.

In addition, the Department of Agriculture assists and promotes consumer co-operatives and the Food and Drug Administration seeks to control matters such as harmful additives in food, dirty and adulterated food produced under insanitary conditions, mislabelling, insufficiently tested drugs, injurious drugs, harmful cosmetics, and the like.

(e) The area of finance is sometimes called the nerve centre of

capitalism. The Federal Reserve System was created in 1913. Since the 1930s Congress has established federal agencies to deal with stock market transactions, holding companies, the insurance of bank deposits, and has the legal right (as yet unexercised) to regulate insurance companies doing business in interstate commerce. Branch banking and bank mergers are among the most controversial issues of federal and state government. Controls over money, interest rates, and tax administration are important tools by which administrators in both the public and the private sectors, working together, may safeguard the health and stability of the economy. Few people realise that the work of even the Federal Bureau of the Budget is more concerned with economic issues than it is with administration in the narrow sense.

(f) Then there is the field of transportation. Outside of the United States most of the means of transportation are government-owned and operated; here this is only occasionally so, the concern of government being largely with regulation in the public interest.

The federal government entered the field of transportation in a major way shortly after the Civil War, fostering the continental expansion of the railroads. Later it similarly aided airlines, paying subsidies (often in the form of lucrative mail contracts); now it regulates all forms of transportation. The Interstate Commerce Commission, created in 1887, is the main federal transportation regulatory agency, dealing as it does with the railroads, waterways and the trucking industry. Other federal agencies regulate aviation and ocean shipping.

At the municipal level, local transit and commuter services are among the main areas of activity, but in a large city such as Chicago or New York, almost every form of transportation must be dealt with. Finally, government itself also sometimes provides transportation services, especially at the municipal level where local transit systems may be government-owned and operated.

(g) Communication is another prime government responsibility. At the federal level a single commission now regulates radio, television, telephone, telegraph and cable communications. As in the case of transportation, communication in other nations is characteristically government-owned and operated and is a main avenue in the spread of public enterprise. In this country private ownership under public regulation is the rule. The 1962 legislation covering the ownership and operation of outer-space communica-

tion satellites, involving the private-public issue, was one of the hardest fought congressional battles of recent years.

(h) Public works is one of the largest areas of government responsibility. Next only to education, which occupies more civilian public employees than any other singly function of non-federal government, is municipal government's concern with engineering and public works: streets, roads, bridges, sewers, public buildings, transportation, major urban renewal programmes, and the like.

At the federal level the Tennessee Valley Authority and the atomic installations at Oak Ridge, Los Alamos, and elsewhere are spectacular illustrations of a similar concern. The long-standing and continuing rivalry between the Army's Corps of Engineers and the Interior Department's Bureau of Reclamation over the engineering and public works functions in the federal government is a classic case in the conduct of public administration. If urban renewal and land-use problems are to be solved, it will be partly because engineering has become and for years will remain a major activity in public administration.

(i) Finally, there is the field of welfare in a broad sense (the largest part of which is public education), partly a federal and state function but predominantly a local one. Everywhere the attempt is to keep it semi-autonomous and divorced from politics. At the federal level Congress created the combined Department of Health, Education, and Welfare in 1953, which quickly became one of the largest agencies in Washington. It is also one of the most controversial, for it is faced with problems such as welfare payments to the hard core of the continuously, even permanently unemployed as well as to those who are temporarily on relief, and the issue of what is called socialised medicine. Concerns such as these were once the responsibility of the family, private charities, or local authorities; now increasingly they are matters of federal responsibility, making the field of welfare a growing area of politics and administration.

Broad as the foregoing coverage of the political economy seems to be, the full impact of government's role in the economy cannot be more than dimly sensed from so simple an outline. And yet some of the boundaries do stand out. Except for the Atomic Energy Commission, none of the agencies mentioned under this classification is directly concerned with national security and defense.

The government, being enormous in size and world-wide in extent, has a great many levels of executive performance: The President, the Cabinet, Prime Minister, Ministers, departmental Secretaries and independent agency heads, undersecretaries, assistant secretaries, bureau chiefs, assistant bureau chiefs, co-ordinate division heads, section heads, area office heads, area office department heads, regional coordinators, and office managers, to mention only the most obvious ones. From the President down to the section head in a field office having supervisory responsibility, therefore, the chain of executive command is continuous.

Alongside these various levels of operating organisations are the so-called staff or facilitative services, the work of which is often partially operational as well as primarily of a service nature to the line official at the appropriate level. These service functions have to do with house-keeping arrangements such as personnel administration, finance, supply, and sometimes research and planning.

With literally hundreds of thousands of executives in American governments at all levels, the ratio of public executive employment to total executive employment in the United States tends constantly to increase. Because of the technical nature of government's work and the constant need for planning, leadership and co-ordination, it is in this crucial area that executive leadership must be strengthened and improved if public administration is to make significant advances.

Authority and Administration

Executive work at all levels of organisation has common needs and requirements. Every aspect of administration is important to the total result and must be meshed with every other aspect of it. Especially important, however, are policy determination, programme planning, supervision, co-ordination, motivation, and communication. Leadership runs throughout this composite process, supplying incentives and motivation and providing the basis for delegation and its counterpoise, co-ordination.

What, in this complex, is the role of authority? It is not position, nor is it legal right, nor is it bossing people, nor issuing orders. Rather, authority is influence with people, a form of voluntary consensus. Thus, said Mary Parker Follett, leadership and authority are plural because many people are involved. Chester

Barnard, former head of the New Jersey Bell Telephone Company and later head of the Rockefeller Foundation, confirmed this view when he remarked that a "superior" is not an "authority" nor does he have authority, strictly speaking because authority lies in the "potentiality of assent" flowing from a widespread loyalty to the common goals of the organisation.[1] In fact, in the accomplishment of the objectives of the programme, officials among the lower ranks of the hierarchy may have even more actual power than those at the top. According to Ordway Tead :

> The real basis for authority is not in the person. It is not something for the executive properly to arrogate to himself and to become self-important about. This is what Miss Mary P. Follett meant when she said "authority belongs to the job and stands with the job." The authority lies not in any single source, including its prestige or status in the hierarchy. It lies rather in the capacity, understanding, judgment and imagination shown by the one "in authority."[2]

The authors of a study of actual business practice sponsored by the Harvard Business School, concluded that few large modern corporations are "dominated by a single man who deals with his subordinates one at a time.....The trend is obviously toward the development of some kind of team effort at the top management level." The concept of the leader as "one who helps the organisation to do is in fact vastly broader in scope than the concept of the leader as one who holds the helm alone.....In most of the companies studied, we found that the task of top management was no longer a one-man job." And finally, showing the wide influence of the human relations approach in administration, in a more real sense than is commonly supposed, "the administrative leader is trying to integrate the needs of the organisation with the requirements of the individual for growth and personal development." The greatest potential of administration, continue these authors, is the human potential, and the greatest expansion of resources to be anticipated in coming decades is the effective release of human talents and energies in ways that are both productive and personally satisfying.[3]

Individuals and Careers

The picture of the bureaucratic world conveyed in the preceding section suggests that bureaucrats, by and large, are made by the contagion of their operating environment. To put it somewhat differently, nobody has good reason to think of himself as a career man unless he has tested his fitness for public administration over a considerable time. But he would not begin such testing without being guided into the civil service by some image of what it is—a brotherhood pledged to the general welfare; a life reverberating with the excitement of great decisions; a respectable profession; or simply a steady job.

That image is greatly affected by what qualifications are asked of the aspirant upon entry, by the general nature of the prescribed entrance requirements. Thus the career man is molded in part by what he believes he should be like as he passes through the portals of government service. In part, however, he is also influenced, and perhaps even more strongly, by the rules of proper behaviors observed by those exercising public functions. We shall now turn to a consideration of these two formative forces in the making of career men, beginning with standards of selection and taking up next the canons of conduct that govern the bureaucracy.

Standards of Selection

Practical Examinations

What is to be found out in the entrance examination about those who will eventually compete among themselves for key positions in the top cadre of the bureaucracy? Should they prove themselves experienced in "management" or at least informed about it? If they are asked to demonstrate experience, they must have gained such experience elsewhere. Here the first question is, Where could they acquire experience pertinent to the responsibilities of higher civil servants? The next question is, How satisfactory would recruitment of middle-aged experience be? And the third question is, What would the mind of this kind of entrant be like? But similar questions are raised when we substitute knowledge about "management" for experience in its practice. Obviously, the acquisition of such knowledge at the price of a fuller orientation toward the nature and the needs of our civilization is a doubtful investment.

By contrast, for sharing in the direction of government agencies a broadly trained mind is better than one filled with expert knowledge of a special field. The typical department combines in its functions a number of different specializations. Thus the principal thing in directing it is a capacity for looking beyond each specialization and for correlating all in the formulation of departmental policies and programmes. The talent needed in this activity cannot be expected to come forth when entrance examinations are closely geared to the practical needs of particular administrative operations or even of particular positions. Indeed, then there will be little room for the career idea—a life's work with increasing responsibilities which do not culminate in a few routine promotions. On every score, therefore, it is distinctly preferable for these purposes that the entrance examinations focus on those resources of mind and personality that are of great value on every level of responsibility but of greatest value on the top levels. In the United States recruitment has long been in the grip of an examination system stressing particular lines of work. Progressive liberation from this system is only a recent accomplishment, one still far from completed.

The Legally Trained Mind : Germany

We say earlier that the question of what the "university man" should bring into the public service has been answered differently by different nations. The particular answer determines to a large extent the characteristics of the bureaucracy, for the "university man," gravitating to the points of greatest responsibility, has a strong effect upon the entire administrative system—in working methodology as well as in mentality and moral fortitude. One answer has been called here the German answer, although in fact it is an answer common to many European countries ranging from Denmark to Greece nd relied upon also in other parts of the world. This approach makes a predominantly juridical study programme the normal road of entry into the higher civil service, without ignoring additional paths for specified alternatives such as economics.

Juridical study, depending on what it actually is, can do more than merely lead to legal knowledge. Traditionally, juridical study in Germany proceeded with a background of Roman law—that great disciplinarian of logical and impersonal thought. Hence juridical study was also an induction into both the spirit and the mechanics of objectivity, into a manner of analysis, into the art of consistency. Moreover, legal study had a bearing upon how to deal with conflicting interests, which is the heart of public affairs. The recognition given to such fields as political science, economics, and history made the juridical course of study a still more useful preparation for the assumption of top responsibilities in public administration.

The requirement of completed juridical study could not fail to infuse into administrative responsibility a deep concern with legality. For the exercise of governmental powers such concern is no less important than efficiency. It concentrated on both the sufficiency of legal authority as a basis of administrative action and the observance of legal safeguards built around the citizen's interests. Thus in the entrance examination for the probationary service the aspirant could not afford to be ignorant of constitutional law or administrative law, but he was not expected to know much about technical approaches to work measurement, as contrasted to its general theory and use. Similarly, it would be highly unlikely that three years later a candidate for the final examination might be pressed for an enumeration of the "principles of management", although he would not commend himself to his examining commission if he knew nothing about the history of Prussian administration, the theory of taxation, or the practical significance of a point of procedure before the administrative courts. On balance, public administration gained greatly by being conducted in accordance with impartial rules, but simultaneously it became rule-minded.

"Gentleman's Education" : Great Britain

The British entrance examinations for the Administrative Class, on the other hand, favour a good record of study, without undue limitation in subject-matter field. The classics, history, literature, and languages have long rated high. The social sciences—in today's sense—were welcomed relatively late and less warmly. As a result, intellectual strength ordinarily has been in greater supply than a forward-looking comprehension of where the world was going.

Needless to say, the British entrance examinations do not presuppose any special knowledge of public administration. The evidence of academic attainment looked for would be equally desirable for men meant to use their heads anywhere, as in research or in mapping the general course of action in business. Greater infusion of the social sciences into the examination pattern has been urged in recent decades by informed critics. One response is the new degree in politics, philosophy, and economics at Oxford. Even this degree, however, lies considerably closer to the British concept of learning than does a corresponding social science degree in the United States.

Institutional Traits

Expressed in institutional traits, the member of the higher civil service in Germany will generally lean on his assistants from the next lower career group to attend to the operating methods of public administration. He will ask questions when there is a special occasion, comment on new developments he has learned about, and insist on prompt remedies when something has gone wrong. Otherwise, however, he will leave these matters in the capable hands of the men of the middle groups of the service, who are the direct supervisors of departmental activities. To the higher civil servant, "management" is an inseparable part of performing each of the functions of the department. In this work he will regard it as his essential responsibility to assure himself and his minister at the helm of the department that its activities, including actions proposed by the minister himself, are in accord with law.

He will also employ his judgment and experience in shaking down the departmental operating methods into craftsman-like written procedures and regulations. Roman law being a teacher of economy of phrase, the regulatory language of German public administration is comparatively concise. In these matters it is of great consequence that the administrative mind and the legal mind are in the same rather than different organisational boxes. Perhaps mainly for this reason, economy in imposing controls, internal as well as effective upon the public, is a traditional feature of German administrative practice.

When not absorbed in a specific legal job, a legally trained mind functions as the "generalist" face to face with the functional specialists of the department—by getting them together and uniting them on a combined type of action, such as a departmental programme. But acceptance of the "generalist" on the top level of thé administrative system is still more explicit in England. There the higher civil servant is meant to contribute to the direction of his department and to the supporting planning process a mind prepared to probe into policy as well as operating issues and to convert findings into recommendations for action. That mind draws consciously on its cultural orientation, gained at the university. This is also the ideal pursued in the new National School of Administration in France. By comparison, the American civil servant on the higher levels of responsibility tends to remain a specialist in the administrative process. He is the man who knows how to put policy into effect but who is less often its initiator.

Routes into the Higher Service

European civil service developments since the end of Second World War, generally speaking, show a strong inclination to maintain and strengthen the higher career as a key group in the administra-tive system. To illustrate, in England the novel route of entrance into the Administrative Class which was adapted from wartime experiments with officer selection has proved to be more than a temporary expedient. Originally popularised somewhat mislead-ingly as the "house party," the new evaluation procedure has been shaken down to a set of group tests combined with intellectual, psychological, and general interviews as well as with written exercises. Known as Method II, this alternative to the traditional literary examination has won praise for leading to a more incisive probing of the candidate's personality. On the other hand, most entrants coming directly from the universities have continued to make use of the older method. Graduates from Oxford or Cambridge are still clearly ahead in winning placement in the Administrative Class. In the last twenty years, however, there has been a measurable broadening of the social basis of England's undergraduate population, with the subsidised scholar becoming much frequent in the old as well as the newer universities.

As a counterpart within the civil service itself, provision has been made in recent years for the conduct of examinations to enable civil servants in the lower grades to move into the Administrative Class as well as the Executive Class. Moreover, the Executive Class—the key management group below the Administrative Class—has been given enlarged responsibilities. This, in turn, has strengthened its co-operative bond with the Administrative Class and minimised the danger of undesirable insulation on either side.

In Germany, as in the past, the aspirant for the higher administrative career enters the probationary service from the university. There he has usually completed a type of juridical study which carries with it more of an introduction to the social sciences and public affairs than does law-school training in the United States. If he qualifies in the entrance examination, he will be moved about for three years from one work situation to another in the judiciary as well as in the administrative system, in each instance under the eyes of a senior who contributes his judgment of performance and prospects to the personnel record.

As in Britain, great reliance is placed on such practical learning under guidance for making trained minds into resourceful civil servants. At the end comes the final examination. Its outcome usually tells the aspirant whether and how soon he may expect an appointment "on trial" ad subsequently a permanent appointment. To provide added opportunities for specialized study, the Administrative Academy at Speyer has been built up in the post-war period to a centre for advanced training.

Training Preferences

Democratization was one of the fundamental goals of the French civil service reform. The spirit of the Resistance had been the spirit of the whole people, and the political as well as social exclusiveness long characteristic of the higher career seemed less tolerable than ever. The first classes enrolled in the new National School of Administration gave themselves such names as *France Combattante* and *Croix de Lorraine*. The halls were named for officials—including a woman—who by acts of self-denial had given their lives for France during the war. The only exception, the Council Room, bears the name of the chairman of the administrative committee in-charge of the short-lived School of Administration founded in 1848. Such evocation of personal sacrifice is hard to extend into an administrative setting, but the available evidence points to the presence of high public spirit among the sixty or seventy graduates whom the National School has annually contributed to the civil service.

Competition for admission to the National School is very sharp, both from the level of advanced education and from within the service. Once admitted, the candidate passes through a three-year programme of preparation that represents a very original combination of familiar concepts. During the first year he is sent out to struggle through the administrative brambles in the field, perhaps as far away as a Moroccan outpost. What is particularly noteworthy is that he is constantly held to the doer's direct responsibility toward the outside world, in contrast with the performance of staff work, where he could easily creep into the shadow of others. The next year is spent at the National School, where he faces a tough curriculum of courses and seminars. The study method is aimed for the most part at developing the student's skill in using broad knowledge to come forth with practical answers to policy questions in a week or two. In the third year he is meant to draw on his first-year experience in order to test the analytical competence he acquired during the second year. This begins with an observer's assignment in private enterprise, to see still another work environment and to learn about both the employer's and the employee's point of view. Thereafter, the student devotes himself to the kinds of projects, in conference sections or individually in one or the other department, that will occupy him after graduation.

As in the grooming of aspirants for the higher career in Great Britain and in Germany, the National School deals with public administration in the wider context of public affairs, rather lightly by American standards. It would be surprising should the new Advanced School of Public Administration in Italy move in a different direction in this respect, but greater emphasis on management subjects is evident in the recruitment for administrative responsibilities in Switzerland. Somewhat ironically, this is one of the results of the absence of a general higher career service. To fill the void to some extent, commercial training has been made to substitute in part for university study in the home service.

Such substitution is made easier because in defining and applying standards of selection great leeway is left to the individual departments. On the other hand, the Swiss regulations of 1955 prescribe that the candidate's "qualities as superior" be given due consideration, in addition to "abilities and character, experience, previous accomplishments, and conduct." Moreover, Switzerland has improvised another part-way solution by filling many of the top career posts at home from the ranks of the foreign service. It is in the foreign service only, specifically the diplomatic grade, that completed university study is recognised as a general requirement. According to the regulations governing admission to the diplomatic grade of the Swiss foreign service of 1955, the entrance examination for the two-year probationary term is to test the university graduate's "general education, his alert interest in political and cultural questions, and his ability to express himself concisely and accurately," together with his knowledge of Swiss constitutional law, international law, history, and economics. One subject reserved for emphasis in the final examination is the history and the importance of Swiss neutrality.

Canons of Conduct

Restraint versus Privacy

In Plato's outline of the best form of government the guardians held an honoured place in the city-state, but their lives were governed by the public interest. For one thing, being maintained out of the resources of the state, they were not permitted to acquire property. Nor were they allowed the ordinary satisfactions of matrimony and parenthood. Although encouraged to have offspring, who might prove guardian material, they were neither to rear nor to educate them; both would be done institutionally. These rules were not intended to make guardian service tougher. They were meant to keep the guardians free from the distractions of personal responsibilities and private concerns.

Civil servants today are not under so severe a regimen, but the conditions of their status include considerable restraints, placed upon them principally in the name of compatibility. Where their public role and their private interests collide, the resolution of the conflict, as a general guideline, is accomplished by appropriate containment of these private interests. Exactly how to draw the line of compatibility has been a matter of historic evolution as well as of prevailing concepts of public necessity.

Related to the spread of democratic government, the tendency has been to reduce, as far as possible, the restrictions upon the civil servant's privacy that flow from his official position. That is particularly true of his civic rights—his participation, like every other citizen, in the political process, especially in elections, as we shall see later in separate paper. More recently, however, a countertendency has asserted itself, which, without directly touching the civil servant as voter, has greatly sharpened the compatibility requirements imposed upon him. This countertendency had its origin in Second World War and the vastly increased security-consciousness of governments as they faced a world divided and filled with unrelenting antagonism.

The Napoleonic Shadow : France

In the administrative system shaped at the start of the nineteenth century in France by the strong hands of Napoleon I, authority was made the taskmaster of efficiency. Authority was also the source of the legal relationship between the state and the civil servant—a relationship determined unilaterally. The discretionary implications of a unilateral determination of the civil service relationship, made solely on the authority of the state, have lived on into the twentieth century. They echoed in the stormy history of French civil service syndicalism as an extralegal counterdrive. They were a motivating factor in the dispatch with which the Fourth Republic adopted the "general statute of the civil service." As recently as in the closing period of the Third Republic, the carry-over of the French civil servant's official capacity into his private capacity was stated as follows :

> The duty of the civil servant consists essentially in devoting his work to the public service. He cannot content himself with doing his work like an ordinary worker, who goes off when his task is finished and has no connection with his employer outside the hours spent in the shop. The civil servant is attached body and soul to the public service. The status of civil servant does not leave him for a single instant even when distant from his office.[4]

Needless to say, this doctrine flew into the face of the rank and file of civil servants when they advanced their collective interest on the model of the labour movement. In full force, they were able to threaten cabinets and to negotiate parliamentary promises without being much bothered by the state's proprietary stake in their souls. On the other hand, it is equally true that the state's superiority in the civil service relationship was limited by legal principles. These legal principles had been developed in the judicial decisions of the Council of State, acting in the capacity of France's supreme administrative court. The easy and inexpensive access to the machinery of administrative justice was of equal value to each civil servant, however humble his position. It contributed to the gradual consolidation of the civil service relationship in terms of legal standards that could not be brushed aside by a superior acting in the name of the sovereign employer.

The Professional Spirit : Germany

The basic rule of conduct for the German bureaucracy was laid down in the civil service act of 1873. Section 10 read: "Every civil servant is obliged to fulfil conscientiously, according to the constitution and the laws, the duties of the office conferred upon him and to prove himself in his behaviour inside and outside the office worthy of the esteem which his profession requires." Very much like the French doctrine, this fundamental provision was construed consistently to mean that the civil servant was at no time as unrestricted as the private individual. Only a few years before Hitler in 1933 displaced republican government, the traditional concept was restated by Prussia's Supreme Administrative Court when it declared that the civil service relationship "embraces the whole personality of the civil servant. Never is he merely a private citizen."

One important distinction between the German and the French doctrines should not be overlooked. The German civil service act did not impose rules of conduct by higher authority. The governing criterion for the civil servant was to show himself "worthy of the esteem which his profession requires." The appeal was to the professional spirit of the civil service, to "pride of outfit," in military language. Moreover, disputes over infractions went to the independent disciplinary courts, which drew part of the bench from the bureaucracy by permanent appointment. Thus the case law of conduct applicable to the civil servant was essentially the judgment of his peers.

This correlation of basic principle with the living ethics of the administrative profession proved persuasive in other countries, too. One example is Switzerland, where the issue of self-restraint outside as well as inside the office, in the German manner, was still hotly argued in the public debates that accompanied the adoption of the civil service act of 1927. In the years afterward, the propriety of the concept and its compatibility with legitimate civic interests have been accepted even among the spokesmen of the rank and file. The law reads as follows : "In his behaviour on and off duty, the civil servant must prove himself worthy of the esteem and the confidence which his official position requires."

After Second World War it was Germany's turn to borrow from Switzerland. The old Section 10 was no longer good enough. The new version in the civil service act of 1953 formulates the traditional rule thus :

> The civil servant shall dedicate himself to his profession with full devotion. He must administer his office selflessly and according to the directions of his conscience. His conduct inside and outside the office must do justice to the esteem and confidence which his profession requires.

As developed by the German disciplinary courts, the case law of professional conduct, binding upon all civil servants, has crystallized answers to many specific questions. To begin with the most obvious, the bureaucracy must always be conscious of its essential task—to function as an agency of the general interest. The tenor of the German decisions was apparent in one of the leading commentaries on the civil service law (1931) as follows : "In his official capacity the civil servant must pursue the common good, and not only remain impartial but not even endanger his impartiality or give occasion for distrust of it." Or, as the German civil service act of 1953 puts it: "The civil servant...must perform his task impartially and justly and bear in mind in the conduct of his office the well-being of the general public."

But the act made plain that the necessary neutrality of the civil servant in the conflict of political, economic, and social interests stops short of any indifference toward the basic form of government. In the language of the act, "By his entire conduct the civil servant must profess his attachment to the free, democratic order in the sense of the Basic Law and exert himself for its preservation."

Sense of Propriety

Doubts about the civil servant's impartiality might arise from any political partisanship—a subject to be discussed later. But doubts could also be prompted by any careless involvement in money deals and other economic transactions based on knowledge or "contacts" acquired in official activities. In these matters a civil servant was expected to think twice and not simply to adopt the profit philosophy of private enterprise. Indeed, cautions applicable to him would also be applicable to the members of his immediate family. The safest line for him, on this point as on others, was to stay meticulously outside the shadow of doubt.

Despite all straight-laced righteousness, the law of conduct remained remarkably free, nevertheless, from the excesses of petty moralising. For instance, unless unusual circumstances put a special slant on the matter, the disciplinary courts showed themselves disinclined to get into such questions as whether Jack was a privileged visitor in Mary's apartment. Moreover, with commendable firmness they refused to place women civil servants in a separate category in this matter. If the men were not to be asked questions, neither were the ladies.

Obligations of the Sovereign Employer

Still more important, German civil service law recognised a counterpart to the obligations of the career man, a counterpart consisting of the obligations that fell upon the state. The state was duty-bound to return the fidelity of its servants by being faithful to them. For example, let us assume that Herr Müller, in a condition of acute depression brought on by a string of trying experiences in the office, had submitted his resignation, taken to his bed, and refused to respond to any inquiries from his department. Let us assume further that the resignation had been acted upon, with the result that Herr Müller was released from the service. But was he? If he changed his mind and sought reinstatement, the department could not simply hide behind the resignation as an accomplished fact. The critical point would be what the department had done to establish the seriousness of the intent underneath the resignation and how much concern it had shown for the condition in which Herr Müller had been during this period. Short of a showing that the state had actually lived up to its duty of fidelity in the particular instance, the department could not expect the court to let the matter rest on the strength of the resignation.

The state's duty of fidelity toward its civil servants carried with it a duty of care, in the sense of attention to their well-being. This, for instance, implied an obligation in law for the sovereign employer to provide working conditions that would not impair the health or safety of his employees. Although temporary overwork in unforeseen emergencies was not exceptional, the state's duty of care would not permit unreasonably strenuous assignments. According to the Supreme Court, the degree of consideration to which the civil servant was entitled depended in part on his general physical condition and the particular circumstances. Thus a partly disabled veteran was not to be employed in such a way that his handicap might become more serious.

The Ideal of Impartiality : Great Britain

From the very beginning, the British civil service has been in the keeping of the crown. That is to say, the bureaucracy came to share in the peculiar combination of detachment from party positions and of constitutional permanence reflected by the monarchy as the symbolic bond connecting not only the peoples of the British Commonwealth but also the strands of national tradition. This combination of detachment and permanence was strengthened, not weakened, by the fact that the monarchy was linked with the dynamics of political decision. For the authority of the crown is exercised constitutionally by the cabinet, which in turn is the executive agency of the legislative majority in the House of Commons. Because it is meant to be at the full disposal of the government of the day, whatever the party emblem, the civil service must attend to the affairs of each government with equal solicitude.

The concept is illustrated in an apocryphal story recounted of Maurice Hankey, long the career head of the cabinet secretariat. When he was told that the Labour government wanted a draft bill providing for the abolition of the House of Lords, he paled but calmly inquired whether he might take until Wednesday noon to do it, in view of the importance of the subject. Equally to the point is what Clement Attlee, from his exceptional experience as former prime minister and long-time leader of the parliamentary Labour Party, wrote in 1954 :

> I do not think that this remarkable attribute of impartiality in the British Civil Service is sufficiently widely known or adequately recognized for what it is—one of the strongest bulwarks of democracy. I am often at pains to point this out and did so at a recent conference of Asiatic socialists in

Rangoon where I told them, to their surprise, that the same men who had worked out the details of Labour's Transport Act were now, at the behest of a Conservative Government, engaged in pulling it to pieces.[5]

The axiom of impartiality and the supporting rules of conduct grouped around it were essentially the product of civil service self-policing in Britain. As in Germany, the nature of the thing, out of itself, furnished a practical guide. It was a guide implicit rather than explicit, accepted as plain enough without much legal specification, and regarded as too little in danger of abuse by superiors to warrant the sort of judicial review which in France is supplied by the Council of State and in Germany by the disciplinary courts. In Herman Finer's words :

> No law or general administrative code lays down a scheme of disciplinary misdemeanors and accompanying penalties. A Civil Servant has no legal action against dismissal. His superannuation rights are ultimately determinable by the Treasury, for its interpretation of the Acts is not challengeable in the Courts.[6]

Disciplinary Procedure

What the British civil servant can demand is that he be given a bill of particulars in support of any charge against him before disciplinary action is taken. If this bill of particulars is actually the results of an inquiry into the facts thorough enough to satisfy a judicial body, subsequent court review might not add much to the fair disposition of the case. Such inquiry may be entirely informal or by official appointment of a special panel.

Without being required by law, examination of disciplinary charges by special panel is not an infrequent occurrence. When the conduct of members of the Administrative Class is in question, the facts normally are looked into by a specially appointed board of inquiry composed of senior civil servants. Reports by such special boards, together with an occasional Treasury memorandum, have taken the place occupied elsewhere by other authoritative pronouncements. Although, in the British view, the scope of the civil servant's obligations away from the office is governed by a presumption of privacy which is different from the French and the German, the inferences to be derived are alike.

This is evident from the so-called Gregory case in 1928, which had its origin in speculative activities involving foreign currency. There the board of inquiry declared :

> The first duty of a civil servant is to give his undivided allegiance to the State at all times and on all occasions when the State has a claim to his services. With his private activities the State is in general not concerned, so long as his conduct therein is not such as to bring discredit upon the Service of which he is a member. But to say that he is not to subordinate his duty to his private interests, nor to make use of his official position to further those interests, is to say no more than that he must behave with common honesty. The Service demands from itself the highest standards, because it recognizes that the State is entitled to demand that its servants shall not only be honest in fact, but beyond the reach of suspicion of dishonesty... . A civil servant is not so to order his private affairs as to allow a suspicion to arise that a trust has been abused, or a confidence betrayed... .
>
> Practical rules for the guidance of social conduct depend also as much upon the instinct and perception of the individual as upon cast-iron formulas; and the surest guide will, we hope, always be found in the nice and jealous honour of Civil Servants themselves. The public expects from them a standard of integrity and conduct not only inflexible but fastidious, and has not been disappointed in the past. We are confident that we are expressing the view of the Service when we say that the public have a right to expect that standard, and that it is the duty of the Service to see that the expectation is fulfilled.

Restraint of Economic Self-interest

A comparable case of conflicting public and private interests occurred in 1936, when a special board of inquiry probed the conduct of Sir Christopher Bullock, then permanent secretary to the Air Ministry. The heart of the case was a number of informal conversations spread over some two years between Sir Christopher and representatives of Imperial Airways in connection with a government contract. During these conversations Sir Christopher had made allusion to his desire to leave the service and to his availability for either the chairmanship or a directorship with

Imperial Airways—an arrangement apparently much to the company's liking. Moreover, at the beginning of the contract negotiations he had suggested to the Secretary of State for Air that the king bestow a high honour upon the chairman of the company. In its detailed report the board of inquiry declared Sir Christopher's actions "intrinsically improper." It found these actions "completely at variance" with the standards of conduct of the civil service despite the fact that none of the actions had actually influenced the negotiations for the contract. The prime minister accepted these findings, and Sir Christopher was dismissed.

How does a career man take such a blow? A clue is supplied in the personal statement that Sir Christopher made to the Press, given out at the same time that the report of the board of inquiry was made public. The discharged officer did not flinch. But while giving recognition to the board's "impartiality," he said :

> I do not seek to shirk responsibility for consequences which have flowed from my own actions. But it is easy to be wise after the event; and fortunate is he...who can honestly say that, if every private and informal conversation he has held were sifted and resifted months, even years, afterwards in the rarefied atmosphere of a solemn and formal inquisition, no passing phrase uttered in an unguarded moment could be held injudicious, no word or deed be called in question in some degree by absolute standards of taste or propriety. Whatever judgment your readers may pass on my mistakes, I hope they may be charitable enough to temper it with that reflection.

Perhaps Sir Christopher had a stronger point in a somewhat different sense. In sitting with representatives of private enterprise around the same conference table, civil servants were faced with a novel test of career ethics. In a way, what in this instance had happened would have been perfectly normal behaviour among businessmen. With government becoming increasingly a negotiator in the economy, rather than functioning solely as a regulator, old questions begged for new answers. Not surprisingly, the Bullock case was followed in 1937 with the issuance of the official Memorandum on the Subject of Acceptance of Business Appointments by Officers of the Crown Services.

Without contradicting the conclusions reached in the Gregory and Bullock cases, the rank and file has generally been in favour of keeping official duties from spilling over into the private life of the civil servant, especially upon his freedom of organisation. Thus, when Clause V of the Trade Disputes and Trade Unions Act of 1927 blocked affiliation with the labour movement, W.J. Brown, the general secretary of the Civil Service Clerical Association, pressed his opposition as follows :

> The first thing which is clear is that the private view of the civil servant does not absolve him from his obligations to the government as his employer. Outside his official duties the position of the civil servant is that of the private citizen—no more, no less. There ought to be no compulsion of civil servants to act otherwise than as ordinary citizens. Most emphatically he is not obliged by virtue of the fact that he is a civil servant to endorse the view of the government of the day. Nor is there anything in the position of the civil servant which disqualifies him individually (or collectively with his colleagues) from having relations with bodies outside the service provided always that these relations do not involve any failure on the part of the civil servant to carry out the duties for which he is paid.

This statement, however, was not meant to be a plea for the civil servant's "right to strike." Indeed, such a "right" has never been claimed by the Civil Service Clerical Association. The range of substitutes for the "right to strike" has been outlined in the preceding discussion of civil service unionism.

Statutory Requirements : United States

A different approach to the matter of civil service conduct is represented by the example of the United States. In the federal government, and to an even greater extent in the several states, the absence of an institutionally recognised higher career has arrested the formation of a professional sense of service ethics. By comparison, the new city-manager profession in local government, product of the twentieth century, soon took the initiative in adopting a code of ethics for its members. Historically, the United States Civil Service Commission saw its role in shielding the merit rule against the pressure of the spoilsmen. Consequently, civil service regulations have been more concerned with keeping those under the merit system politically sterilized than with fostering a career point of view that could be trusted to acknowledge implicit restraints of conduct. The result has been a sprouting of explicit requirements laid down by legislative enactments, helped along by the indigenous tendency that "there ought to be a law" whenever there is a question.

What are the expressly prohibited actions? They are defined casuistically and often ambiguously. In the first place, no one who represents a private concern or is directly or indirectly interested in its profits or contracts may act on behalf of the government in transacting business with the concern. In turn, a federal officer or employee may not receive private compensation for services rendered in relation to any contract in which the government is a party or directly or indirectly interested, or in relation to any proceeding, claim, or other matter in which the government is directly or indirectly interested. Moreover, he may not aid in the prosecution of any claim against the government nor do so for two years after leaving his public position in cases involving a subject directly connected with those he dealt with previously. No federal officer or employee may receive pay for services performed by him for the government from any source other than the government, except as may be contributed by a state, county, or municipality; and no contribution may be made from private sources toward his salary. Without authority, he may not release officially received confidential information or use it privately, especially for speculation. He may not ask or accept any money, check, promise, or gratuity with the intent to have his action on any question before him influenced by it. Finally, he may not engage in business activities that are incompatible with the duties of his office. As the Attorney General has put it in one of his official opinions, a government officer or employee "cannot in his private or official character enter into engagements in which he has, or can have, a conflicting personal interest. He cannot allow his public duties to be neglected by reason of attention to his private affairs."

Government Employment as Privilege

The legislative treatment of civil service conduct has been a mixed blessing. It had a dampening effect upon the development of a high ethical sensitivity out of the resources of the bureaucracy. This is not to suggest a lack of common virtues in the civil service. Quite the contrary—the merit system and "clean government" have come to be practically synonymous. But ordinary honesty is one thing, and alert awareness of professional canons of behaviour, settling subtler things, is another. The subtler things were not touched when in 1954 all federal departments were instructed to set up within themselves special machinery for internal inspection.

One further factor that discourages the crystallization of civil service ethics is the tendency of American society to keep authority and office within the range of common man's rules. This is a thoroughly democratic tendency. The desirability for the official not to stand apart is asserted inside as well as outside the civil service. Civil service ethics seem an exotic thing when the ordinary man's ethics have an aura of wholesomeness and sufficiency about them. But the "free-enterprise system" is not a good guide for official morality. A close parallel, if not an inference, is the far-reaching axiom that government employment is at the sovereign employer's pleasure and hence legally a privilege. In other words, government employment is not a source of rights unless such rights be expressly granted by legislation.

In this matter, ironically, the shadow of Mr. Justice Holmes looms large, although, for once, it is an obnoxious shadow. In one of his lightest judicial quips, while still on the Massachusetts bench, Holmes helped to squelch an action brought by a fired policeman by telling him that he "may have a constitutional right to talk politics, but he has no constitutional right to be a policeman" (1892). Instead of vanishing with time, this line of thought has held the ground. The idea is widely accepted today that the work relationship of the civil servant is dominated by the legal concept of privilege and that the scope of the privilege is freely shaped as well as modified by the sovereign employer. If in the definition of his status the civil servant is thrown back upon the concept of privilege, he cannot use the constitutional shield of due process. In the language of a judicial decision later affirmed by an evenly split Supreme Court (1951), the due-process clause "is not applicable unless one is being deprived of something to which he has a right," and thus the clause "does not apply to the holding of a government office."

Security Requirements

The doctrine of privilege has the most sweeping effects in the sovereign employer's freedom to dismiss a civil servant or reject an applicant for government employment for lack of "suitability."

The absence of a general basis of rights is made more dangerous when it magnifies the striking power of discretionary authority in judging the civil servant's conduct from the angle of loyalty and security. When the appraisal of derogatory information is not governed by specifically stated, generally applicable criteria but is left to each agency; when fair procedure, in spirit as well as in form, cannot be taken for granted; when public pressure may be brought to bear upon an agency that insists on placing fairness above a record of speedy disciplinary action; and when the security officer of the individual agency has reason for keeping himself on the safe side by the widest margin—under these circumstances, civil service tenure may come to rest on shaky foundations. The oddity of the situation is nicely portrayed when the drama critic of a Washington newspaper runs the following item in his column (1956):

> *Safety Note* : Still trembling under security threats, government employees have been phoning this desk to learn whether the Chinese film "Yang Oh" ("The Heroine"), to be shown at 12.30 and 2.30 Saturday at the Colony, is likely to be contaminating.... This department is assured that the picture was made in Hong Kong, has an historical setting and has been shown openly on Formosa.

This tidbit suggests the strange ways in which contagion may affect unwary victims. Once the clues get thicker, the attentive eye and ears of the government, such as the Federal Bureau of Investigation, collecting all the straws, will have little difficulty in coming up with a report that cannot be ignored. Faced with its presence but not its full contents, the object of the report will feel as did Professor Albert S. Coolidge of Harvard University, whose partisan interests were deemed incompatible with his sitting on a committee of the Library of Congress to administer his late mother's benefactions in the interest of chamber music. Wrote Professor Coolidge in a letter to the *Washington Post* (1956):

> On February 17 you printed...a letter...pointing out that the FBI has scrupulously refrained from evaluating, inter-preting, or drawing conclusions from the factual information which it was its duty to supply the Librarian of Congress about my past record. It has simply collected with impressive

thoroughness every incident which might be open to a derogatory interpretation. I well understand this, and have been at pains not to appear to blame or criticize the FBI.

I also well understand the frustration and despair of the man whose livelihood depends upon securing loyalty clearance, and who cannot command anything like the resources of the FBI in ferreting out facts and incidents tending to establish his loyalty, integrity, and political awareness.

Support of the Internal Security System

But the mater does not end with the individual immediately affected. The entire institutional environment, in due course of time, becomes saturated with the zest for suspicion. If its logic cannot afford to relent, this campaign is bound to demand of every civil servant the full measure of co-operation irrespective of his mental reservations as an individual. That, indeed, was proposed by an eminently respectable special board of inquiry in a report which found a distinguished scientist, Dr. Robert Oppenheimer, a security risk, said the report :

> There remains also an aspect of the security system which perhaps has had insufficient public attention. This is the protection and support of the entire system itself. It must include an understanding and an acceptance of security measures adopted by responsible government agencies. It must include an active co-operation with all agencies of government properly and reasonably concerned with the security of our country. It must involve a subordination of personal judgment as to the security status of an individual as against a professional judgment in the light of standards and procedures when they have been clearly established by appropriate process. It must entail a wholehearted commitment in the preservation of the security system and the avoidance of conduct tending to confuse or obstruct.

An obligation of this kind cuts deeply into the web of personal relationships as well as the civil servant's sense of justice. This is true especially when he persuades himself that the security system makes extravagant demands without compensating for these by adequate personal safeguards. He may feel that the idea of a watertight system is based on illusion and that steps toward achieving such tightness are comparable to the bizarre proposition to inflict preventive custody on all citizens in order to keep them from committing offenses.

Thus it may be said that the contemporary drift is toward a definition of requirements of conduct more comprehensive and more restrictive than would have appeared possible only twenty years ago. The fluidity thus introduced into the concept of civil service tenure can bring about serious abuses, with the appraisal of derogatory information so dependent on the goodwill of superiors. If the blight spreading in the law of civil service is not checked, the prospects of working for the government are bound to become less appealing for all but the least articulate or the most conventional aspirants.

References

1. Chester Barnard, *The Functions of the Executive* (Cambridge, Mass.: Harvard University Press).
2. Ordway Tead, *The Art of Administration* (New York : McGraw-Hill).
3. Learned, Ulrich, and Booz, *Executive Action.*
4. In the introduction to the French civil service contributed by Aubert Lefas to Leonard D. White (ed.), *The Civil Service in the Modern State* (Chicago : University of Chicago Press).
5. "Civil Servants, Ministers, Parliament and the Public," *Political Quarterly*, XXV (1954), 309.
6. *The Theory and Practice of Modern Government* (London : Allen & Unwin, 1932), II, 1444.

2

Work Specification and Orientation

The Generalist and the Specialist

Everyone in the world is unique in fingerprints, in important organic features, and in experience. Psychologists verified decades ago as environmental in source many differences in attitudes and personalities among children of the same family brought up in what had been presumed to be practically identical circumstances. That no one is exactly duplicated makes every person have some of the values that attach to rarity. Individuality gives one place in society. It is a proper occasion for pride and dignity. At the same time this means that anyone and everyone is limited in point of view and experience. Because he is what he is, he can speak only within very narrow and tentative terms on behalf of mankind in general.

The advance of civilization is a long march in the direction of further differentiating people, making all persons more and more unlike each other in knowledge, background, concerns, and skills. Primitive peoples have only a few dozen kinds of skills and small cultural inheritances. They and their customs change very, very slowly. Change in highly advanced societies goes on at faster and faster speeds in more and more directions.

I attended a college where, still actively teaching, was the professor who taught the first "political science" courses offered anywhere in the world. In my lifetime and a few decades more, political science has developed specialized fields within itself:

political theory; constitutional and administrative law; municipal government; state government; politics; comparative government; international relations; public administration. These fields of political science are now themselves broken into sub-fields. There are specialists in particular foreign governments, in international law, in comparative public administration, in international organisations, in public purchasing, in public authorities, in police administration, in natural resources management, in urban and rural zoning, and in many other sub-fields and sub-sub-fields. Very few now would claim to be "generalist" political-scientists, and any one would readily confess vast ignorance about the areas occupied by professional colleagues.

The price of specialization of every kind is parochialism. To be especially informed about anything is not to be similarly informed about everything else. A way of looking at problems is an infinite number of ways of *not* looking at them.

Civilization marches onward in the first instance as people specialize their efforts and thereby learn things and contribute to the doing of things otherwise not possible. At the same time, as one's knowledge increases in a specialized way, by study or situation and assignment, one's general ignorance increases disproportionally. This could result in such confusion as to stop the advance of civilization and cause its devolution. Unless we can make all of our specialized learnings, functions and interests harmonize in the sense of being at least mutually tolerable and many of them actually complementary, the march of civilization will become a descent into chaos.

Making civilization possible—maintaining social order in the face of more and more differentiated preoccupations—is the supreme responsibility of government. Government's instruments are politics and public administration in the broadest possible meaning of the latter term.

There are, and can be at this stage of history, no individuals who can be described as being even approximately true "generalists." Even philosophers are nowadays specialized into schools and fields, and most of them are not themselves philosophers; they are only familiar with certain philosophical literature. In any case, the synthesis which is to be achieved in an on-going society is dependent on actionists rather than on professional intellectuals. In many cases the professional intellectual, indeed, is so unlike the body of people who comprise the workaday world as to be perculiarly disqualified for political and quasi-political leadership.

But if there are no true generalists, there still are and always will be persons who are relatively more of the generalist sort than the vast majority of their contemporaries. Then, too, it is possible to organise and carry on institutions especially designed and staffed to achieve general ends.

Government is the primary, indispensable institution capable of maintaining an advancing state of balance in a condition of advancing complexity. It is charged with the extraordinary function of making *general* sense out of a dynamic proliferation of special occupations and preoccupations. There are some social illiterates who vociferously call for "minimum government" without realizing that they are advocating minimum civilization.

Neither the synthesising role of government nor the synthesising process is much understood. Too many think of government as properly having to do with "order" conceived in terms of avoiding violence. The pursuit of order does, indeed, involve capacity to deal with incipient riots, rebellion and international warfare. But it always has also involved order as between diverse interests and concerns of divisive character short of immediately violent import. As civilization advances, these features of society grow in much the same proportion as that illustrated by the translation of slings and catapults into hydrogen bombs and space stations.

Government as an ordering institution, in terms both of violence and of social synthesis of much more subtle sort, is most familiar to the general public in verbiage related to constitutional structures. Nations which are quite different from each other in actual processes and in the values they serve sometimes have quite similar constitutions, and acquaintance with constitutions, therefore, provides little understanding of government. Yet there are at least a few persons in any particular democratic country who are justified in feeling that they understand its basic structures.

In the United States, for example, the general roles of the Congress, the President and the Supreme Court are consistent enough and familiar enough so that very many citizens tend to feel that they understand their government in terms of these three main organs. Hence once the point is made that all three deal not merely with present and potential violence but with order in terms of an expanding complexity in things known, things being done, occupations, interests and aspirations, the way in which general policy decisions are made on a basis of congressional and Presidential consideration is readily perceived. The interaction of Congressional committee members coming from all parts of the nation, individually embodying differences in experience and responsibility, is rather vivid. The interaction of these legislators with the constituents who elected them and who can return them to private life is readily assumed. The relatively specialized concerns of the committee originally considering a measure are seen as influenced by other committees or they are modified also by awareness of the need to secure concurrence of the other House and by thought of the possibility of Presidential veto and judicial review.

It is not hard to see that this process of interaction is, in small, much like a nationwide process of interaction between the whole body of voters. It is like it, yet more manageable and more illumined by special access to relevant information. And in the end, even though not completely satisfactory to any citizen, it is usually acceptable to all citizens, just as while not just what any member of Congress or any member of the Executive branch would most like, it is as acceptable to them all as any feasible alternative would be.

It is nothing less than amazing how often it is true that this governmental product is generally acceptable. Whereas general consensus would be almost never possible on matters of such complexity and import, consent is almost invariable. When consent is not evident, the government modifies its course. But the cries of outrage are about things believed to be contemplated, not about things actually done.

In important part this is true because of refinements achieved in the application of statutes by administrative organs. This constant decision-making, operating phase of government is not at all well understood popularly.

The bureaucracy has its own representational characteristics, its own synthesising roles. Persons from all parts of the country, with highly varied professional and occupational responsibilities in scores of agencies with hundreds of bureaus having thousands of divisions with tens of thousands of smaller units, impinge upon one another, competing, deferring, influencing each other and adjusting actions in terms of citizen demands and complaints.

The whole result is a highly important contribution to social co-ordination. It is a synthesising, generalizing product of interaction between specialists in agencies with specialized responsibilities. In a good many cases it may be very little more than this. But even these cases are developed under the discipline of persons and bodies having positively generalist abilities and clearly general responsibilities. These persons and bodies are the frankly political ones, at least potentially partisan. There would be no synthesis of a kind appropriate to popular government without them.

In spite of the fact that training and work assignments specialize the members of the bureaucracy, and that any individual politician is also to some extent a specialist in responsibility to one party, a specialist in geographical peculiarity, and a specialist in terms of his own background and personality, some persons lend themselves more readilty than others to generalist roles. Persons differ in degree of specialization in outlook, differ in degree of capacity to deal in relationships between specialized functions, knowledge and concerns. "Specialist" and "generalist" are relative—not absolute—terms.

No one is a complete specialist, wholly unable to have any perception or any sympathy for other persons and for considerations not really his own. And of course no one is equally interested, informed and understanding with reference to everybody and everything.

But people in general are certainly very much more specialist than generalist in outlook, and in recent decades there has been a growing faith in "experts." There has also been an increased tendency on the part of experts in many fields to assume or assert some special right to dominate public policy in areas of their own expertise. There has been, similarly, a general failure to recognize that the importance of generalizing competence in persons and in institutions has gone up in a geometrical ratio as specialization has proliferated in a rapid arithmetical ratio. The familiar dictum is increasingly true : "The expert should be on tap not on top."

We should direct more attention to the fact that a Prime Minister needs to be more competent as a generalist, less competent as a specialist, than his ministerial colleagues. Similarly, more attention should be paid to the facts that all ministers have roles of more generalist sort than any civil servant has, and that the need for generalist qualities and performance rises at each upward level in the bureaucratic hierarchy. There should also be more recognition of the need ministers have for generalist-type aides.

No matter how specialized in training and interest a civil servant administrator may have been initially, each promotion upward constitutes a vesting in him of successively larger responsibilities for enforcing the general point of view of his minister and his government. The higher he goes, the wider the scope of personnel and functions subordinate to him, the more crucial is his function as administrative agent of a still higher authority.

There is in this phenomenon of hierarchal responsibility a certain ambivalence. The executive represents his subordinates to a degree and up to the point where he has transformed their views so as to relate them to the broader context within his purview and has so put those he accepts before his own superior. When the higher authority promulgates a decision, it becomes his duty to support that higher authority, to interpret its decision to his subordinates and effect their willing and understanding implementation of it. One incapable of this ambivalence is an incapable administrator.

It is generally true that the more thoroughly professionalized a function is, the less administrative competence will be exhibited, and the more constant will be a stubborn parochialism. Most scientists, engineers and medical doctors, for example, tend to remain emotionally champions of their respective professions, no matter how much their elevated hierarchical positions may require of a general responsibility exercised in broad terms. It is this stubborn allegiance to specialism that is at the root of most performances called "bureaucratic" in the invidious sense of that word.

The higher one goes, the less particularly relevant is any kind of earlier, special orientation. Some highly trained professional persons who have become distinguished administrators have discovered this. A friend once asked the head of governmental research in the United Kingdom how valuable he thought this training in science had come to be for him in his high administrative post. The administrator answered quickly out of prior reflection, "It gives me nothing in my present position except a readier acceptance of me by my subordinates."

Authorities had once organised a conference in the U.S. Office of Naval Research participated in by heads of all the naval laboratories. Triggered by some remark by a professional educator, each laboratory head rose in succession to assert that his university training had no particular bearing on his current and recent tasks.

In a lecture to principal executives of the U.S. Public Health Service, it was once sought to provoke illuminating discussion by saying something like this : "All of the professional staff of this service are either medical doctors or engineers. All of the service-wide administrators are medical doctors. Yet if being a medical doctor qualifies anyone to be head of the Public Health Service we might just as well put all the names of the medical doctors in a hat and select as head of the Service any man whose name we draw from it. You know, and I know, that this wouldn't do. I suggest that if a medical doctor makes a good head of the service he does it in spite of being medically trained, rather than because of it." To our surprise, we started no argument at all. Everyone who commented expressed agreement. In any case, the Ministers to whom the heads of the Public Health Service have been responsible would all have agreed, and their point of view is more valid than that of the medical specialists. The Public Health Service does not exist for the sake of the doctors but for the sake of the public, and the politicians as a body are the only appropriate judges of who can best serve the general interest in any particular post of general responsibility.

Ministers and heads of government, of course, are the crucial politicians who should serve with least justification attaching to expert competence. We frequently err in this respect in the United States—not because Presidents do not know better, but because the halo of expertise is politically more potent with us than it should be. We, therefore, tend to put farm spokesmen in the position of Secretary of Agriculture, labour spokesmen in the position of Secretary of Labour, bankers in the Secretary of the Treasury post, and businessmen in the position of Secretary of Commerce. This is one reason why we have too few able politicians with experience qualifying them for consideration as possible Presidential nominees.

In Britain, they do better in this matter. Their method is one that puts politicians in domestic political posts and gives long and varied political experience to an impressive number of persons.

The point is that even any top civil service position requires so much of political competence (in a non-partisan sense), requires so much of generalist capabilities, that any man in such a post who thinks of himself as an expert is already at a position higher than any he is properly fitted to fill. At that level he should be—and should think himself to be—primarily an administrator and a public servant.

In this particular matter, India seems to be at a stage which we in the United States were beginning to leave several decades ago, even though (or possibly because) in these same decades we have carried the phenomenon of specilization further in more directions than any other society.

In the nineteen-twenties all American hospitals were administered by doctors—and in numerous and important respects very poorly administered as a rule. Today there is a large and respected body of hospital administrators without medical degrees, and the administration of hospitals has been greatly improved. Non-medical administrative officers also now hold high place in national and state public health services although not yet so extensively as in private services.

Similarly, in the nineteen-twenties there was a considerable fad for engineers as administrators. Public ignorance of one sort had combined with professional ignorance of another sort to confer or to claim for "engineer" as for "doctor" more sweeping significance than the terms actually signify. In that period most of the city managerships then being established were filled with engineers. The climax of this movement was the election of an engineer—Herbert Hoover—as President of the United States. We hear almost nothing of engineers as administrators nowadays. The great majority of the city managers of today were not trained as engineers. Urban redevelopment administrators, who in recent years have come to head up multimillion-dollar reconstruction programmes in our most progressive cities, are not usually engineers. They hire engineering firms to do engineering work, and everybody is happier that way. The man here who insists that only engineers can administer programmes importantly involving engineering technology only betrays his own failure to understand administration.

There is no one "right" source for an administrator because of some technical character in the activities to be directed. Whatever the programme is, it involves vastly more than any one kind of training or experience may be counted upon to provide. Nor is it an iron law of administration that promotion should always be made by elevating someone already within the particular organisation. A good high level administrator is always a *rare bird* and such rare birds are developed from many different sources.

A really good cadre of administrators in any large organisation will consequently represent a great variety of backgrounds, and some will have been brought in at high level from outside. The president of one of the world's great mercantile organisations told me that they always were on the lookout for a good executive wherever they would find him. They continually experimented with likely prospects from other fields and sometimes bought another company just to obtain an executive they could not otherwise hire. This company's intelligent practices were not so exceptional as many laymen and specialist claimants would be inclined to believe. Diversity of background on the part of an administering cadre makes for vitality and competence. Diversity of experience on the part of single administrators is often also a feature common to the preparation of many of the ablest ones. Yet this consideration provides little more basis for an iron law of selection than does professional membership. Good top administrators are rare birds.

There is another way in which the general point may be made. This is in terms of the problem of communication. The more an expert specialises in some aspect of some function or subject-matter the lower is his actual position in the hierarchy of that function or subject-matter, whereas his unique achievements may confer upon him higher and higher repute. The consequence is, speaking illustratively, that a specialist so differentiated from his own professional colleagues that even they find difficulty in understanding what he is saying may be the very one who tries to communicate with the Prime Minister or President about his field of work. This can only frustrate both the specialist and the President or Prime Minister. A very great deal of the organisational frustration of professional people—scientists in particular—derives from this misguided kind of effort at communication.

It might be demonstrated that no expert as an expert should

ever try to communicate with anyone responsible for general policy. Rather there should be efforts to develop well-filled-in hierarchies of specialists in the principal areas of specialism with persons in the upper levels of such hierarchies being more expert in exposition than in the particular subject and function being described and explained. One trouble is that experts don't like that position and the role it involves, since thereby they lose the eminence of uniqueness : in specialization and particular achievement and are charged with being "superficial." They may lose face with the general public and—more often, more certainly, and more devastatingly in terms of professional pride—they lose face with their professional colleagues. And yet an occasional C.P. Snow illustrates the possibilities.

Another illustration of less general applicability is provided by a story one is assured is true about the problem of communication between physicists engaged in one part of the Manhattan Project out of which came the atomic bomb. The story is that these physicists had so specialized in sub-sub-fields of physics that they did not understand each other. It was essential that they should communicate, and, therefore, an English professor was brought in, charged with talking successively to the physicists until he could serve as an interpreter.

Because of this problem of communicating about and synthesising in action more and more things, facts, functions, people, interests and aspirations, changes in political and administrative arrangements will be required from time to time in all nations and between nations.

In this country, for example, some structural changes within ministries and between the national and State Governments may be rather soon required.

We do not know, of course, just what changes may be most useful here, or when they should be instituted. But by referring to the experience of my own country, we may be able to illustrate the process of administrative development. All these have to do with elevating consideration of the general interest over what Jefferson called "local egoisms" and what now are also "specialist egoisms."

First of all, of course, has been the rather fortuitous emergence of a two-party system to serve as the continuing instrument of majority government.

Secondly, there has been a long and continuing clarification of the dominance of the nation over the states. Climaxed unmistakably in the Civil War, the national power has been exercised with moderate persistence to enforce racial equality in reluctant communities.

Thirdly, there has been a great growth in delegation, thus keeping the way clear for political leaders in administrative posts to handle more and more important matters by developing and utilizing the capacities of subordinates. Both the President and the Secretary of State gave personal attention to every patent issued in the Washington administration, for example.

Now patents are better handled four or five or more levels lower in the administrative hierarchy.

Fourth, the development of a civil service has been gradually supplemented with a system of personal aides around ministers and civil service administrators.

Fifth, rather more consciously than in earlier periods, administrative structures have been designed to be competitive in the first instance, co-ordinative in the second instance. In other words, structures are now somewhat intentionally designed to identify and pose issues, as well as to resolve them.

Developments of the third, fourth and fifth kinds just listed have been intended to improve the bureaucracy's service to Ministers.

One of the important gains sought is that of providing ministers with more varied subordinate viewpoints—giving them more chance to understand what the issues are, and what alternative action possibilities there can be.

There is here, we think, too much tendency to advise ministers through a single kind of channel from subordinates. Too few issues are presented to him from within the ministry; he hears about issues too exclusively from disturbed citizens.

If proponents of several viewpoints derived from differentiated responsibilities have, and use, free access to the minister, they will give him perspective, which is the essential basis for judgment. In successive cases they will also give him a fairly clear picture of his ministry and how it operates, the points of view dominant in it, and how much it is achieving. All this will be enhanced if he learns how to ask all concerned more and more searching questions.

The general point is that the staff of a ministry should be structured somewhat more to maintain open channels for competitive viewpoints.

It is as much a Secretary's duty to advise the Minister according to his own judgment in the first instance as it is to carry out the Minister's judgement when that judgement has been definitely expressed. Too often in a Western country and in India alike those who serve Ministers recommend the action toward which they guess their Minister to be inclined. Too often they do not argue when a decision is being considered.

Secretaries should be valued on these principal points :

1. Frank and independent advice in the first instance;
2. facilitation of opportunities for others to get before the Minister views different from those of the Secretaries;
3. careful maintenance in all important matters of written records showing clearly who recommended what and what decisions were made.

(It should be remarked here that too many decisions are made only in conversation with no proper written record; too many "notes" accompanying papers are devoid of any real content). A fourth important basis for evaluating a secretary is his success in building competence and confidence in subordinate staff. Improvement in the top structure and in the performance of Secretaries is one thing; their displacement by specialists would be to go in the opposite direction.

An auxiliary point, already suggested, requires explanation. It is that personal staff of high competence and status should be provided for ministers and for civil service administrators at an increasing number of hierarchical levels.

Staff facilities available to the President of the United States outside of Civil Service personnel have been made vivid to newspaper readers in the weeks just preceding and following the inauguration of President John F. Kennedy. On a smaller scale, staff of a similar sort is a resource of the heads of departments and agencies. As the Presidential level, staff authorization comes from Congress, often simply in Appropriation Acts but sometimes in special statutes. At the Cabinet and Agency level concurrence in the number of places open to non-civil service appointment is usually a prerogative of the Civil Service Commission. But in all these it is properly believed that the identity of persons chosen is wholly for the Minister or Agency Head to determine. If the practice should be attempted here it might be more acceptable and safer, for a few years, for the Public Service Commission to have the power of vetoing—but not nominating—such appointees.

At the ministerial level, the purpose would be to provide him assistance in using civil servants, enabling him to obtain information consciously couched in terms appropriate to the ministers' special responsibilities. A personal secretary or two cannot begin to give adequate service. Alone as a politician in his ministry, a minister and a deputy minister normally cannot learn nearly enough fast enough.

At the level of civil servant administrators, the need is to help the civil servants formulate materials in terms of more institutional wisdom and less in terms of merely personal wisdom than now is the case.

One can illustrate this matter by pointing again to experience in the United States. In the Ministry of Agriculture there the minister used to have occasions wen he wanted in relation to some special problem the distilled wisdom of, let us say, the Bureau of Agricultural Economics. The request for advice would go to the Chief of that Bureau, whose personal secretary would pass it on to a Division Head whose personal secretary would pass it on to a Section Head, who would assign the matter to a single economist. The economist would write an anonymous individual view of the subject in question. It would be transmitted through the Section Head to the Division Head, thence to the Bureau Chief, and finally to the minister who would find in it as a rule nothing clearly helpful or even relevant to his original query. It did not reflect the wisdom of the Bureau as a whole. These were all intelligent persons, but they were not staffed to serve their minister well. Since then, the development of personal staff around ministers, bureau chiefs, division heads and section heads has become rather a commonplace resource of great value.

Beyond such devices, of course, is the problem of having civil service administrators who are truly actionists. There is a tendency, born of frustration, to turn to experts for high administrative posts because the civil servants are not selected enough and trained enough in terms of ability to lead institutional action programmes. There is a related tendency to over-intellectualize administration at the expense of workaday-world effectiveness. Both tendencies are in the wrong direction.

The potent focus of concern, we are convinced, is to provide ministers with better institutional resources. Instead, the subordinate functional specialists and the experts wish somehow to compel him to take their judgement. The responsibility is to equip him to make for himself the best judgement of which he is capable in terms of his higher, broader responsibilities.

The problem is one of the greatest magnitude, with the dimensions of feasible civilization at stake. The expert is at the core of the forward movement. Yet if his point of view becomes dominant, the bounds of civilization will prove tragically confined. We must find ways to make general sense out of things. We must have more persons committing themselves to more general functions and concerns. Then society can achieve through its institutions a kind and degree of wisdom unattainable by individuals however much they dedicate themselves to generalist performance.

3

Dynamics of Bureaucracy and Government

We already have some idea of the nature of the administrative functions and of the role played by the modern bureaucracy in the conduct of a government's functions. But "bureaucracy" is a word often used without exact indication of the meaning ascribed to it. This profile paper seeks to make clear the principal meanings of the word and, in doing so, to show the several aspects or dimensions of bureaucracy.

The ambiguity of the word "bureaucracy" is often exploited for deliberate befuddlement. We must distinguish :

1. bureaucracy as a particular form of organisation, more specifically as a general design for the conduct of public administration, and

2. bureaucracy as an ailment of organisation, an ailment obstructing good management.

We must also distinguish :

3. bureaucracy in the sense of "big government," an establishment of vast proportions which is joined in countless ways to the social and economic order, for better or worse, and

4. bureaucracy thought of as a blight, always for the worse, falling on liberty. Bureaucracy is considered a blight by those who are ready to indict modern government for the responsibilities it has assumed.

Bureaucracy—Understanding and Misunderstanding

Judging by the way it looks and sounds, "bureaucracy" is not the sort of word that grows out of the talk of ordinary people. For that matter, it is not likely to take hold in the common man's vocabulary. There must be millions who have never heard of "bureaucracy." But everybody who has heard of it either suspects or knows that "bureaucracy" is a bad word or a word for a bad thing. That much is clear to him even though he may hesitate when asked to tell exactly what the word means.

Perhaps, while forming his answer, he will think first of a similar word—"democracy." Possibly he knows the roots of that word as well as its meaning—that is, government by the people, or popular rule. Putting two an two together, he may come up with the answer that bureaucracy means government by bureaus, or public agencies. With that he would be right in a way. He may add that bureaucracy is bad because government by public agencies would make these agencies the masters of the people.

In not a few countries, however, particularly those of continental Europe, statesmen and editorial writers as well as scholars speak of bureaucracy as one may speak of the weather. There the word means simply the body of regular government employees mostly in the specific sense of the civil service, especially the higher service. In this bland meaning the word is also applied to the administrative system as a whole. Nevertheless, even in these countries it is not flattering to be called a bureaucrat, in the sense of acting in a bureaucratic manner. For, as with Americans, a bureaucratic manner means such things as doing everything by regulation, ignoring better reasons, and being coldly aloof from the outside world. In contrast with the United States, however, European references to bureaucracy—in particular the bureaucracy —are ordinarily free from derogatory intent or implication. On the whole, unlike American usage, the term has come to be emotionally neutral in Europe.

Origins of Word

Although "bureaucracy" may be counted among the notorious words of our age, its origin is not entirely clear beyond the hint of French ancestry. The first half of the word has been traced to the Latin *burrus*, meaning a dark and sombre colour—a colour suitable for solemnity and possibly also to cloak evil deeds. In Old French a related word *(la bure)* meant a certain kind of cloth used on tables, especially in places where public authorities were holding forth. In other words, even the officials of distant times apparently did not deem an honest table good enough to support their elbows. From the tablecloth, the table covered with it got the name *bureau*, and next this word was applied to the office room itself. It has been claimed that the creative mind first to envisage the public offices as the operating government by speaking of it as *bureaucratic* was Vincent de Gournay, an eighteenth-century French minister of commerce. In all probability he intended to express the critical point of view of private enterprise.

Although a hideous example of teaming French with Greek, and obviously not meant to win friends for officialdom, the new word gained a footing because of its nice argumentative edge. It soon spread to other countries. Not surprisingly, it came into considerable vogue in nineteenth-century Germany, where a highly developed civil service, steeped in the spirit of authority, encountered the liberal surge. As a matter of fact, the Germans were so taken with the French term that before long they gave it Teutonic braids by spelling it *Bl̦rokratie*. But the real flowering of the word in many languages is a recent development. Equally recent is the systematic description and analysis of bureaucracy both as an arm and as part of the mind of modern government, public administration in the context of the industrial society. This is a field of study which in its origins is largely identified with the work of the German historian and sociologist Max Weber.[1]

Government of Bureaus versus Government by Bureaus

In speaking against administrative tyranny in the alleged defense of the people, a versatile politician knows how to clinch his case by thundering about bureaucracy. All that may have happened is that one of his constituents failed to get what the particular governmental agency was not authorized to let him have under law. But the cry of bureaucracy rings loud and true irrespective of the merits of the case. Yet, if popular rule employs administrative machinery to make itself effective over the wide range of present-day governmental activities, the citizen has no good reason to act as if this machinery were the product of diabolical cunning. Measured by quantity, modern government—

whatever the degree of popular rule reflected in it—consists of the performance of continuing functions by public agencies to a much greater extent than at any time in the past.

In the practical experience of the citizen, government has become indeed largely one of public agencies, one of bureaus. He deals with these agencies, for the most part, when he has any dealings with government. Government of bureaus, in this sense, is different from government by bureaus. There is no government by bureaus when the administrative system acts in accordance with the decisions of the representatives of the people and accounts to them for what is being done. Obviously, government of bureaus is much more appealing than a government operated by commissars, investigators, bosses, or crooks. Moreover, if we think of *bureau* in the sense of an office table, especially a desk, bureaucracy appears to be the equivalent of government from behind desks, or "desk government." Who would not rather be governed from behind desks than from the back room of the corner saloon or the boudoir favoured by the chief of a junta?

Desk Government

Certainly, to modern man the desk is not a symbol of either elevation or authority. On the contrary, it is as common as the income tax, which touches high and low. Today uncounted millions spend their working hours seated behind desks. With but slight exaggeration it can be said that this has become the productive posture of the white-collar breadwinner everywhere. In addition, with the advance of automation, the chair, if not the desk, increasingly becomes also the companion of the man who watches the machines. Modern society is turning into a "sedentary society" in which the chair serves as both the means and the symbol of production. In social ranking, then, the man at the desk is a reasonable facsimile of everybody, and he is likely to do something useful.

"Desk government," obviously, is a phrase without terror. It suggests forethought and planning, analysis of the facts, considered decisions, direction and co-ordination on a rational basis, predictability of performance, and assurance of results. It alludes to the contribution of the mind, highly esteemed in the era of science and technology. It carries a connotation of knowledge and even of insight. No doubt, twentieth-century government with its great burden of responsibilities should be informed as well as imaginative, capable of assembling and interpreting the data essential for policy-making, and sophisticated in designing longer-term programmes. In short, modern government cannot afford to be less than intellectually resourceful. If this is the mark of bureaucracy, we should clamour for more rather than less bureaucracy.

Despite its possible merit, however, bureaucracy is seldom praised; and it is often slighted by those who, openly or secretly, plead a special cause. Specifically, even before the time of De Gournay two camps had existed, separated by one of the enduring dividing lines of politics. On the one side were those who regarded government as basically allied with their interests. On the other side stood those who looked upon government as an impediment to the pursuit of their interests. Denunciation of bureaucracy, naturally, was a promising tactic for this second group—most frequently the spokesmen of private enterprise when they were anxious to stay the arm of government regulation. To them, bureaucracy essentially meant government and all its works. In fact, the more efficient government showed itself, especially in the discharge of its administrative functions, the less could leaders of private enterprise say in its favour, because it was then that much more dangerous.

The same hostile predisposition shows up when the folklore of the contemporary business civilization presents large-scale private organizations as wholesome and productive and corresponding structures of public administration as heavy-handed and wasteful. For instance, many Americans are inclined to view as national assets such giant corporations as General Motors, Standard Oil of New Jersey, and United States Steel, without including formations of this kind under the heading of bureaucracy. Conversely, as Harold D. Lasswell has pointed out, there is no general cartoon figure presenting government as a constructive or beneficial factor. In most of the invective directed at bureaucracy we may, therefore, find upon close examination a bias based upon narrow self-interest.

It is clear, then, that "bureaucracy" is an ambiguous term. We saw that it could mean quite different things. It might mean, first, the type of organization used by modern government for the conduct of its various specialised functions, embodied in the administrative system and personified more specifically by the civil service. Bureaucracy might mean, second, a mechanistic and formal approach in carrying out such functions, literal and "inhuman" to the point of indifference toward the effects achieved. This is a common failing of large-scale organisation, whether public or private. Third, bureaucracy might mean one or two other things or both at the same time. On the one hand, it might mean the kind of government that shoulders a large burden of responsibilities in support of the economic and social order. On the other hand, it might mean a political condition in which the executive branch plays a role increasingly more important in relation to the role of the legislative and judicial branches. This is decried, we recall, as the "welfare state," but it is also spoken of sympathetically as the "service state." And, fourth, bureaucracy might mean government subject to control, not by the electorate, but rather by a group of power-hungry, visionary functionaries. Each of these meanings calls for closer examination.

Bureaucracy as Structure of Organisation

Concentration of Responsibility

To speak of bureaucracy as designating a particular structure of organisation suggests technical rather than ordinary man's language. For it is not likely that the proverbial man in the street would be fascinated with anything as abstruse as structures of organisation. This is a subject closer to the heart of the specialist, who must know which organisational structure is best suited for particular purposes. A subject about which specialists must know is of equal interest to the scholar, who feels he should know first, or more about it, so as to teach the specialists.

One concept of the bureaucratic type of organisation gained considerable currency during the second half of the nineteenth century in the German terminology of public administration. That concept came to mean about the same thing Americans have in mind when they talk of single-headed departments, in contrast with organisations headed by collegial bodies, such as boards and commissions, with each member essentially the equal of every other, including the chairman. More specifically, in accordance with this terminology, a bureaucratically organised agency was one directed by a civil servant who alone was responsible for the actions of his subordinates; these simply exercised the authority of the man at the top. In the same way, a departmental system organised on such principles was referred to as "bureaucratic" in character. Implicit in the turn was a strong suggestion to the effect that this structure imparted efficiency. If the French were torn between indignation and amusement over *bureaucratie,* the Germans managed to drain the word of all satire and to make it the label of a system of superior accomplishment.

Another meaning of bureaucracy is more familiar and more recent as applied to organisational structure. It refers to a type of structure manned by trained personnel who are grouped in specific command relationships. Bureaucratic organisation in this sense is equally and conspicuously serviceable for a large variety of public and private purposes in industrial societies.

Hierarchy and Control

The type of organisation called bureaucratic in this now widely used sense has several unmistakable characteristics. They include—as principal factors—hierarchy, jurisdiction, specialization, professional training, fixed compensation, and permanence. Hierarchy is perhaps the most important. As a concept applied to the doing of things, hierarchy signifies a scheme of interlocking superior-subordinate relationships. In such a scheme John Doe may be the boss of a number of underlings who—short of exceptional circumstances—defer to his authority as if he were king. Each of these underlings, again, may command still others, and so the scheme goes down to the very base. But John Doe is far from being king, for normally he gets his orders from somebody higher up; and , even if he were at the very top, the presence of restrictive considerations will usually prevent him from issuing the sort of orders closest to his heart. But if John Doe is at the top and issues a particular order to be implemented throughout the organisation, he can be reasonably sure that everybody, from one level of internal control to the other, will get busy doing what the order demands.

The advantage of hierarchy as an organisational device is obvious from this bare outline. Through the scheme of interlocking superior-subordinate relationships even the largest organisation can be held together and be made to act as a single, cohesive body. Yet the responsibility for direction from the top is not over-extended, because every order, travelling down, is reinforced by the way it secures attention on successively lower levels of control. In turn, confusion is reduced, because each human being within the organisation ordinarily knows precisely from whom he gets orders and to whom he is to pass them on.

The performance of superiors in transmitting orders received by them to their subordinates can be observed and controlled with relative ease. It can be stimulated by prospects for advancement and threats of disciplinary action. As a result, instead of losing force because of the distance it has to cover in moving throughout the organisation, each order from above gains new force as it proceeds from one superior-subordinate relationship to the next lower one. In the chain of superiors each puts his own authority behind the order. Equally important, not only does hierarchy make it easy to transmit orders which set in motion specific actions but it is as effective in conveying to all parts of the organisation a general sense of direction, a common approach, a basic point of view, and even an operating doctrine. Hierarchy, then, enables an organisation—even one in which large numbers of human beings have been brought together—to move toward specified goals with the least amount of floundering and friction.

Jurisdiction and Specialization

As a characteristic of the bureaucratic type of organisation, the concept of hierarchy is linked with that of jurisdiction. This term, in the organisational context, refers principally to two things. First, it indicates a formula recognition that the individual organisation is committed to discharging particular functions and these alone, usually in relation to a defined geographic area. Second, jurisdiction is made part of the internal division of labour within the organisation.

For example, a municipal department of welfare as a matter of jurisdiction will indicate that it is available for the handling of applications for public assistance; but it will not undertake to furnish supervisors for playgrounds, playground supervision being outside its jurisdiction. The welfare department would also make a distinction between an application coming from a resident of the town and one being mailed in by a resident of a neighbouring town. The bureaucratic type of organisation will thus gain increased efficiency by sticking to what it is equipped to do in terms of its jurisdiction, without trying to do other things. In addition, the external jurisdiction—that is, what an organisation is to do—will be translated into internal jurisdiction in the sense of detailed assignments for all components of the organisation, down to what each individual at his working place is meant to do, such as the filing clerk in the receiving branch of the day-care division, for instance.

Jurisdiction amounts to an acknowledgement of readiness to do certain things and not to attempt others. Thus a basis is established for identifying the particular specializations that the organization requires for the accomplishment of its ends. The chain of superior-subordinate relationships provides a convenient pattern for so grouping employees possessed of a specialized competence as to make best use of them. Different kinds of specialists are needed for different kinds of agencies—for example, social workers, cartographers, bacteriologists—but most agencies cannot be without specialists having to do with effective conduct of administration. For this reason the bureaucratic type of organisation must value professional or technical training. An ordinary man of good will, lacking such training, will simply not get in—unless he has "pull."

Fixed Compensation and Permanence

Even more significant for the nature of bureaucratic organisation is the fact that ordinarily no one active in it is at the same time the owner. Typically, everybody is an employee working for a fixed compensation, which in nearly all instances is unrelated to the measured or assumed success of the organisation and the actual pressure of business. The compensation, as a rule, is paid on the basis of a set schedule from a general treasury. It is not paid by individual superiors at their discretion, nor is it raised in the form of fees collected from applicants or customers, in the sense that the pay depends on how much money has been taken in. Those making up the organisation do not view it as a tangible asset at their disposal, for they lack control over it, especially over the physical means by which the product of the organisation is turned out.

Finally, the bureaucratic type of organisation reflects considerable long-run continuity. The survival of a private business firm is ultimately subject to the selective test of the market. This test, however, is usually less strenuous to a large economic organisation that supplies a sizable share of the total demand. Public agencies exercising functions deemed to be in the common interest enjoy still greater tenure. This is true even though antagonistic public sentiment, retrenchment, or changing circumstances may have sharply contractive effects, leading to the liquidation of entire departments in extreme cases.

Professional Point of View

As a type, bureaucratic organisation indicates sophistication in both design and operating method. Calculated to increase efficiency of performance, it is the product of applied reason, an expression of rationality. It is on these grounds that both the structural perfection of the bureaucratic type of organisation and the increasing use of machine processes as a manpower substitute are often referred to as rationalization in other countries.

But the characteristic of rationality comes in view from still another angle. With the evolution of the bureaucratic type of organisation in modern public administration, a foundation was laid for the formation of a body of civil servants who worked for the government as a lifetime career. The very presence of this professionally trained body exerted a rational influence upon the way in which government reached decisions. It is thus understandable why the factor of rationality has been emphasized as both the characteristic working approach and the outstanding contribution of the modern bureaucracy. In the unrestrained interaction of political forces the strongest pressure would usually win out. But in a technological civilization as complex and sensitive as ours a crude test of political strength is not a satisfactory source of public policy. A moderating influence is needed, which gains its persuasiveness from the knowledge of pertinent facts. Hence the existence of a screening operation, singling out for proper attention the pros and cons of competing alternatives of action, is a highly welcome thing. Governed to a considerable degree by professional standards and likely to value a reasoned approach, the modern career service, under favourable conditions, can function as a significant support of rational consideration in politics.

Bureaucracy as Rigidity of Organisation

It seems hardly plausible that bureaucracy could be an ailment of organisation if—as we saw—the word also connotes a specific type of organisational structure that commends itself for its strength. The explanation must be found principally in the fact that the bureaucratic type of organisation gives rise to certain tendencies that pervert its purpose. Some of its strength—and in extreme cases all of it—is drained off constantly by vices that paradoxically spring from virtues.

In trying to spot the symptoms of the organisational ailment widely called bureaucracy, it may be best to go back to the main characteristics of the bureaucratic type of organisation as outlined in the preceding section. Let us begin again with hierarchy, in the sense of a scheme of interlocking superior-subordinate relationships. It was said earlier that such a scheme is singularly well suited to make all those within even a large organisation move as one body. Things go in channels, as the insider expresses it—that is, in channels of command or control. The things that flow down in these channels are orders, and the things that flow up are either responses to orders or raw materials for still further orders, such as reports on conditions which may call for guidance or proposals for action to be taken higher up. But the very efficacy of control, including the way in which it shapes the attitudes of all participants, inevitably carries with it a loss of mental flexibility. A conveyer-belt psychology spreads throughout the organisation like a curse.

Hierarchy as Deadening Influence

This loss of mental flexibility takes many different forms. For one thing, those within the organisation may be so overawed by orders that they do not move unless explicitly directed. Adoption of this point of view, moreover, adds to the convenience of the participants, especially if a special effort is needed to explain to the superior each instance in which action was taken without direction. In such a setting, personal initiative is not encouraged. Doing things on his own may in fact expose the "eager beaver" to sharply critical reaction. As a counterpart, orders may not be questioned by those meant to carry them out even though it is clear to them that the situation under their eyes requires a different solution. In addition, hierarchy can stimulate a division of those within the organisation into strata or layers which come to function as particular interest groupings, each with its own work outlook and its different degree of allegiance to the organisational purpose.

As a result, when there is no bond between them, it becomes perfectly all right for the subordinate to let the superior make a fool of himself.

Hierarchy can, therefore, turn into a deadening influence, prone to reinforce set ways and traditional arrangements. The best justification for doing a thing in a particular fashion is that "it is done that way". The traditionalism fostered by hierarchy induces a transfer of personal responsibility to authoritative images. "I was told to do that" is the best of reasons. But the next best is that the boss likes it this way and would so do it himself. There is a civilian counterpart of the tragicomic figure of the British commander-in-chief who on the eve of the charge of the Light Brigade at Balaklava, as with every other strategic or tactical decision, first asked himself how the great Wellington would have done it.

The symptoms of the bureaucratic malady show up also in the assertion or denial of jurisdiction. Assurance of being well prepared to perform certain functions may induce an organisation to advance extravagant claims in support of its presumed monopoly of satisfactory service. In public administration this attitude accounts for the familiar spectacle of bitter wrangles between different departments over which has actual jurisdiction in the matter. Conversely, when the subject is "hot" because of public controversy, each department may fight with equal determination to have another department accept jurisdiction.

Quite the same thing can be observed in the way individuals within an organisation seek to build up their jurisdiction from motives entirely unrelated to the goals of the organisation. Expansion of one's recognised sphere of action brings with it an enlargement of his personal importance within the organisation. Greater personal importance is prized for psychological reasons quite apart from the prospect of gains in formal status or economic benefit such as promotion or a raise in pay. But unless it helps in "empire-building,"everyone may find it best to "stick to his assignments." The bureaucratic fires that shoot up elsewhere need not be noticed, much less attended to, for they singe somebody else.

As a characteristic of the bureaucratic type of organisation, specialization has a multiplying effect upon institutional competence. Each needed specialisation available in the organisation increases its resourcefulness. But one must not overlook the spirit of self-isolation that so often grows spontaneously in the occupational attitude of the specialist. In the sheltered precinct of his specialization he alone knows best; he is, therefore, best satisfied if he can keep out of the way of the formal authority higher up in the organisational structure. Authorities are all too likely, as he sees it, to impose their uneducated will upon him, which he regards as downright interference.

Yet, on his own, the specialist often makes recommendations inadequately related to the particular policies of the organisation of which he is a part. Typically, the specialist strains against having his occupational contribution trimmed to the operating decisions made at the top of the organisation. This explains why in the activities of an organisation the specialist is often happiest when he can concentrate on his "own business," determined not to worry about other things. As far as he can, he will try to get around the demands of the policy-makers in the organisation who press him to come forward with a result to their liking. The same situation arises in the relationships among representatives of different specializations. The economist, for example, concerned with better forecasts of trends, may be anxious to keep the tight-fisted fiscal officer out of his hair, while the fiscal officer tries his best to avoid the personnel director, who wants to talk with him about the agency's need for additional staff.

Disengagement from the Public Interest

Making a living on fixed pay, based upon a schedule largely indifferent to individual performance, can inspire both a desirable determination to do an honest day's work, without demoralizing servility, and an undesirable withdrawal into personal interests at variance with the aims of the organisation. Those within a large bureaucratic organisation are not, as a rule, personally affected by the fluctuating fortunes of the organisation, especially when it enjoys a reputation for institutional immortality. The working force may feel about its part in the organisation as one feels about having a part in the morning and evening ride in a crowded bus. There is no common spirit. One day is like the other. As far as personal exertion is concerned, all one needs to do is to get by.

Despite the superiority that it imparts to the bureaucratic type of organisation, the drive for rationality which is guaranteed by it may have a negative effect when it stimulates self-sufficiency. Rationality is linked not only to a tested methodology of analysis but also to an objective point of view. Objectivity in examining issues, as an occupational habit, puts value on a retreat from active partisanship. Indeed, in the realm of public administration the career bureaucracy can serve as permanent instrument of government under conditions of changing party control only by acknowledging and practicing the virtue of neutrality. Such neutrality is the premise for loyal support of any lawful government. On the other hand, neutrality may foster a personal disengagement from any kind of political choice, including even the difference between constitutional and unconstitutional means or ends in the actions of the government of the day.

Thus the career bureaucracy, presuming to be rational instead of partisan, may come to show callousness in matters of constitutional principle, disdain for party contest, unresponsiveness to changing political leadership, arrogance in trusting its own judgment, and, ultimately, even a yen for trying its own hand at governing when there is political stalemate. The principle of institutional neutrality can be perverted into a neutralization that commits the civil servant to nothing but astute defense of his public status.

Bureaucracy as Characteristic of Modern Government

Rise of "Big Government"

Much of this book deals with bureaucracy in the sense of a type of organisation utilized in the conduct of public administration and with the mode of operation of the bureaucratic type as well. As shown in the preceding section, however, the bureaucratic type of organisation is not easily separated from its pathology. For this reason more will have to be said about bureaucracy as an ailment of organisation. The two interrelated aspects, in turn, cannot be fully understood unless they are placed in the context of modern government, the kind of government characteristic of predominantly industrial societies. The conspicuous thing about this kind of government is that within less than a century it has developed into "big government," pushed into a role supporting the machine economy and heavily concentrated populations. True enough, the pace of development, affected by political traditions and economic necessity, was not the same in different nations; but ultimately government everywhere had to lend an organizing hand to stabilize the emerging industrial order.

Pressure and Counterpressure

"Big government" is the result of many things associated with industrialisation and urbanisation. Something had to be done to reduce the unequities as well as the instabilities of the industrial drive in the raw. Something had to be done to make it possible for massed populations to exist in the congested city. Something had to be done to sustain social security as a protection of breadwinners and as an economic defense of purchasing power. Government was, therefore, induced to undertake numerous activities that an agrarian order and rural living had been able to do without. In fact, the urban structure of todays' industrial society costs the general taxpayer many times the amount he contributes in support of the rural way of living. But the expansion of public functions, though promoted by the push toward industrialization, has also carried into rural life many new services as well as many improvements in old ones.

Considering the nature of the development, it is ironic that the most clamorous opposition to the expansion of governmental functions has come from the spokesmen of free enterprise, mainly the new industrial leadership. Both regulatory and service activities initiated by government have been denounced as "creeping socialism" and the like, with little regard for the fact that these functions, by and large, have been assumed reluctantly to mend the holes torn in the social fabric by the industrial revolution.

Whose Government?

As we saw earlier, statistical evidence tends to demonstrate that one of the strongest periodic prompters in the growth of "big government" has been calamity. Adversity apparently not only drags government to the centre of the stage but also keeps it there after the emergency has ended. Is it to be assumed that public preference and the aims of statesmen, even under popular rule, may not challenge prevailing views about what is proper for government until the country is in the grip of an emergency? Or is it to be assumed that electorates acquiesce in "bigger government" once it has got bigger and that nothing much can be done about it? Each question is disturbing in its implications. The growth of governmental functions appears to have much to do with concepts of what the industrial order requires for its own continued health. It evidently has less to do with ideas about distributive justice and the happiness of men.

If big government were to be rejected categorically, the rejection would extend equally to the whole of the industrial foundation of our civilization. This is like setting the clock back. Indeed, for the large body of men big government has increased the worth of the state precisely because of the enlarged public concern with their welfare. But big government is good only in proportion to its actual performance. From this angle the question of general efficiency in public administration is something in which today almost everybody has a personal stake.

Changing Group Positions

If the enlarged presence of government in the affairs of industrial society be called bureaucracy, then bureaucracy is as much the shadow of industrial society as is big government itself. Conversely, if big government is to be condemned, then bureaucracy must be condemned for the same reason, irrespective of whether or not the administrative system in fact shows integrity and efficiency. On such grounds we might even insist—as some spokesmen of private business have—that an efficient civil service is the worst, because good men in government offices are not easily pushed over.

But it should not be assumed that the lines of partisanship can be drawn so simply. Political attacks upon bureaucracy—in particular, the bureaucracy—have often come from those who sensed in it an unsympathetic predisposition toward them. Thus such attacks have frequently come from organised labour. Moreover, depending on time and circumstance, private business may actually look upon government as its partner or its defender. Upto the Civil War, for instance, American government, especially in the eastern seaboard states, was deeply involved in economic planning and the promotion of private enterprise. Henry Clay's "American System" was meant to rest squarely on an alliance between government and private business. Needless to say, under such auspices it did not matter how big government was as long as it was big enough to do its part. In somewhat the same manner, private business generally looks upon government with less critical eyes when government acts in the role of a large-scale dispenser of contracts. This is true of wartime conditions, for example, when government becomes the key customer of private enterprise. But we may also notice the spirit of partnership in the contractual relationships between government and private business in the vast and expanding field of research and technical application, in its present-day scope the most recent addition to big government.

Censure of the Executive Branch

Big government, with its stress upon continuing administrative functions, gives increasing importance to the executive branch as the logical place to lodge these functions and to provide general direction and co-ordination for them. As a result, the civil service has physically grown in a substantial manner. These two interrelated facts have furnished grist for the mills of those who regard both as adverse to their own interests.

On the one hand, the executive power has been portrayed as usurping control of the government and outflanking the position of the legislative branch. There is superficial plausibility to the charge, but the facts, for the most part, are not on its side. In particular, this line of criticism neglects the enhanced importance of the legislature in supplying statutory guidance to the executive establishment and in imposing political accountability upon it. Moreover, it was usually the legislative branch itself which gave the executive power the task to assume leadership in the formulation of basic policy proposals so as to make for more effective legislative consideration and action.

The civil service, on the other hand, could be presented, with some poetic license, as a hydra growing new heads faster than anybody could hope to cut them off. The permanent officialdom has often been prictured as engaged in unproductive routines when not indulging in its favourite sport of bullying the helpless citizen, as both intolerably meddlesome and bogged down in inertia. This seemed to come to light in the limited ability of large-scale organisations to give adequate attention to the human aspects of each particular case to be dealt with. The magnifying effects can easily be imagined when it is borne in mind that it has become a common experience for contemporary man to be a frequently-unwilling visitor in government offices.

Bureaucracy as Indictment of Modern Government

A New Absolutism?

As modern government was called upon to widen the range of its responsibilities in the interest of industrial society, it extended its administrative operations to the point of touching ever larger parts of the public. As a result, the impact of today's career bureaucracy has become one of the familiar facts of life for the ordinary citizen. But some obstinate questions remain unanswered. Are we on the road to a new absolutism more ruthless than the old, which was often moderated by the philosophical currents of enlightenment? Can we be sure that nations or leaders can maintain control over the growth of government?

It is no acknowledgement of defeat or despair to allow such questions to stand instead of brushing them off as pointless. As an act of caution it may profit us to doubt when doubts alert the mind to dangers that otherwise might be ignored. Blind confidence that "things will work out somehow" is not a good guide. On the other hand, inability to answer large questions conclusively need not lead to a loss of that sturdy confidence that stems from mature reflection and an experimental approach to practical problems.

Effects of Reckless Criticism

It is quite a different matter to indict modern government for alleged encroachment upon inalienable liberties. The central premise of this denunciation appears to be the liberty claimed by some to ignore the obligations of man toward fellow man, especially in the pursuit of private gain. Thus there will be those who use "bureaucracy" as a word from the dictionary of contempt. Whether viewed as political power that somehow got into the wrong hands or as a conspiracy of irresponsible officeholders eager for complete control, "bureaucracy" then adds upto only one thing—a damnation of government for its capacity of enforcing change unwanted by the critic or of resisting change demanded by him.

The indictment flung at modern government for embodying and promoting bureaucracy is addressed to the contemporary role of government in the life of industrial society. It has little reference to the institutional characteristics and the working processes of public administration, but it has done much to lower the esteem in which government is held. It has exerted a detrimental influence upon both the performance of the administrative system and the behaviour of civil servants.

References

1. Max Weber (1864-1920) has gained a growing following in the United States as well as in other countries, although some of his concepts and conclusions have caused critical comments, in part on the basis of assumptions about his purposes and intent; a considerable body of his writings is now available in English. One should add, however, that the line of prophets of the "administrative state" includes other great names, such as Italy's Gaetano Mosca, whose work has not yet found the recognition it merits, perhaps because he is often placed in the company of the "elitarians"—the school of thought which, like "honest" John Adams, Jefferson's most profound antagonist, sees nature or the "facts of life" in alliance with government by the few, by an elite. For a brief appraisal of Mosca's theories see Fritz Morstein Marx, "The Bureaucratic State," *Review of Politics*, I (1939), 457 ff.

   In the United States one of the foremost pioneers to focus attention upon the administrative structure of modern government was Frank J. Goodnow (1859-1939). Turning to the next generation of American scholarship, we must name Leonard D. White, who has further added to the esteem earned by his research in his recent studies devoted to the history of federal administration. In the sphere of comparative government a landmark was set by Herman Finer with the publication in 1932 of his *Theory and Practice of Modern Government*, including an admirable treatment of the background as well as the significance of public administration. Carl J. Friedrich's contribution in this area has been equally outstanding and influential, as has Arnold Brecht's. In the sphere of the sociological theory of bureaucracy Robert K. Merton has done distinguished work, and the number of those worthy of mention has considerably increased during the last few decades.

4

Approaches to Public Service Adaptation

I

Introduction

The purpose of this section is to open discussion on the topic "Adaptation Strategies for the Public Administration—Strategies and Institutions." The kernel of this discussion is to probe what fundamental condition or set of conditions ought to underpin a strategy for public sector adaptation so that it may be successful. In order that the discussion should be as comprehensive as possible. I have interpreted the topic in a broad and fairly fundamental sense. However, the chapter is not designed to be a comprehensive and detailed coverage of the nature of and need for public service change nor of the prerequisites for effective public sector adaptation. Also, it should not be regarded as a framework within which all the discussion in our session is contained. We will be dealing with the subject in the context of democratic government.

The issues referred to are mainly those which have been raised and debated in the context of the public service change programmes of a number of countries with which we have been associated. They are also issues which, to one degree or another, have surfaced in various international discussions on public service adaptation.

Before dealing with what adaptation strategies and institutional requirements are desirable for effective public sector change it will be necessary to consider the nature and purpose of what change is likely to be required. It is obvious that the choice of basic strategy for public service adaptation will be influenced by the nature and extent of what change is required. What needs to be changed will depend, in turn, upon a variety of considerations. Thus, in this chapter we will be focusing on three key questions or areas of analysis. They are :

(i) what factors or considerations are likely to influence both the kind of adaptation which may be necessary in public administration and the basic strategy which is likely to be required before effective change can be realized?

(ii) in consequence, what critical features of public administrations are likely to be in need of change/adaptation?

(iii) against the background of these two questions or areas of analysis, what is likely to be required in a strategy to bring about the needed change or adaptation?

Consideration Likely to Influence Both the Adaptation Requirements and Choice of Strategy to Accomplish Change

I see five areas of consideration which may influence and shape both the adaptation requirements of public services and the choice of strategy which will be required to accomplish this adaptation effectively. These areas are not mutually exclusive; there is a degree of overlap between them. They are :

First consideration : The environment within which public administration operates.

Second consideration : Some general trends in society and in community perception of public administration which are likely to give rise to the need for adaptation in public administrations.

Third consideration : The key roles of public administration.

Fourth consideration : Some problems which arise in the effective discharge of its central roles by the public administration.

Fifth consideration : Various difficulties in the way of public service change programmes.

I believe that, when combined, the overall effect of these five areas of consideration is that in many public administrations some fundamental readjustment rather than minor continuing institutional fine-tuning is required; and that this can only be accomplished effectively if there is on-going and visible political commitment to and central government institutional responsibility for the adaptation programmes. In saying this we do not wish to ignore or diminish the need for on-going adaptation of public administrations to meet changing requirements and situations. A continuing fine-tuning or adjustment process is obviously required, and it is important that it be undertaken effectively. However, a strategy for day-to-day adaptation only will in large measure be indigenous to various agencies and will hardly be sufficient to accomplish the fundamental readjustment I refer to. Whereas, a strategy designed to cope with the fundamentals can, we submit, also have a built-in dimension designed to deal with the need for on-gong adjustment.

To expose some of the issues which arise under each of these considerations I would now like to take them one by one and expand upon them.

First Consideration : Environment within which Public Administration Operates

The environment within which public administration operates and the relationship of the public administration to that environment is an intangible but, nevertheless, important determinant of the pace and direction of public sector change and of the strategy which is likely to be required to accomplish effective change. It is obviously a very wide subject and all I attempt here is to raise some points which are of immediate relevance. Our starting point is that the public sector, in democracies, operates under the aegis of elected representatives of the community; its prime operating purpose is to serve that community. Most communities are at once disinterested and interested in the functioning of their public administrations. While the public sector may appear to be a self-contained and almost self-deterministic management entity, ultimately it is not so—certainly not so at the boundaries of its advance and development. The environment for public sector development is very much conditioned by the sense of community purpose within which it operates and by the linkage which its political controllers have with that community. Insofar as public service change goes, this linkage tends to be of a conservative nature. For instance, in many democracies fundamental public sector change which is likely to impact upon the role and functioning of ministers (as elected members of the government) or perhaps upon the distribution of powers and functions below the national levels will not readily be decided upon by members of the government or by the government itself without first obtaining 'feedback' from the community—perhaps through a referral of the matter to Parliament. In effect this means that all far-reaching or fundamental public service adaptation has a parliamentary/political dimension operating on behalf of the community.

Second Consideration : Some General Trends in Society and in Community Perception of the Public Service which are Likely to Give Rise to the Need for Adaptation in Public Administration

The ability of governments to perform well, and indeed to survive, over a period of time will depend, partly, on their ability to fulfil the demands which society makes upon them at a given time and to influence these demands. This requires of governments an ability to formulate in advance and anticipate policies of relevance to the demands of society and to adapt their policies in the medium-term to take account of changes in these demands. It also requires of governments an ability to deliver these policies, in programme form, to society. A government served by a public administration which has a weak and cumbersome system for formulating and implementing policy cannot expect to meet this requirement satisfactorily. This situation is compounded by the fact that societal and community requirements of government are changing constantly. The relationship of government to society, likewise, is changing. These changes give rise to some general trends which call for adaptation in public administrations. I wish to refer here to some of these trends which are evident nowadays so that perhaps we can arrive at some general understanding of what adaptations may be required within public administrations. The broad trends which we wish to highlight are as follows (the other in which I have listed them need not necessarily designate their importance or relative priorities) :

1. *The increasing complexity of society and the growing realisation or acceptance of this complexity for government operations :* Nowadays, policies formulated under the aegies of governments do not automatically fall within the confines of any one sector. There is a need to take account of interactions between sectors which have in earlier times been self-contained and thus dealt with separately : Also, there is a need in various cases to introduce new sectors or dimensions which did not exist previously (perhaps to reflect the changing values of society or its higher sensitivity as a result of increasing levels of education). This leads to a situation where the policy formulation process is becoming increasingly more complex and it is very often necessary to trace or project the consequences of various policies in areas other than those at which they are primarily aimed or from which they have arisen.

In addition, there is the growing experience amongst governments of international interdependence. Many policy areas nowadays facing governments, such as monetary, economic and trade systems, communications, environmental pollution and maritime exploitation, require solutions of an international nature. National policy making capacities are being required increasingly to develop their activities within the context of international commitments and norms. This requires more flexible procedures and also procedures which will be able to cope with the conflict which can arise between growing international interdependence on the one hand and the realisation of internal national policy objectives, on the other. It requires systems and procedures under national governments which can carry and rationalize the interests of national governments with those thrown up by international interaction. This trend has implications for the policy formulating and policy decision-making activities of governments.

2. *Diminishing understanding by electorate of the full implications of government policies :* Hand-in-hand with the increasing complexity of policy issues which fail to be catered for by government action is the decreasing ability of the average elector to grasp and understand fully these complexities. Consequently, much of what is being developed by governments in the name of electorates is being allowed to happen on the basis of an act of faith by various electors. This leads to a diminution of the situation in a democratic system which holds that the electorate should be able to evaluate

a government through an awareness and appraisal of the results of that government's actions while in power. For instance, important results may come about from a policy decision n areas such as environmental and educational policies many years after that decision has been taken, thus leaving the elector with no chance to make his views known within the time limits and to the group responsible. There are broad implications for public service adaptation here. They have to do with two broad areas : first,with ensuring that the machinery of government is equipped to ensure full consideration of both the short-term and longer-term consequences of various policies—particularly when the political system is inclined to press for short-term solutions which correspond with a particular electoral cycle; second, with the capacity of the public administration to articulate adequately the various implications, both short- and long-term, of complex policy issues so that these can be communicated adequately to the electorate by the politicians.

3. *Apparent divergence between the policies and objectives of government and the needs of society* : The situation may arise from time to time in certain countries where some sections of society believe that government and the political system are not responsive to their needs and do not offer meaningful choices about the matters which concern them most. Needless to mention this is important and it behoves government to deal with the matter—either to correct it if it has occurred or to guard against it. The relevance of this to public service adaptation arises from its implications for communication and dialogue between government and the community. It has implications for the flow of information between government and society and *vice versa;* this is turn, of course, has implications for the structures for policy making, the consultative procedures which are associated with policy formulation and planning, and the methods and effectiveness of the systems used to disseminate information on various policies to the public. Related to this matter is the demand which is being made in some cases for a more real involvement of the public in the formulation of policy than is provided by the conventional political system. This has implications for governments in relation to the nature and purpose of the institutions for discharge of the functions of government at sub-national levels.

4. *The increasing range of government responsibilities* : Public administrations have historically been responsible for the provision of goods and services where the mechanisms of the free market are not interested or are considered unable to produce the desired results. These responsibilities tend to grow and expand as a result of many influences—not the least of which is the increasing concern with the distribution of income and resources within societies in support of groups such as the elderly and unemployed or unemployable, which lack economic bargaining power. This implies that an increasing range of social demands must be met through the political/governmental system rather than the private economic system. For whatever reason, it is almost a world-wide experience that the responsibilities of governments have been increasing both in terms of their range and depth. This is leading to rapid growth in the scale, complexity and costs of public administration and in the need for many more public administrators with a wide variety of expertise and skills. Given finite resources there is thus an increasing need for public administrations to operate more effectively, efficiently, and productively. Matters such as optimal resource allocation, cost-effective programme choice, efficient productive and cost-effective public sector operations are of paramount importance and will be increasingly so.

The four general trends just listed will, when combined, have important implications for public sector adaptation in the areas of :

— structures, institutions, and expertise for policy formulations;
— institutions and systems for communication and dialogue between government and the community;
— institutional systems, procedures and practises leading to effective productive, and efficient administration.

Third Consideration : Key Roles of Public Administration—Implications for Public Service Adaptation

The organisation, structure, personnel and operating systems of the public service must derive from and be equipped to discharge the key roles of public administration. While the nature, ordering and interaction of the various roles assigned to public administrators is a complex topic, suffice it here to refer simply to the three basic roles of public administration. They are :

1. the formulation of policy on behalf of political decision-takers at various levels;
2. the implementation in an efficient and effective manner of settled policy; and
3. the review and monitoring of the implementation of policy.

These three roles, which can of course be subdivided into several other responsibilities and tasks, are probably the starting point for any evaluation of the need for public service adaptation. They raise many questions with implications for adaptation. For instance, what structural, institutional and personnel requirements are necessary for effective policy formulation? What parts of the public administrative system should be concerned with each of the three roles we have outlined? In particular, what aspects should elected government ministers (and by definition their immediate ministries or departments) be directly responsible for? What can or ought to be farmed out from the direct purview of ministers? Is it possible or desirable to free the senior staff of departments and ministries to concentrate on policy issues by the devolution of the greatest possible volume of executive detail to agencies and executive units? If so, is this a desirable development? What review, monitoring, and co-ordinative mechanisms, operating on behalf of the collective government, should exist? What operating systems and conditions will bring about the most effective and efficient implementation of various public service programmes to achieve the aims of settled policy?

Obviously the answers to all of these questions would give rise to many detailed studies and analyses. My point in raising them here is to daw attention to the fact that the effective discharge of the roles of the public service requires adaptation and change not only at the levels of individual agencies but also at the highest levels of policy formulation and political decision-taking, and in horizontal and vertical directions in relation to public service ministries and agencies. The following section will outline further aspects of this matter.

Fourth Consideration : Some Problems which Arise from the Effective Discharge of the Central Roles of the Public Administration

When one considers the key roles of public administration in further depth, and against the background of the first and second considerations I have raised, it is possible to isolate various problems areas which I believe require public service adaptation in various countries. For the purpose of this paper I have grouped the possible problem areas into four broad bands. They are as follows :

Problem Area 1 : Policy Formulation

I have referred earlier to various issues which arise in connection with policy formulations. So, I will do no more here than pose some basic questions which lead to public service adaptation. They are : How can governments ensure that their critical responsibility for overall policy formulation is adequately catered for? In particular, what is required in order that, in making important strategic decisions, governments can take fully into account the future needs of society and the probable medium to long-term consequences of their action? In many important areas, many years may elapse before major government decisions are fully realised or their impact fully felt. It is very difficult, but yet necessary, for governments to be able to assess through their institutions and personnel what the future needs and values of society are likely to be and how the policies they are now formulating will meet these needs. These questions give rise to three categories having repercussions upon adaptation programmes :

- *(i)* effective institutionalisation of planning procedures and systems;
- *(ii)* the provision of appropriate expertise for policy formulation and planning; and
- *(iii)* the adjustment of administrative responsibilities so as to allow ministers and other senior government officials more time to consider and perhaps be concerned mainly with major policy issues.

Problem Area 2 : Co-ordination

There is in all governments a need to have on-going co-ordination on behalf of the government as a whole on matters such as planning and finance. This tends to be made more complicated today, as mentioned earlier, by the tendency for the policy and programme areas of government to cut across various functional boundaries which grew up in earlier and less complex times. A problem which arises as a result is how governments, through their structures and operating systems, can better co-ordinate the activities of their various departments and refocus these as required to deal with problems which extend across certain departmental boundaries or affect the government as a whole. An important consideration in this area is the distribution, at the political level, of functions of government over various ministers. Another important consideration is the question of what links and relationships ought to exist between the "line"ministries and agencies responsible for carrying through programmes in various policy areas, and the central ministries responsible for the government overview (including the processes through which plans are synthesized and decided upon and resources are raised, budgeted, allocated and controlled). The task of co-ordination has not been made easier by *(i)* the need growing for more specific consultation by government with the social partners, particularly the employer organisations and trade unions; and *(ii)* the demands being made by various communities for more decision-making at local levels which raises the question of what the distribution of functions of government should be at sub-national levels (regional, local and community for example) in order to achieve the best balance between centralized and decentralized policy-making and implementation.

Problem Area 3 : Public Programmes—Choice and Efficiency in Implementation

There is the perennial and increasing problem of demand for government services and programmes exceeding, insofar as resources are concerned, the supply. This presents a problem for governments in relation to management of public expenditure in the face of a demand for government activities and output which is growing faster than available revenue. This problem area has obvious implications for many areas of public adaptation. For instance it requires, within the public service, a managerial capacity backed up by appropriate expertise which will :

— improve the mix of public sector programmes so that outmoded or outdated programmes are eliminated or at least phased out and existing on-going programmes are accurately focused on the needs and demands of the community;
— ensure that scarce public resources are not used on programmes which, for whatever reason, do not achieve their objectives;
— improve the efficiency with which resources of all kinds are used on the actual processes of governments themselves, particularly in those areas where goal-oriented performance indicators do not exist.

This managerial capacity will require improved procedures for planning and implementing programmes; adequate means of assessing their effectiveness; better management systems to control their progress; improved procedures for setting priorities and for the identification and discontinuation of ineffective or obsolete programmes.

Problem Area 4 : Personnel and Expertise

Personnel development and personnel management are vital elements in a strategy for public service adaptation. The effectiveness and efficiency of the public service very often depends upon the calibre of its personnel; institutional solutions will only be effective if adequate personnel exist within them. Both specialist and management skills are required. Nowadays an important component of personnel management within the public service is the increasing role which organised labour plays in agreeing upon various courses of action to be pursued. This, in many cases, extends the dialogue on change between management and staff outside of the immediate ministry or agency environment.

Fifth Consideration : Some Difficulties in the Way of Public Service Change Programmes

It is desirable, before one refers specifically to the key strategy to be adopted for public sector adaptation, that account is also taken of difficulties which may exist in the way of public service change programmes. In the course of this short paper it is not possible to do more than indicate that the process of change is invariably slow and difficult; it has to encounter and overcome many difficulties. Amongst the various difficulties which may be encountered in various public adaptation programmes the following are important :

(i) The Reconciliation of Administrative Desiderata with the Political Dimension :

Many of the problems we have been sketching lead to the need for a review and change in the distribution of functions over various ministries. While the distribution of functions between ministries can be viewed as an administrative matter, the identification of the ministry and minister means that the distribution is also an act of distribution of power at the political level. Neat administrative solutions are, therefore, not always possible. Also, even with agreement as to distribution at political level, it is difficult to formulate meaningful goals and objectives, let alone establish clearly the main purpose of a department which constantly has an organic and adaptive relationship with a wide range of society. There is, therefore, an innate tendency in public service organisations to resist a precise definition of objectives and this factor raises great difficulties in attempts to assign roles and measure organisational effectiveness.

(ii) The Need for a Constant Stimulus for Change from Outside in Public Service Organisation :

In many countries the desire for public service adaptation begins with the setting up of a "reform committee" and the subsequent publication of its report. The desire for change reaches a high point around this time but quickly diminishes. There is a constant requirement to revitalize this stimulus, not least at the political levels. The creation of specific machinery—but closely linked to central government—for conceiving of and implementing innovation in the fields of organisation and personnel development is of fundamental importance.

(iii) The Reinforcement of Normal Resistance to Planned Change in Periods of Environmental Stress :

While there is a growing body of theory and practice on resistance to change, one matter which remains as an important consideration is that, as the demands of the environment increase through, for instance, the need to counter increasing inflation, to cope with the energy crisis, or to reduce persistent unemployment, the organisational response is to reinforce existing institutions and behaviour rather than accept planned change.

Critical Features of Public Administrations which are Likely to be in Need of Change

I wish now, on the basis of the preceding analysis, to draw attention to certain features of public administrations which may be in need of change. I do so not to discuss in depth the nature of each of these features, but to form a basis for reaching some conclusions on what central adaptation strategy will be required. Not all of these features, perhaps, will be in need of change in any one country. They are, however, a cross section of the various changes that may be required in a wide-range of public administrations and countries. I wish to isolate five features. They are as follows :

1st Feature :

The nature and extent of the linkage and relationship which ought to exist between parliament and the executive—and through the executive to the public administration. This includes the answerability of ministers to parliament, the field of public accountability and parliamentary review mechanisms.

2nd Feature :

The role and functioning of ministers as members of the elected government/executive. This includes the desirability or need for the devolution of responsibilities from the direct purview of ministers and the direct role and responsibilities of ministries *vis-a-vis* agencies.

3rd Feature :

The distribution of functions at the level of Central Government. This includes both a political and administrative dimension—political in relation to the distribution of powers as between ministers, and administrative in relation to the appropriate grouping of functions for organisational purposes. It also includes the relationships which ought to exist between line ministries and central staff ministries.

4th Feature :

The allocation of powers and functions of government at sub-national levels, *i.e.,* below the level of national government, particularly at regional, local and community levels. This includes the sharing of power by governments with tiers of elective administrative responsibility below the level of Central Government.

5th Feature :

The internal structure, organisation, operating systems and expertise requirements within ministries. This includes those considerations which apply to the efficient and effective internal management and organisation of ministries and agencies.

When we discuss, in an international forum such as this, the question of managing change in the public administration it is important to present the change area in its widest perspective before attempting to draw conclusions on what strategy should be required to bring about the public service change. Thus, the five features I have outlined range over the full spectrum of public administration as I perceive it—from Parliament through government and the executive to the community. My understanding of the forces at work, within democracies, in relation to these features leads me to conclude that public administrative change of this nature is such that it is likely to be accomplished effectively only if there is on-going and visible political commitment to the adaptation programme.

What is Likely to be Required in a Strategy to Bring About the Needed Public Sector Change or Adaptation

The precise strategy for accomplishing administrative adaptation will, naturally, be shaped by the realities, mores and customs of the particular country for which it is intended. This notwithstanding I think we can generalize in relation to public administrations for democratic governments and say that one can do very little in fundamental public sector adaptation without impinging upon the role and functioning of ministers, their relationship to Parliament, and the distribution of power amongst and below them. All these matters have important political dimensions at the level of parliament and Central Government. In addition, a dimension external to the public service agencies themselves also occurs in the form of, for instance, organised labour and its reaction to change. Many attributes are required, of course, for effective realisation and implementation of the change— not the least of which is the capacity and perception of those officials responsible for orchestrating and implementing the change programme. Of all of them, the single most important attribute, however, is the need for visible and on-going political commitment to the programme. The effective change agent or agents will almost certainly either come from a political source or, at least, be reinforced by it. The basic strategy for change needs to involve, at the very least, government but preferably parliament as well. This may be difficult to achieve since, from the parliamentary or political points of view, public service change tends to be a residual matter since the community in the form of the electorate tends not to demand change and output directly from the public service adaptation programme. On-going political commitment needs to be more than an occasional exhortation or statement of intent from government sources. It needs to include a number of important requirements such as, for example, the following :

— the designation of a specific government minister to have responsibility for initiating and managing public service change and the provision of adequate strategically placed institutional machinery and personnel for this purpose;
— the specific fostering of parliamentary interest through debates on appropriate occasions;
— a continuing overview of the adaptation programme on behalf of parliament (indirectly) and government (directly) by some group or source which is independent of the permanent administration;
— the programme for administrative change to be an integral part of the wider planing and decision-taking systems of government so that implementation of the change programme is not seen as a separate "once-off" event outside the normal government decision-taking mechanism.

A basic question is whether a strategy for public adaptation of the type discussed can be developed and implemented successfully without these four requirements. We believe that, in democracies, it is highly unlikely that it will.

II

This section focusses on two issues : the problem of reforming administration so that the bureaucracy in its political decision-making is more firmly responsible to the elected representatives of the people and more responsive to community needs and values, and the interlocking problem of the politics of the reform process itself.

Where a government announces its intention to undertake a reform programme, its purposes are usually explained in terms of the need for greater efficiency. The process of reform, apart from the stress on efficiency, is usually described in value-neutral terms. The programme or the enquiry, it is claimed, will result in the job being done better or more quickly or more cheaply.

However, if one looks more closely at the reasons for the establishment of such programmes and enquiries, it is clear that underlying the urge to change the administration, there is a dissatisfaction not so much with the way in which decisions are carried out, as with the decisions themselves. The 'hidden agenda' of most reforms is to ensure that different decisions are taken and different outcomes in the community result.

Thus, most of the major enquiries into reform of the government machinery in OECD countries in the past twenty years have been initiated after a change in government. The new government declares itself dissatisfied with the efficiency of the civil service, but in fact is equally or more dissatisfied that the decisions made in the civil service do not appear sufficiently to reflect the new government's policies and priorities.

Proposed changes in organisation design, changes in the groups of people recruited into the bureaucracy and changes in mobility, promotion or reward systems cannot be considered purely on technical or managerial grounds. Such changes result in different decisions being taken about the allocation of public resources. They result in shifts in power within the bureaucracy and in gains and losses among different groups, both within the bureaucracy and in the community at large—in short, in the re-allocation of public resources and benefits.

This is not to say that there are no managerial or technical reforms that are needed in public administration or that a great deal of reform of this nature has not taken place. My aim is to stress, however, that many of the really important reforms of administration are basically political in character and that this political aspect is often hidden because the political nature of administration is hidden. This results in confusion about the true nature of reform and often leads to its defeat.

This paper, then, seeks to look at the political role of the bureaucracy, both in the exercise of administrative power and in the relationship of the bureaucracy to administrative reform. In brief, the paper outlines the essentially political role played by the bureaucrat, whether consciously or unconsciously, in the modern State and the widespread breakdown of the mechanisms of accountability and responsibility back to the people. The paper goes on to argue that administrative reform movements have become increasingly concerned over the past decade with this problem, but since such administrative reform is one aspect of social reform and results in a redistribution of power as well as re-allocation of public resources and benefits, those who stand to lose by the process may be expected to resist it and will be in a particularly powerful position to do so.

Politics and Administration

Questions concerning the relationship between politics and administration and the role of the public servant in a democracy are, of course, time-honoured themes of public administration. The problems raised are, however, far from solved and indeed, have become more pressing. The growth in the range, complexity and pervasiveness of government functions has meant that democratic control of bureaucratic activity has become at once more important and more difficult. Government has moved into virtually every aspect of economic and social life. This is a growth that, despite the nostalgia of some conservative critics, has continued in response to popular demand and has been carried out with popular approval. It carries with it, however, a number of problems not fully resolved, one of which is how such increasing power of government is to be exercised responsibly, and how those who exercise it are to be held accountable. In simple terms, our everyday lives are increasingly affected by government and what government does is increasingly determined by bureaucracy and bureaucrats.

Discussion of these issues has been confused by widespread adherence to the convention that politics and administration are separable and separate. In countries adhering to the Westminster system it remains official doctrine; in the United States it was associated with the name of Woodrow Wilson and the view of the bureaucracy as a machine ready to be used by whatever group of politicians was democratically elected; in some European countries it is associated rather with the view that public issues can be resolved in terms of some objective standard of justice or of legality or of technical practicality.

The adherence to this convention in public discussion has been little shaken by the fact that the distinction has for many years been rejected in the theoretical and academic literature. As one author wrote nearly forty years ago :

> "...The concrete patterns of public policy formulation and execution reveal that politics and administration are not two mutually exclusive boxes, or absolute distinctions, but that they are two closely linked aspects of the same process. Public policy, to put it flatly, is a continuing process, the formation of which is inseparable from its execution. Public policy is being formed as it is being executed, and it is likewise being executed as it is being formed. Politics and administration play a continuous role in both formulation and execution. . . ."[1]

The framework for decision-making that administrators develop and the decisions they have to take, do much to determine the distribution of goods, services and benefits that the government provides. The questions which they are asked to advise on, analyse or decide, are questions of choice between courses of action which alter the well-being of different groups in the community. On such questions claims of objectivity can have little meaning because, by their very nature, they require value judgments. Thus, on the same issues and on the basis of the same facts, different departments, all staffed by 'objective' and 'impartial' public servants, will fight for very different solutions with very different effects on the community.

Administrative decisions then, are based not just on fact, but also on the values of the decision-maker or of the institution (often incorporated in the informal rules of the institution) in which he or she works. This value component of administration is essentially political and cannot be treated as technical or scientific.

In the formulation and execution of public policy the role of the administrator is little different to that of the elected politician. The two are distinguished by the different arenas in which they perform and the different resources (in terms of expertise, time and legitimacy) that they bring to the performance of their roles, rather than by the types of decisions they participate in reaching.

It has, however, served the purposes of both administrators and politicians in many countries to maintain the myth of the separation of politics and administration (and thus, incidentally, obscure the purposes of administrative reform). The myth allows politicians to concentrate on electoral politics and other aspects of their roles. It allows administrators to engage in politics and in policy-making without being held accountable politically for the outcomes of their actions.

Administrative Responsibility

Nevertheless, as awareness has increased of the important decision-making role of the administrator, reformers have become increasingly concerned about the mechanisms by which the administrator is held responsible to the public for those decisions. The problem of responsibility is, of course, not a new one. Writers on administration have often asked how in a democracy, those who make government decisions or perform governmental actions, are to be made responsible or answerable to the electorate for those decisions or actions (or inaction). Or to put it in the obverse way : how is the public to exercise control over actions which are taken in its name? In respect of elected politicians the answer is relatively simple (though both incomplete and unsatisfactory) : it lies in the ballot box at election time. In respect of permanent officials it is more complex. In most OECD countries it has lain in two mechanisms, though the precise constitutional and administrative arrangements and the balance between the two mechanisms has varied greatly. Firstly, there has been a reliance on the authority ultimately exercised over senior officials by elected representatives (and then, in turn, on the hierarchical arrangements through which senior officials exercised authority over the rest of the bureaucracy). Secondly, there have been, in particular in European countries, systems of judicial and administrative tribunals, to which aggrieved citizens could turn for the review of bureaucratic decisions inconsistent with legislation or government policy. The extent of such review has also varied greatly.

Insofar as the first of these mechanisms of control is concerned, the conventional picture of how the bureaucracy fittec into the system of liberal parliamentary democracy may be simplified into a fairly straightforward one. The line of responsibility was clear. The public servant was responsible to the minister, the minister was responsible either to the parliament or, in some cases, to the elected President (in which case the ministry also in some countries had to maintain the confidence of the parliament). The parliament and the President were responsible to the people. The public servant, in theory, had little or no independent power of his own. He was responsible to his minister and the minister, through the elected representatives of the people, was responsible to the people. This is, of course, a much oversimplified characterization. It also clashes with the classical view of a somewhat more independent (almost-quasi-judicial) bureaucracy still evident in some countries —particularly where the establishment of the bureaucracy preceded the formation of the institutions of democratic government. Nevertheless, in an oversimplified form, it is the traditional democratic view of the role of the bureaucracy.

The mechanisms underlying this system of control have, however, become increasingly ineffective. One of the reasons for this lies in the diminished role of representative assemblies or parliament in most Western democracies (the United States being a major exception). This diminished role is most clearly seen in the case of those countries subscribing to the Westminster system of government. When shifting alliances in parliament exercised real influence over the composition of the ministry, it was possible for parliament to extract information on the acts of officials and to enforce some degree of accountability on them through their ministers. However, the party system means that it is now ministers who, through control of the majority party, dominate parliament, not parliament which is the arbiter of a minister's fate. Not only is a government whose party has a majority in parliament virtually secure from parliamentary defeat, regardless of its administrative actions, but the doctrine of ministerial responsibility, once the instrument of administrative accountability, now can be and is used to shield administrative actions from serious parliamentary scrutiny. Ministers are in alliance with their officials in calling upon such conventions as ministerial responsibility and the anonymity of officials, to ensure that parliament's role in the scrutiny of administration becomes more and more limited. In many European countries there has been a similar decline in the power of parliament *vis-a-vis* the bureaucracy, and while the mechanisms differ from country to country (*e.g.* in a number of countries the increase in delegated powers has been an important factor) in nearly every country there has been a reduction in accountability of officials directly or indirectly to parliament. (It is, incidentally, interesting to note that most reform plans aimed at the revival of parliament, begin with a plea for more staff for parliamentarians, that is, a call for a parliamentary bureaucracy to control the executive bureaucracy!)

This has left the minister or Cabinet member as the lynch pin in the system of democratic accountability. After all, it may be argued that he is himself an elected representative or has been directly appointed by an elected representative. It is his function to know and direct what is going on in his administration and then be held accountable for it at election time. This picture of a minister in control of the activities of his department or ministry may have been a realistic one in a limited number of countries in the nineteenth century. The range of government activities for which ministers were responsible was relatively small, the numbers of officials relatively few. It was possible for a minister to be aware of nearly all government activities and he might be expected personally to know the relatively few public servants of any authority who worked in his ministry and what they were doing. These conditions have clearly changed and the weakening of ministerial control over the bureaucracy has moved increasingly to the centre of concern of many administrative reforms.

The relative strengths that ministers (or political executives) and their senior civil servants bring to the decision-making process have often been discussed. On the one hand academic writers tend to stress the strengths that the bureaucrat brings to this relationship. First, there is the simple fact that political executives are so outnumbered ('one person against the vast Department,' as one British Cabinet Minister put it). Secondly, there is the expertise and accumulated knowledge that the bureaucrat, as opposed to the temporary appointee, brings to bear on the subject (again the same minister described the problem graphically in saying : "The danger of the British Civil Service to our democracy lies in its excellence").[2] Third, there is the considerable control that the bureaucrat has over information flows to the minister. Fourth, as against the minister's often shifting commitment to often incompletely articulated policies, there is the bureaucrat's firm adherence to the departmental 'line' or ideology.

On the other hand, public administration practitioners, even when they admit these factors, stress that the minister's imprimatur is required to give any decision legitimacy, and that in any dispute over policy, the political executive has the last word, and the official must accept that last word.

While this latter view might be true (if the political executive has the stamina and perseverance to overcome the bureaucratic obstacles likely to be placed in his path), the question that remains to be asked is how important that last word is. The first word, *i.e.* the setting of the framework in which policy options are formulated and the actual formulation of those options, is usually far more important than which option is chosen. And the setting of that framework is usually in the hands of civil servants. As one former British head of the Treasury has written :

> "Obviously I had a great influence. The biggest and most pervasive influence is in setting the framework within which the questions of policy are raised. We, while I was in the Treasury, had a framework of the economy basically neo-Keynesian. We set the questions which we asked ministers to decide arising out of that framework and it would have been enormously difficult for any minister to change the framework, so to that extent we had great power. I don't think it was used maliciously or malignly. I think we chose that framework because we thought it was the best one going. We were very ready to explain to anybody who was interested, but most ministers were not interested, were just prepared to take the questions as we offered them which came out of that framework without going back into the preconceptions of them."[3]

Similarly the Norwegian budgetary process has been described in the following terms :

> "It is in the nature of the process that the choices of civil servants who collect and analyse the mass of data on which the national budget is constructed are of fundamental importance to the outcome... by allocating to them the prero-

gative of asking questions that need to be answered politically the process enables civil servants to control the direction in which the government's attention moves. Only in a very limited degree to members of the government have the time and motivation to consider areas of the budget about which no questions have been asked...not only do they (civil servants) control the general framework in which decisions are made, but they also define the important questions, influence the direction of politicians' attention, and argue for their proposed solutions with esoteric knowledge that it is difficult to refute."[4]

This is not to say that ministers have no power—they have a great deal, and on some issues bureaucrats have little say. But bureaucrats also exercise very considerable power, and while ministers are held personally democratically accountable for their power, permanent officials are not.

It is important that this political role of officials be recognized. As David Marquand has noted :

"There is nothing odd or distressing in politicians basing their decisions on a value judgment. One of the reasons why it is better to be governed by politicians than by civil servants is that civil servants are apt to disguise their value judgments as judgments of fact. Politicians are slightly more honest about bringing this out into the open."[5]

Whether civil servants do indeed hide their value judgments in this way, or as is more probably the case, more subtly through institutional rules and apparently value-free decision-making processes, it is important to note that their values and political views are not randomly distributed or a statistical reflection of the views of the community as a whole. The Chairman of a recent Royal Commission into Australian Government Administration, in commenting on a career service that since its outset has been regarded as 'politically neutral' and recruited 'on merit,' noted that :

"...the people who compose the bureaucracy...are selected by processes which give greatest weight to qualities most likely to be possessed by those with privileged social background and access to privileged educational institutions. The composition of the bureaucracy, therefore, reflects not the

> structure of Australian society as a whole but that of the already privileged sections of it. The unconscious presumptions which influence its patterns of thought tend, therefore, to lean heavily towards preservation of the status quo."[6]

Studies of other countries indicate that much the same conclusion could be reached throughout most of the OECD.

The view that must be taken of government is that it is led by two elites, one political and one administrative, and a principal concern of major administrative reform efforts in recent years has been to make the latter more responsive to the former. As the above quotation suggests, this is a particularly acute problem for left-of-centre or reform governments. Nearly all of the government MPs on a committee of the United Kingdom House of Commons examining the civil service, supported a minority report which put the problem in the following, somewhat striking, terms :

> "We regard the resolution of the struggle for power between the executive, by which we basically mean the Cabinet, and the bureaucracy, by which we mean those top civil servants who claim to be policy advisers, in favour of political power and authority and against bureaucratic power and authority as a central need of our age. It is part of the struggle for democracy itself."[7]

This concern (or 'struggle') has resulted in proposals for changes in a number of areas to re-inforce the accountability of the administration to the political leadership. One approach has been to try to boost the power of ministers themselves. This may be done, for example, by building up their personal staffs, or restructuring ministerial responsibilities so as to include more elected ministers in the executive, or providing additional support of them while out of office so that they will enter office with a clear commitment to electorally endorsed policies whose administrative feasibility has already been examined.

A second approach is to change the views or flexibility of senior administrators, *e.g.* by giving greater attention to the 'education' of the bureaucracy after the appointment of each new government, by greater flexibility in and government control over the promotion of senior officials ('politicization,' perhaps, of the bureaucracy), though hopefully in a more flexible manner than in Belgium, or by different methods and criteria of administrative recruitment.

A third is by wholesale changes at the senior levels of the bureaucracy after each change of government, on the United States pattern. This undoubtedly provides major support to the elected leadership, but as the practice extends and political leaders must search for high degrees of competence as well as loyalty in their senior appointees, the process can become self-defeating. As one United States writer points out :

> "Presidents have fewer old-style patronage jobs to dispense and more highly qualified political executives to recruit. Yet the very competence and specialized clienteles of political appointees can produce layers of officials who are indistinguishable from the organisation men of the bureaucracy. The more appointees talk about 'their' programmes and agencies, the more a president may worry about controlling government actions that will go down in history under his name."[8]

That is to say, that once the number of political appointees in the bureaucracy (or, for that matter, on personal staffs) grows, they become divorced from the elected person appointing them and develop their own loyalties to the programmes they are administering, their working colleagues and their clients in the community.

Administrative Responsiveness

The problems of ensuring 'responsible' decision-making are not, however, confined to the senior or 'policy-making' levels. Policy is made at all levels of the bureaucracy and decisions at all levels influence the allocation of public resources. The work of middle-ranking or junior civil servants is usually not simply the application of rules to cases, but the difficult interpretation of policy, which in itself is policy-making. At each level of the bureaucracy, the civil servant defines 'policy' as the decisions made at more senior levels and 'administration' as what he or she does. The work now done by the civil service is very different and the methods used are very different from Weber's characterization. This has led to a renewed concern with the 'problem of implementation,' one aspect of which is the problem of ensuring that decisions made by those lower down in the bureaucracy are consistent, at least broadly, with the intentions of those at the top.

One way that has been proposed to meet the problem of accountability at the lower levels of the bureaucracy is to recognize that there are limits on the control that elected representatives can exercise on the bureaucracy, to concentrate this control on the central issues of government (especially budgetary issues) and to devise other means of control over the remainder of the administration. An approach similar to this was put forward by the Royal Commission on Australian Government Administration :

> "The concept of the administration as simply an extension of the capacity of a Minister fully responsible and accountable to Cabinet and to Parliament for matters within his portfolio is unrealistic and misleading. It is necessary, therefore, to acknowledge and delimit the area of responsibility of officials and to establish the means by which they are held accountable for their actions within it."[9]

The second of the traditional mechanisms for ensuring responsible administration referred to above, namely the review by the judiciary or by tribunals, of administrative decisions, does in some ways act as a device to ensure that decisions made by officials dealing with the public are not made in arbitrary disregard of local conditions and are made in keeping with laws passed by or policies determined by the government (which in time has come to mean elected representatives, since the origins of such review in most countries, of course, predate democratic institutions). However, such review mechanisms apply only to individual cases and this is also true of the function of ombudsmen. Many of the most important decisions of officials are not of this nature, *e.g.* decisions on the details of how a particular assistance scheme is to be advertised, administered, accounted for and evaluated may make a very major difference as to which groups of individuals will benefit from it. In any individual case the policies and rules may be applied fairly, but it is in the making of the detailed policies and rules at each level of administration that the administrator's values most intrude and where they may most differ from the community.

Some have suggested that responsibility at the public servant/ client interface, instead of being upward through the hierarchy to the minister or president should, within the confines of broad ministerial policy, be outward to the community that the administrator serves. A wide variety of measures are grouped under the head of increasing responsibility to the community—or at the least, responsiveness to social needs. These include decentralization, and regionalization of administration, reduction in the anonymity of public servants and their participation in public debate, systems of appeals against administrative decisions and various forms of community participation.

A *sine qua non* of such responsibility is, of course, a considerably greater degree of openness than at present exists in most administrations—it is impossible to devise mechanisms for holding officials responsible for secret decisions, the very existence of which is unknown to the public. Officials are anxious that discussions of 'open government' and secrecy should be conducted in terms of efficiency rather than accountability and defend the *status quo* on the grounds of the need for confidentiality if advice is to be given freely and frankly. It is not at all clear that greater openness will have the dire effects predicted, as the long experience of Sweden and the recent experience of the United States indicates, it may result in better decisions being taken. But the desire for secrecy really needs to be seen and evaluated also in terms of the distribution of decision-making power. As Weber noted long ago :

> "Every bureaucracy seeks to increase the superiority of the professionally informed by keeping their knowledge and intentions secret. Bureaucratic administration always tends to be an administration of 'secret sessions' : insofar as it can, it hides its knowledge and action from criticism... . The concept of the "official secret' is the specific invention of bureaucracy, and nothing is so fanatically defended by the bureaucracy as this attitude. . . ."[10]

As important as all the other measures is the present concern for the establishment of a bureaucracy which is more representative of the community it serves. Reformers argue this case not only on the grounds of social justice (i.e. equality of access to employment in the public service and to positions of power) but also on the grounds that a bureaucracy which is representative of the major social groups and classes will make decisions more responsive to their needs. The evidence for this latter belief is mixed, as the socialization pressures of the bureaucracy often overcome the initial allegiance of the bureaucrat to class or social group. It does seem, however, that the socialization pressures to conform to bureaucratic norms and procedures are particularly powerful on a single individual and that where the bureaucracy contains larger numbers of persons from say, disadvantaged groups, they are more likely to act in accordance with the norms of those groups. The demands for a more representative bureaucracy may to a degree be met without major change in existing institutions as overt and systemic discrimination against individuals from currently disadvantaged groups is diminished. Eventually, however, we may see a real clash between the proponents of the need for representativeness and sensitivity to community needs and the upholders of a narrower definition of professional expertise.

Clearly there is a tension between this concept of 'outward responsibility' and the more traditional one of 'upward responsibility.' Unless the area of administrative discretion where the administrator is responsible to the community (or his or her client group) is carefully delineated it could (and does) result in the administrator putting his or her own preferences, or the interest of a special group, ahead of the policy of the government which represents the community as a whole. This objection would have greater force if traditional lines of responsibility were effective; once the current degree of discretion, under the cloak of ministerial responsibility or similar doctrines, is recognized, it seems likely that systems of 'direct' responsibility can be devised which will increase rather than diminish democratic control.

Where many of the proposals for increasing responsibility of administrators, at whatever level, to the populace stop short is in the development of a system of sanctions. To Bentham responsibility was accountability plus liability. The sanction on the elected representative is his or her failure to be re-elected. It is also easy enough to devise sanctions against public servants who on examination (perhaps by an administrative or judicial tribunal) are found to have acted capriciously, arbitrarily, in a deliberately discriminatory manner, or unfairly in a particular case. It is far harder to devise methods of acting against public servants who, in good faith, take decisions which frustrate or delay ministerial policies or are not in keeping with social needs. How are these matters to be judged (excluding such extreme measures as the installation of political cadres in the bureaucracy or the institution of people's courts!) without a complete breakdown in administrative procedures, and what sanctions are appropriate?[11]

In the end, this discussion of the difficulties of increasing the responsibility and responsiveness of the administration suggests that while reform in this area should be pursued, a degree of 'irresponsible' administration may need to be accepted, as some authors have argued for many years. The question, then, is to whom should such power be entrusted? If we wish to pursue a democratic course it would seem that everyone should have opportunity to exercise this power at some stage in their working lives. This would take us away from regarding the bureaucracy as a 'closed shop,' as a career service and regard it instead as a permeable institution in and out of which many people move during their working lives. Public employment has now grown so that it is in excess of 15 per cent of total employment in most OECD countries and in excess of 20 per cent in about one third.[12] This continuing increase must cause a reformulation of recruitment rules that seemed to apply well enough when only one person in twenty was in the government work-force.

The stress on responsive administration can, therefore, take us a long way from traditional concepts. There are, of course, other qualities sought in administration apart from responsibility and responsiveness—in particular professionalism and expertise. The mood in many OECD countries appears to be, however, that the pendulum has swung too far towards an entrenched professional bureaucracy, albeit chosen on the merit principle. Its critics claim that bureaucracy now makes political use of appeals to 'merit' and 'professionalism' (terms which are defined by the bureaucracy in a narrow and self-interested manner) to beat off attacks on its power : the bureaucracy in many countries insists that it alone should determine its own methods of recruitment and advancement, and politicians attack this position at some political risk. The failure of government to deal adequately with many of today's complex economic and environmental problems, and a more educated and less deferential populace, more willing to question decisions from those whose authority has traditionally been accepted, have both been factors in breaking down the special position of the bureaucracy. Its critics claim that the pendulum has a considerable distance to swing back towards representativeness, reponsiveness and responsibility before professionalism and expertise are endangered.

Resistance to Reform

Most recent reform attempts have, in fact, dealt extensively with one or more aspects of responsibility, accountability and responsiveness. In Britain the Fulton Committee was limited by its terms of reference but did critically review the processes by which top administrators were recruited; more recently, however, the House of Commons Expenditure Committee has stated that the 'installation of special advisers (to ministers) should become an accepted feature of administration[13] and urged other extensive changes to bolster ministerial control, while the British Labour Party has adopted a policy of increasing ministerial power, enlarging personal staffs of ministers and changing selection procedures for senior civil servants.[14] Two commissions on administration in Denmark have sought to increase the Minister's role in policy-making. The recent United States reforms have as one of their major aspects the establishment of a senior executive service which will allow administrators to be moved around far more easily, breakdown loyalties to programmes and agencies and effectively give political executives greater control. The current Canadian Royal Commission on Financial Management and Accountability has seen as central to its task :

> "examining two key accountability frameworks that underpin democratic and responsible government in this country today. These are the way in which Parliament holds the Executive to account for the conduct of its administration of government and the way in which the Executive in its turn holds the senior managers of the public service and Crown agencies to account for their administration. These are two separate but interrelated systems of accountability and control that provide the foundation for responsible government."[15]

Consideration of this aspect highlights the political nature of administrative reform. It is clear that if reforms of the nature discussed in this paper are carried out, and the same may be said for much other administrative reform, some decisions that are now taken by one set of politicians or administrators will be taken by another. Some groups who now have a relatively easy path to top administrative positions will find that path harder, while others may find it easier. Some sections of the community with easy access to the bureaucracy will find that access more difficult. Insofar as different decisions will be taken, some sections of the community will stand to gain and some will stand to lose. There will inevitably be a redistribution of the rights, benefits and resources that government provides.

Equally inevitably, many of those who stand to lose by reform—whether they are in the bureaucracy or in the community at large—will resist it. They will not normally use the arguments of self-interest, but rather will dwell on the difficulties of any scheme of reform (while overlooking the deficiencies of the *status quo)* and emphasize fears of change as opposed to a comfortable familiarity with the existing situation. Since there are for virtually every situation, conflicting principles of administration that can be drawn on, they will find no shortage of arguments in the professional literature.

The problems faced by reformers in this respect were well identified by Macchiavelli :

> "And one has to reflect that there is nothing more difficult to handle nor more doubtful of success nor more dangerous to conduct than to make oneself the leader in introducing a new order of things. For the man who introduces it has for enemies all those who do well out of the old order and has lukewarm supporters in all those who will do well out of the new order. This lukewarmness arises partly from fear of their adversaries who have the laws on their side and partly from the incredulity of mankind who do not put their trust in changes if they do not see them in actual practice. Thus it arises that whenever those who are enemies have the opportunity to go on the attack they do so forcefully and the others put up a lukewarm defence, so putting themselves and their cause at risk at the same time." (I 1 Principle, Cap. VI)

One major hurdle for reformers is that arguments against reform is mounted in traditional public administration terms seeking to elevate efficiency, financial stringency and strict adherence to rules into ultimate values. Reformers very often accept a managerial and technical framework of discussion rather than a social or political one which would place these undoubted administrative virtues into perspective (*i.e.* would set them against the overall societal goals being sought through the administration). As long as reformers allow their opponents to set the terms of the debate they are likely to lose it. They need instead to validate other concepts to be used in assessing reform, such as a resulting increased equity of access to publicly provided goods. The processes which are in traditional terms most efficient may result in the most inequitable outcomes.[16] This willingness of reformers to allow their opponents to set the terms of discussion is, in part, related to their desire to avoid charges that they are 'politicising the administration,' still a damaging accusation in most OECD countries. (It is to be noted that conservative politicians such as Michel Debre, first Prime Minister of the French Republic, in changing the administration in a direction they prefer, often claim to be 'depoliticizing' the decision-making processes).[17] Perhaps reformers would do better to demonstrate that the administration is always politicized and to concentrate the debate on the question of which political values should predominate within it.

Basically, the resistance to administrative reform is a political resistance. It is not only that administrators are reluctant to change processes and procedures with which they have grown familiar, but rather that those groups who stand to lose their privileged position become aware of this danger and fight to retain it. Since they are in positions of privilege and responsibility they are the very people who are best able to resist reform.

Political Strategies for Reform

This suggests that the first prerequisite of major reform is a strong political commitment by the government of the day since in the end, it is only the political leadership which has the resources to win the battle. A government which regards civil service reform as a minor task on its agenda and is not prepared to put political energy behind it and to use up political capital in its achievement, is unlikely to succeed. Unfortunately, the history of many of the major commissions of enquiry, *e.g.* Fulton, Glassco, Coombs, is that by the time they have reported, the government that appointed them has lost either interest or office.

The impetus for administrative reform often lies in a government's desire for social reform. Even though most other aspects of social reform must be carried out through the administrative machinery, governments will often espouse administrative reform but then pay only lip-service to it, since it is more difficult and tedious and less glamorous than other areas of reform such as education, housing or health. But unless government sees administrative reform as a central task, social reform will be much more difficult to achieve.

While some groups will lose in administrative reform, clearly others will gain. Those who stand to gain will, in general, tend to be less powerful than those who stand to lose, but their support is important nonetheless—if for no other reason than to demonstrate to the government that there are political advantages in pursuing reform. Reformers are, therefore, likely to be more successful if they can build up alliances for change both within the bureaucracy (which can be achieved by strategies which do not confront all the powerful institutions but are designed to win support of some of them), or within the community (*e.g.* among business or trade union groups). The success in some countries of plans for a more representative bureaucracy is in no small part due to the way in which the support of women's and minority groups has kept pressure on elected representatives. In other countries, where these groups are less well organised and their electoral weight is less, similar reform proposals have made only slow progress.

Even with political support and alliances for reform, it seems clear that there must be some reform agency within the government that is preparing the agenda for reform and supervising its implementation. That institution cannot be part of the traditional bureaucracy, since it asks too much of human nature that the bureaucracy should provide the impetus for its own reform. One of the reasons for the failure of reform has been the strange methods by which it has been undertaken. Special commissions or committees have been established, which have issued reports and recommendations, but they have usually then been disbanded. This has left the task of actually undertaking reform with the bureaucracy itself and it is not surprising that the pace has been slow. Thus, as the Australian country paper for this Symposium notes, the ministerial committee whose responsibility it is to consider and implement the recommendations of the Royal Commission on Australian Government Administration is serviced by a group of senior officials—but this comprises the heads of those departments which have most to lose by the implementation of the report.

In those countries where there are continuing agencies concerned with reform, these too often become absorbed into the bureaucracy itself. Implementation has been described as the 'Achilles heel' of administrative reform[18] though this is, in some ways, misleading as implementation cannot be separated out as one aspect of reform—without implementation there is no reform. There is no such thing as a 'good' reform plan which failed because of obstacles to its implementation, because it is those obstacles which are the whole object of reform and the reason why it was necessary in the first place. The plan neglected problems of resource and cost. Reform must be seen as a process in which policy planning and implementation cannot be separated.[19] Experience demonstrates that the process of reform must be supervised by those with a commitment, not just to the letter, but to the spirit of the reforms. There has, for example, despite changes in procedures, been little difference in the social composition of those recruited to become Britains' senior administrators as a result of the Fulton reforms and it will be interesting to follow the progress of the United States Senior Executive Service and to see to what extent the aims of mobility and flexibility have been achieved in ten years' time and to what extent civil servants have found that they can comfortably administer the system only by informal maintenance of many of the existing rigidities and the introduction of new ones.

The realization of major reform, it seems, will only be successful if those who carry it on, rather than being concerned with their advancement in the bureaucracy, have a vested interest, at best in terms of personal fulfilment and at least in career or financial terms, in seeing reform implemented as intended. It also suggests that those who staff a reform agency will need to have different values from those pre-dominating within the bureaucracy. 'Smooth' implementation of reform with little conflict would lead one to suspect that little real reform is taking place.

The advocates of administrative reform are very often motivated not so much by an interest in administration as by a desire to build a better society. They are moved by existing inequities and injustices, and believe that administration is important and that administrative reform can result in better and more equitable conditions, not only for those in the bureaucracy but for the community at large. The task they set themselves is a considerable one and it cannot be achieved unless they pursue strategies designed to win them political, bureaucratic and community support.

References

1. Carl J. Friedrich, "Public Policy and the Nature of Administrative Responsibility," *Public Policy,* Vol. 1, 1940, pp. 3-24 (Cambridge, Harvard University Press).
2. Barbara Castle, "Mandarin Power, An Attack on Civil Service Methods and How They Stifle True Political Decision", *Sunday Times,* London, 10 June, 1973.
3. Lord Armstrong, *The Times,* London, 15 November 1976.
4. J. Higley, K.E. Brofoss, K. Groholt, "Top Civil Servants and the National Budget in Norway" in M. Dogan (ed.), *The Mandarins of Western Europe* (Sage, 1975).
5. David Marquand, "A War of Ideologies," New Society 17 (18 February 1971), p. 271, quoted in Mattei Dogan (ed.), *The Mandarins of Western Europe* (Sage, 1975).
6. H.C. Coombs in C. Hazelhurst and J.R. Nethercote (eds.), *Reforming Australian Government* (ANU Press, Canberra, 1977).
7. *Eleventh Report from the Expenditure Committee of the House of Commons,* p. 79, HMSO, 1977.
8. Hugh Heclo, *A Government of Strangers* (The Brookings Institution, Washington DC, 1977).
9. *Report of the Royal Commission of Australian Government Administration,* AGPS, 1976.
10. M. Weber in H.H. Gerth and C. Wright Mills (eds.), *From Max Weber : Essays in Sociology,* p. 233 (Routledge and Kegan Paul, London, 1948).
11. For this point and the analysis of a number of other problems relating to responsibility I am indebted to R.S. Parker, especially in "The Public Service Inquiries and Responsible Government" in R.F.I. Smith and P. Weller, *Public Service Inquiries in Australia* (University of Queensland Press, 1978).
12. OECD, *Public Expenditure Trends,* June 1978.
13. *Eleventh Report from the Expenditure Committee of the House of Commons, op cit.*
14. *Statements to Annual Conference by the National Executive Committee* (The Labour Party, October 1978), p. 44.
15. *Royal Commission on Financial Management and Accountability,* Progress Report, November 1978 (Supply and Services, Ottawa).
16. See, for example, G. Sjoberg, R. Brymer, and B. Farris, "Bureaucracy and the Lower Class," *Sociology and Social Research,* 1966, V. 50, pp. 325-337.

17. Vincent Wright, "Politics and Administration under the French Fifth Republic," *Political Studies*, Vol. 22, No. 1, March, 1974.
18. Gerald E. Caiden, "Implementation—The Achilles Heel of Administration Reform" in A.F. Leemans (ed.), *Management of Change in Government* (Martinus Nijhoff, The Hague, 1974), pp. 142-164.
19. See B.B. Schaffer, "Comparing Administrations : Researching and Reforming," *Public Administration Bulletin*, No. 22, December, 1976.

5

Motivation and Control in Systems

Behaviour and Compliance Systems

Fundamental for the study of behaviour in any bureaucracy are the interrelated issues of motivation and control. Motivation has to do with the factors that lead individuals to act in a given setting. Types of motivating factors are commonly perceived as being significant in the actions of bureaucrats : a desire for material gain, a desire for ego satisfaction, a desire to avoid mental stress or anxiety, a desire for status recognition, a desire to avoid physical stress or discomfort, and a desire to fulfil internalized social, cultural, or religious norms.

Control is the obverse of motivation. Whereas motivation deals with the forces that lead individuals to act or avoid action in a given situation, control deals with the stimuli that mobilize those forces. In offering a salary contingent on the performance of certain acts, a superior attempts to control—or gain the compliance of—a subordinate by appealing to his (or her) desire for material gain.

The character of a bureaucracy is greatly shaped by the dominant patterns of motivations and control mechanisms that it uses. Etzioni terms the interaction of these two elements a compliance relation,[1] and it is useful to think of the aggregate of a bureaucracy's compliance relations as its compliance system. Etzioni suggests that organisational control can be exercised through the use of physical, material, or symbolic means.[2] He goes on to argue that these means have progressively greater levels of effectiveness. Physical means tend to force compliance and generate little commitment but great alienation. Material means build up self-oriented interests in conforming and generate moderate amounts of commitment and alienation. Symbolic means tend to convince people and generate high commitment but little alienation. These principles apply, according to Etzioni, "all other things being equal, at least in most cultures."[3]

If each successive means of control provides greater commitment, less alienation, and more effective compliance, then why do not all organisations use symbolic means ? Clearly, this relates to the problems involved in getting subordinates to respond to—or be motivated by—symbolic appeals. As Etzioni suggests, there is a general correlation between types of organisations and dominant means used to control their lower ranks. Physical means dominate in prisons and custodial mental hospitals where inmates are present against their wills. Material means dominate in factories and civil service organisations in which routine tasks are performed by personnel interested in financial rewards and security. Symbolic means dominate in voluntary organisations, schools, and religious or ideological-political organisations.[4]

The inclination and capacity to motivate subordinates to respond to successively "higher" forms of appeals depends on more than social role, however, cultures differ in their evaluations of alternative motives, in their assumptions about basic qualities of men, and in their repertories of techniques for interpersonal influence. Different historical experiences generate and perpetuate distinctive myths about how specific groups of men behave and how they must be managed. And different ideological traditions generate an impressive range of techniques for inculcating new values, commitments, and modes of behaviour. Thus a sociologically defined category of worker that might in one setting be seen by superiors as responsive only to physical threat could very well be successfully controlled by symbolic means in a different setting.

The nature and effectiveness of a compliance system is of particular importance in the management of a field organisation that depends on agents who are geographically remote from one another. Since conventional physical surveillance is impossible under these circumstances, alternative compliance mechanisms must be used. Frederick Frey has suggested three compliance mechanisms that have been used to maintain indirect control over the behaviour of physically inaccessible field agents.[5]

The first, *material incentive control*, is achieved by arranging the terms of a field agent's employment in such a way that it is to his personal advantage to fulfil the requirements of his agency. In isolated areas where government activities are at a low level, for example, a man can be hired as a tax collector and be told that he is responsible for the remission of a specific quantity of tax money every year, the understanding being that he can keep anything he collects above the quota. The tax collector thus has a strong personal incentive to carry out the government's tax collection programme as long as he can extract from people in his jurisdiction amounts substantially in excess of his quota. Material incentive control relies on a direct appeal to the motives of material gain. Indeed the mechanism is defined in terms of its motivational basis.

The second compliance mechanism, feedback control, is achieved by requiring the field agent to send in regular reports on his activities. His reports can be checked for internal inconsistencies, and physical verifications can be made on a small sample of reported activities. This system's major limitation is the need to translate the activities of the field agent into measurable quantitative units. A rural extension agent may be required to report, among other things, how many agricultural demonstrations he has performed, how many farmers he has persuaded to adopt a new seed, and how many acres he has induced them to plant with that seed. Where the work involved has a heavy qualitative component, feedback control is frequently unable to provide an accurate accounting of the degree to which field agents are actually accomplishing the agency's goals.

Feedback control can be linked to one or a combination of several motivation forces : the desire for material gain, the desire for ego satisfaction, the desire to avoid mental stress, the desire to fulfil certain kinds of norms. What becomes critical from a motivational perspective is the set of rewards and sanctions that are used in response to more or less satisfactory feedback. Thus, a superlative report might provoke public praise, a financial bonus, a promotion, a reduced set of future targets, an increased set of future targets, or no response at all.

Preprogrammed control, the third type, is achieved by persuading the individual field agent to accept and internalize the goals and methods of his agency. This is generally accomplished through an intensive training programme and maintained by newsletters, periodic reunions, refresher training and other techniques designed to foster and sustain a strong *esprit de corps*. The agent is sent to the field with general instructions and the hope that his high ideals and motivation will lead him to act in ways that fulfil the goals of the agency. He is not assigned specific quantified targets, but is instead told to work in whatever ways seem to foster the broad goals of his agency, given the situation in which he finds himself. He is thus allowed a great deal of discretionary freedom of action and is encouraged to work toward results that are qualitative, as well as quantitative, in nature.

Only a limited range of motivating factors can be associated with preprogrammed control. The conscious appeal is almost always to the field agent's desire to meet norms he has internalized in the process of his training and probationary work. A variety of techniques are used to encourage the field agent to identify his personal self-esteem and social status with the satisfaction of those norms. A considerable sense of elitism is frequently associated with preprogrammed control. A major source of identification with one's cadre derives from the unusual capacity of its members to perform effectively without any apparent administrative control. The Indian Civil Service was a classic case of a preprogrammed field cadre and its successor. The Indian Administrative Service, has maintained the tradition. The Peace Corps is another example of an agency that has relied heavily on preprogrammed control in the handling of its field workers.

Because material incentive, feedback, and preprogrammed control mechanisms are likely to be based on distinctive motivational appeals, there are rather severe limits on the extent to which they can be combined in the management of any one group of field agents. Preprogrammed control, for example, depends on the desire of the field worker to justify the high degree of trust placed in him as an individual and as a member of his cadre. Feedback control, on the other hand, makes explicit the limitations of trust and confidence which are placed in the field agent. Thus when a field agent who has been preprogrammed suddenly finds himself increasingly controlled by feedback procedures, he finds it correspondingly difficult to maintain the spirit and sense of pride which are essential underpinnings of preprogrammed control systems.[6]

Organisation Evolution

The four models of organisation that impinge on Tamil development administration have distinctive approaches to motivation, control, and compliance mechanisms. The interaction of these models in the evolution of administrative processes has been of fundamental importance in shaping the character of bureaucratic behaviour in this setting.

The *dharmic* tradition idealizes allegiance to duty, but sees man as being constantly tempted to forsake his duty because of laziness or a desire to maximize his short-term material gain. Powerful social controls keep these predilections within bounds in village society, but a more overt and menacing form of threat is necessary when one moves to larger jurisdictions. *Danda,* the coercive face of authority, is the necessary complement to *dharma.* Fear and threat are the mechanisms one uses to provoke adherence to duty among recalcitrant and devious subordinates.

The British colonial tradition contains two separate models of motivation and control, one for the top tier of primarily British officers, and the other for lower-level Indian subordinates. The British officer was trained to internalize and value a set of norms that emphasized his honesty, independence of mind, physical vigour, and capacity for decision-making. The structure in which he operated reinforced adherence to these norms by assuring him of high status recognition and very considerable material benefits.

There was little sense, however, that Indians would respond to appeals directed at internalized norms. Rather, the British saw their Indian subordinates as being motivated to act contrary to the interests of the bureaucracy by their desire to avoid mental and physical stress and their desire to fulfil the social norms of family and caste loyalty. Powerful sanctions against such actions were, as a result, felt to be necessary to keep their behaviour within acceptable bounds. The role of the remote, harsh, and punitive father became the model to be emulated by the British official in the management of his subordinates.

The *dharmic* and British colonial traditions mutually reinforced each other in their approaches to compliance systems.

Dharmic perceptions show skepticism of man's voluntary adherence to duty because self-denial is so central to the fulfilment of personal *dharma*. British skepticism was based more on widely shared perceptions of laziness and deviousness as integral features of Indian character. The shared expectations that subordinates could not be trusted fostered and perpetuated a pattern of close an openly abusive supervision among both British and Indian officials. Sustaining fear of a remote, powerful, and threatening authority figure was seen to be an essential ingredient in the task of "extracting work from subordinates."

Mechanisms for exacting compliance of field agents in the colonial bureaucracy reflected the dual character of control in the colonial tradition. Collectors were preprogrammed representatives of the elite ICS cadre who were broadly trusted to implement the goals and norms that they developed in training and probationary service. At lower levels in the hierarchy, however, reliance was placed on an elaborate system of feedback control. Checks and cross-checks, as well as frequent physical inspections, were used in efforts to maintain satisfactory levels of compliance. The Tottenham system of record keeping with its elaborate procedures for keeping track of documents, reflects one aspect of this highly sophisticated set of mechanisms.

A radically different approach to motivation and control permeates the community development tradition. The nature of extension work is not consistent with close supervision and control of field agents through the requirement of detailed quantitative feedback. Rather, the extension worker must be allowed flexibility to meet specific needs of his own villages. Thus, preprogrammed control is the appropriate mechanism of assuming compliance, and the tradition has always emphasized the importance of lengthy training programmes. The most effective motivating force for extension workers is believed to be the ego satisfaction that one derives from guiding a dynamic programme of social and economic change. It was recognized that enthusiasm would wax and wane, but extension-team meetings, refresher training courses, and other mechanisms were available to revive sagging spirits.

The Gandhian transformation of the concept of *dharma* has an important impact on the tradition's approach to motivation and control. Duty, in the Gandhian sense, is not the simple performance of traditionally assigned tasks, but rather the pursuit of what Gandhi called Truth. Though his use of that term is ambiguous, Gandhi seems to have had in mind an ordering of society that undergoes change but retains a fundamental harmony. Thus, each individual must endeavour to follow a path of right action that will be consonant with this pattern of development. Gandhi, of course, had his own vision of that pattern, which he propagated broadly in his writings. The ideology thus encouraged the individual to become familiar with Gandhi's world view and then undertake his own pursuit of Truth.

The community development and Gandhian traditions came together in their common concern for training and indoctrination of agents of rural change. Elements of Gandhian thought and practice permeated the community development training organisations.

Intensive training in the precepts and norms of the community development and Gandhian approaches to bureaucracy was thus given to the vast army of young high school graduates who were hired to fill the ranks of the Gram Sevaks. Before assuming their posts they went to training centres for up to two years of intensive education and indoctrination. They were instructed on technical subjects such as agriculture, animal husbandry, and village industries, but they were also infused with the ideals of planned village development, the importance of felt needs, and the role of the Gram Sevak as friend and helper of the peasant. The training emphasized the values of village change, respect for manual work, selfless action, and team effort. Gram Sevaks were taught skills, that would presumably be useful in advancing those values and told that they were members of a noble group of trained and dedicated workers. They were made to feel proud of their positions and dedication, and were led to believe that they would be appreciated and respected by coworkers and villagers alike.

Community Development Processes

The hiring, training, and placement of thousands of new Gram Sevaks within a period of several years represented a major investment not only in a new and exciting development programme, but also in an approach to bureaucratic compliance that was revolutionary for India. Young men went out to their block assignments with a dedication, commitment, and determina-tion that had never before been seen in the lower levels of the public service. One to two years of training instilled in them new attitudes toward development and new motivations for undertaking development work.

It was considered impractical or unfeasible, however, to provide, extensive training for men who were to fill the middle and upper echelons of the emerging development bureaucracy. The BDOs were to be men who had already gained years of experience in the revenue-dominated district administration of the colonial era. What little training they were given familiarized them with the structure, goals, and ideals of the development effort. DAOs, who were to supervise the burgeoning ranks of AEOs, assumed their jobs on the basis of the seniority they had accumulated in the Department of Agriculture bureaucracy. Both BDOs and DAOs, however, had been trained in, and were practitioners of traditional close supervision and feedback control of field agents.

Thus, when Gram Sevaks and AEOs met their supervising BDOs and DAOs in the field, their expectations and anticipated working styles were strikingly different. Gram Sevaks and AEOs saw their interactions with the villages as being the primary determinant of their work. The block establishment was thought of as a source of support and as a communication channel. Only in unusual circumstances was it seen as likely to impose constraints. BDOs and DAOs, however, brought with them to the new bureaucratic structure the conventional view of their supervisory role, rooted in the colonial and *dharmic* traditions.

The structure of the new community development bureaucracy appeared to be ill-conceived from the perspective of the traditional supervisor. The anomalous position of the AEO, whose role was declined as a member of the block "team" under the dual supervision of the BDO and DAO, seemed to threaten the supervisory power of the DAO. The authority of the BDO over the Gram Sevaks was unclear in light of the presence of extension officers who were also of higher rank than the Gram Sevaks, but only partially under the BDO's control. And finally, both BDOs and DAOs were uncertain about how they would be able to exert their supervisory authority and extract work from their sub-ordinates if standards of achievement were to be established from the bottom, rather than the top of the hierarchy.

The anxieties of the middle- and upper-level supervisors were soon relieved, however, as it became clear that traditional patterns of supervision could still be applied in this new structure. Such integral features of the community development model as targets, reports on extension work, block team meetings, and visits to the field could, they soon discovered, be used as mechanisms of rigorous feedback control.

Though the demise of planning from below may have begun as a result of sincere desires to get the planning process underway quickly, it was accelerated and made irreversible by the need, felt by superior officers imbued with colonial and *dharmic* approaches to supervision, to have clear standards against which to measure the performance of their subordinates. Target figures, designed to be specific goals which the field worker would himself help to define, rapidly became externally imposed norms against which his performance was to be judged.

In the central offices of the technical agencies, planners began formulating new development programmes and assigning targets to the field organisation. Soon the initial anxiety of the middle level supervisor about criteria for evaluating his subordinates was replaced by an opposing consideration. His own performance was being evaluated on the basis of his ability to coerce his subordinates into fulfilling their targets. Thus, the more demanding the levels of performance required of his subordinates, the greater the difficulty he would have in achieving a creditable record. So, as an overall state agricultural target came to be broken down into specific targets for Deputy Directors, DAOs, and AEOs, each officer was strongly motivated to minimize the potential of his region and the capacity of his staff in order to keep his own targets to the lowest possible level.

Targets, then, were not set as a result of what was appropriate to a particular village, but rather as a result of a multistaged negotiation process through which an overall target was broken up into a multitude of smaller targets. Impressionistic attempts were made at each level to allocate the overall target among the smaller units in proportion to their potential, but the resulting targets were, nevertheless, often inappropriate to the needs or capacities of specific villages.

The most glaring problems arose, however, when the aggregate of targets assigned to any one Gram Sevak was considered. When each of the technical officers on the block team assigned the targets among the Gram Sevaks, their resulting workload was many times their capacities. Well over a hundred programmes might require implementation, each with its accompanying educational, organisational, distributional, and recordkeeing components. Some were of real interest and of potential benefit of the farmers; others held out little prospect of benefit, and villagers remained indifferent to them.

The relative merit of the programmes, however, was not a concern of the line officer of the colonial tradition. His interest was with extracting work so as to fulfil targets. In order to achieve maximum response from their heavily overburdened Gram Sevaks, the BDO and DAOs relied heavily on the second and third institutionalized structures facilitating their control requirements.

The periodical report was the second feature of community development administration that was transformed into a tool of intensive feedback control. The field agent operating under a system of preprogrammed control is required to make frequent reports, but their purpose is to provide information on field conditions, not to serve as a means of evaluating his work. They are, as a result, apt to be qualitative, discursive, and concerned with programme failures and inadequacies, though they will frequently also contain reports of successful endeavours. In a feedback control system, on the other hand, the primary function of periodical reports is personnel evaluation. As a result, the formats specify in detail the figures that must be provided on achievements made toward a multitude of targets. Such reports can also be used as sources of information about programme success and supply requirements, but the dangers inherent in such use are obvious. When an individual who provides the figures for a report knows that they will be used to evaluate his work, he is under enormous pressure to falsily his real achievements.

Gram Sevaks writing to their superiors initially for informational purposes soon discovered that their reports were treated primarily as bases for evaluation of their personal performance, and that the evaluation was based on their relative success in achieving targets. The formats on which reports were to be submitted became increasingly quantitative and restrictive in nature, and the character of the reports soon reflected the changing motivational forces operating on field agents. Descriptive, problem-oriented accounts of the trusted representative were replaced by the quantitative reports of the defensive subordinate.

The final item on many report forms—"Have you any special difficulty in the implementation of the programme?"—became a token reminder, ignored by almost all respondents, of a type of superior-subordinate communication that was promised in training programmes but never effectively achieved in the field.

Twice monthly staff meetings supplemented the control function of targets and periodical reports. Here again, the intended role of these forums as opportunities for open discussion of practical programme difficulties was soon almost entirely displaced by the concern of superiors for the achievement of quantitative targets. The presiding officers of such meetings—whether BDO, DAO, or collector—used the occasions to openly criticize and threaten those of their subordinates who had failed to report a minimal performance level. The formal, critical tone of the staff meetings usually taken up, was typical of the proceedings. The Polur DAO stood out as a striking exception in his attempt to introduce consideration of substance and work strategy into his sessions.

Finally, "going out on tour" provided a critical supplement to the supervisor's arsenal of control devices. Team leaders in Mayer's Etawah project were expected to visit the field in order to assist and encourage their extension agents. More familiar to the new BDOs and DAOs, however, was the use of such travelling to check on the accuracy of their subordinates' reports. Records were gone over in detail, the presence of supplies under the subordinates' care was physically verified, and performance on specific targets was reviewed and deficiencies pointed out and criticized. Like the Collector on his tour to Sathanur, many officials viewed these field visits as opportunities to symbolize close supervisory techniques and to stimulate their subordinates to more effective action through the desire, to avoid further criticism and possible sanction. The Ranipet DAO was unusual in his attempts to follow up his criticism of a subordinate with an effort to help that subordinate learn how to deal with his administrative problems.

Response of Workers

The transformation of the compliance system in development administration from the one envisaged by community development planners to the traditional feedback control mechanisms of colonial bureaucracy radically altered the role of the extension agent. Instead of the incremental efforts to change the attitudes and practices of villagers that were to be at the heart of their extension work, attention had to be focused on achieving highly specific targets : meetings held, fertilizer sold, loans processed, permits issued, and acres planted in new varieties.

Since the use of approved extension methods to inform and persuade farmers of the value of so many schemes was impossibly time-consuming—and in many cases unsuccessful—Gram Sevaks, AEOs and others involved in the actual implementation of the multitudes of development programmes quickly developed three basic strategies for coping with the impossible set of demands placed on them : falsifying or distorting reports; neglecting targets they determined to be of low salience; and using resources under their own control to stimulate farmer participation in unpopular programmes. The choice of strategies depended on the nature of the programme, the degree of attention it was receiving in the bureaucracy, the motivation of the field agent, and the supervisory enthusiasm of his superior.

The systematic distortion of reports was the usual strategy followed when the chance of their being effectively verified by superiors was low. Activities that were either not carried out or carried out in a perfunctory manner were inflated into significant achievements on paper. AEOs, for example, were expected to conduct Radio Farm Forums each month. They were required to listen with people of a particular village to the evening radio programme. "For Farmers," and then discuss with the villagers the relevance of the programme's material to their own needs. Though the scheme attracted little attention, and officials in the State Agricultural Information Office did not see it as central to the success of their radio activities, it was still one of the 24 schemes on which the AEO had to report his monthly progress. The standard method of handling this demand was for the AEO to spend, once or twice a month, a few minutes listening to part of the programme in a village where he had to be for other reasons, count the number of villagers listening to the programme and chat briefly with a few of them afterward. He then reported the village, the date, and an acceptable number of participants. That no forum was actually held would not be reflected in the report, nor was the fact likely to be discovered by a superior.

A modified version of this same strategy was frequently

applied to acreage targets. When these became matters of special attention, Gram Sevaks and AEOs were required to list individual farmers, their village, and the number of acres planted in a specific crop. Since such lists could be spot-checked by superior officers, reasonable standards of accuracy were generally maintained. Gram Sevaks were supposed to compile the lists as they made their extension rounds. In theory they were to enlist farmers as participants in the programme, explain a package of practices to them, and help them fill out "farm plans" containing growing schedules and instructions. More frequently, however, such lists were compiled as the Gram Sevaks were approached by farmers for loans and fertilizer permits which were conditional on the farmers planting a certain number of acres in the specific variety. Target deficits were made up by calling together small groups of farmers shortly after planting time and adding to one's list the names of those who said they were, on their own initiative, already planting the variety in question. AEOs received reports and lists from the Gram Sevaks and consolidated them; if the total acreage did not meet their targets, they added names from their own lists of individuals who had come to them for fertilizer permits or seeds.

Though targets could not always be completely fulfilled in this way, a large measure of success could be achieved with a minimum of time invested. With the introduction of new varieties that gave dramatically improved yields, the extension agent's problems fulfilling acreage targets were greatly reduced. For the better varieties, reports of full target achievements could generally be compiled from only a partial listing of acres contracted for by individuals who had obtained seed, fertilizer permits, or loans. The extension agents were aware that some individuals would not, in fact, plant the variety for which the fertilizer or credit was given, but the chance that specific evidence of this fact would reach their superiors was quite remote.

Another strategy used by extension agents was to ignore some targets. As the feedback system evolved, they soon came to realize that whereas deficiencies in reports on some targets brought swift and voluble reaction from their superiors, failure to even submit reports on other schemes produced no adverse reactions at all. They then fell into a pattern of ignoring programmes their supervisor ignored and emphasizing those he emphasized. Staff meetings gave some clues about which schemes fell into which categories, but even more useful was an elaborate and ubiquitous system of "reminders."

As the numbers of programmes, targets, and reports increase within any bureaucracy, the headquarters staff becomes progressively overloaded and, as a result, the processing and analysis of reports becomes less regular, prompt, and consistent. Clerical staffs aggregate figures, analyze discrepancies, and write critical letters relating to programmes of concern to their senior officers; they defer actions on less salient programmes. Harried clerks and officers in subordinate offices soon discover that delay in filing certain reports will produce prompt demands for immediate submission, whereas delay on other reports may cause no response at all.

Awareness that little or no attention was being given to certain schemes and reports soon began to filter down the hierarchies of Tamil development agencies. The greater the work overload and the frequency of late reporting, the more rapidly this awareness reached the Gram Sevaks. Consequently, it became conventional practice to ignore the initial deadline for many reports. The receipt of an "urgent" and then a "most urgent" reminder, however, made it clear that a particular scheme was being followed closely and that a report had best be made.

In addition to simply not filing reports on some targets, extension agents soon discovered that, when numbers of targets were consolidated onto a single periodical form, some of them were virtually ignored at higher levels of authority, so that gross underachievement produced no complaint from their superiors. On more salient programmes, however, moderate underachievement seemed to evoke intense criticism and threats. There was, in short, a *de facto* scale of allowable underachievement which was a function of programmes, salience. Attention to schemes in terms of that scale made it possible for extension agents to further reduce their actual workloads.

The strategy of selective target fulfilment worked, however, only within a large margin for error. Extension agents had little way of knowing when a particular scheme would suddenly become the subject of the collector's special interest or the concern of a joint director in Madras. Nevertheless, it provided a basis for handling an otherwise unmanageable set of demands and reduced pressure, criticism and threats from superiors.

The third and perhaps most powerful strategy available to

extension agents was the use of resources that were in demand as inducements to farmers to help them with their more intractable targets. Gram Sevaks and AEOs controlled the distribution of seeds, fertilizer permits, pesticides, agricultural implements, and production loans. Though some of these items might be ill-suited to the locality or of no interest to most farmers, others were certain to be in great demand. The extension agent would, therefore, condition the sale or distribution of a high-demand articles on the willingness of the recipient to take a low-demand item with it. As a result of such a *quid pro quo*, a farmer might count himself fortunate to have obtained a permit to buy fertilizer at a subsidized rate and an AEO would be relieved to have made progress toward fulfilling his target for the sale of green manure seeds nobody wanted. Neither would be particularly disturbed by the fact that the farmer would simply throw out the seeds.

Rigidity of Control

Mechanisms of intense feedback control, then produced reactions on behalf of extension agents that were counterproductive of real development goals. Deception and coercion replaced dedication and service as the dominant features of extension work.

The tendency of behaviour patterns in a closely supervised bureaucracy to degenerate into a "vicious cycle" is well documented.[7] Close supervision fosters alienation that leads to a decline in work habits that triggers a further intensification of supervision. An especially pernicious cycle developed in Indian development administration, however, when central planning and intense feedback control were imposed on a structure designed to accommodate planning from below and cadres of extension workers who had been preprogrammed to act as autonomous change agents. The cycle can best be understood by first considering the heavy workload imposed on the extension staff.

Two features of Tamil development administration reinforced and aggravated normal bureaucratic predilections to develop new programmes without eliminating older and less productive ones. First, no structural mechanism existed to control and co-ordinate the number and mix of schemes and programmes that were centrally planned and passed down through numerous hierarchies for implementation by Gram Sevaks. Even when a single agency such as the Department of Agriculture developed its programmes, it did so without the capacity to plan and co-ordinate their interrelationship at the local level. Second, traditional compliance practices of colonial bureaucracy were to establish heavy demands on subordinates in order to maintain the pressure and threat that were felt to be essential to effective supervision.

The pressures for more programmes and targets led to the placement of unmanageable levels of demands on Gram Sevaks and AEOs. Consequently, even allowing for the protective strategies employed by the extension agents, increasing numbers of failures to achieve targets were reported up through the hierarchies. The reaction of superiors in the chains of command to these reports was to intensify the application of feedback control procedures. Monthly reports on a series of targets were to be supplemented by weekly or bi-weekly reports on schemes of special interest. Reports of final achievements (such as acreage planted in a new variety) were to be preceded by preliminary progress reports containing detailed accountings of efforts undertaken.

The increasing amount of time extension agents spent in the preparation of ever-more-detailed, ever-more-frequent reports reinforced their tendency to ignore initial requests and early reminders of reports due. Thus clerical staffs spent increasingly more in the preparation of depressingly voluminous and angry reminders of mounting urgency. The remedy, then, simply intensified the problem.

It had other effects as well. First, it led to a pervasive alienation and disillusionment among the field workers. As Gram Sevaks and AEOs discovered that they were not trusted to work under a system of preprogrammed compliance, their self-esteem and motivation to carry out agency goals declined. As targets exceeded capabilities and field agents increasingly relied on adaptive strategies that conflicted with real development goals, their alienation from their role and its symbolic rewards became more intense. This led to a progressive lessening of their psychic involvement in their jobs and a weakening of their sense of identification with the agency and its goals.

As the preprogrammed field agents found themselves increasingly deprived of psychic, status, or achievement rewards for performing well in their jobs, they were increasingly inclined to work at the lowest level of output and effectiveness that could be maintained without antagonizing their superiors. As a result, a self-fulfilling prophecy was created. Middle- and upper-level supervisors, imbued with *dharmic* and colonial assumptions about the laziness and deceitfulness of subordinates, found ample evidence to confirm their views that harsh and threatening techniques were the only effective means of extracting work from subordinates.

In addition, the extension agents' strategies of deception were producing misinformation in reports to higher levels of administration : levels of achievement were inflated and serious problems in implementation of programmes were not reported. Middle level supervisors showed little interest in verifying the accuracy of most reports because the aggregation of inflated figures from their subordinates made their own reports look better in the eyes of their superiors. Even on personal inspection tours of village programmes, supervisors ignored practical problems and concentrated on the specific and quantitative issues for which they were directly responsible. Operational problems brought to them either by extension agents or by specific villagers were treated as self-interested excuses or complaints, which were not representative of actual conditions. Thus, the quantitative indicators that showed up on consolidated reports encouraged the view that programmes were operating reasonably well and could be brought upto the mark with a little more pressure on the subordinate staff. Inquiries into the need for modification of programmes were thus discouraged, and the planners turned their attention to the creation of more new programmes.

Conclusion

In brief, then, the attempt to reform a colonial bureaucracy by preprogramming a band of young workers with the ideologies of Gandhi and the community development movement was swamped by the pervasive domination of colonial and *dharmic* models of compliance systems. The result was not simply a routinization of procedure, but a severe and progressive deterioration of performance, integrity and morale.

Notwithstanding this general pattern of deterioration, some individuals retained allegiance to the idealism of the Gandhian and community development traditions. Some Gram Sevaks continued to derive, as late as 1968, distinct satisfaction from their self-images as altruistic workers concerned with the well-being of the people. Their working patterns, however, departed so strikingly from the norms established in the community development ideology that they had had to undergo tortured changes in views to sustain their motivation. They argued that the need to develop the country quickly, combined with the low level of literacy and knowledge in the villages, had made classical extension efforts impractical. Instead, rational criteria had to be used to define village needs and then villagers had to be forced to try new ways of working. Thus, the focus on targets became a necessary part of the programme. One of the few highly motivated Gram Sevaks in North Arcot sustained his own enthusiasm by reconciling the community development ideal with the realities of a closely supervised feedback control system in the following terms :

> There is no contradiction between extension methods and our actual work. The government gives us only very useful schemes but the people, because of their ignorance and illiteracy, often don't understand them. So it is our duty to make them understand the usefulness of these schemes. In the beginning they won't come forward, but if we compel them once or twice then they will realize the benefits and come forward them-selves.

The DAO from Polur was perhaps the most enthusiastic advocate of using human relations techniques to motivate subordinates. In his efforts to create a sense of personal involvement and enthusiast among his subordinates, however, he found that his attention to their needs and practical difficulties had a very different effect. Just as the colonial mythology suggested, they worked less effectively because his lack of harsh-ness was interpreted as a "weak-kneed policy." In his brief tenure at Polur he managed to dispel that notion, but he was not able to noticeably modify the enthusiasm or commitment of his subordinates.

The Ranipet DAO took a less doctrinaire but perhaps more successful approach to the problem of motivation. By beginning with the normal and expected criticism, he made it clear to his subordinates that he had within him the harshness to command respect. This made it possible for him to then listen to problems and involve his subordinates. Although he was personally concerned with bringing about change in agricultural production patterns, his rhetoric contained little that was designed to stimulate the same concern in his subordinates. He did, however often encourage them to help farmers with specific needs, even at the expense of meeting their targets.

Perhaps the most important counterforce to the pervasive pressures for close supervision, with all of its behavioural consequences, came from a group of senior officers in the Department of Agriculture who had received advanced training in the West, been actively involved in the Ford Foundation's project in Tanjore District or both. They were largely responsible, for example, for a March 1967 meeting of DAOs in which, for the first time, joint directors actively solicited the views of their subordinates. A tone of openness was established and a great deal of information about the actual operation of many programmes, and the effect of many administrative decisions, was conveyed from district officers to the planners in the Madras headquarters.

Three years later, in the course of a brief follow-up visit to North Arcot, I found evidence that this new openness to information from the field had begun to have significant consequences for the agricultural bureaucracy. Many of the most onerous features of the AEOs' work situations had been improved. Though the number of reports they were responsible for had not noticeably declined, they had been given assistants to help in the handling of block agricultural depot accounts. And though the number of schemes and programmes on the books appeared to be only slightly reduced, the AEOs were clear in their own minds that the HYVP was a priority programme and that work on many of the other schemes could legitimately be slighted. As a result of these changes and the general success of agricultural programmes, there was a noticeable improvement in the AEOs' sense of involvement and self-esteem.

The continually worsening plight of the Gram Sevaks was in striking contrast to the modest improvement in the position of the AEOs. The numbers and levels of their targets had, if anything, increased, but nothing had been done to augment the resources at their command. Most simply continued to try to carry out their duty in a proper way. For those who had, three years earlier, still retained an enthusiasm and a sense of hope, the enthusiasm had waned and hopes had, in most cases, turned to despair.

References

1. Amitai Etzioni, *A Comparative Analysis of Complex Organization* (New York, Free Press, 1961), p. 4.
2. Amitai Etzioni, *Modern Organizations* (Englewood Cliffs, N.J., Prentice-Hall, 1964), pp. 59-60.
3. *Ibid*.
4. *Ibid*.
5. *Concepts of Development Administration and Strategy Implications for Behaviour Change* (Massachusetts Institute of Technology. Mimeographed, n.d.) pp. 2-14. The following analysis draws on Frey's typology, though modifications have been made both in terminology and in conceptualization.
6. Etzioni makes a similar point in his *Comparative Analysis of Complex Organizations*. Referring more generally to means used to make subordinates comply, he differentiates between coercive, remunerative and normative power. He then argues that most organisations tend to emphasize only one means of power because when two kinds of power are emphasized at the same time, over the same subject group, they tend to neutralize each other." (p. 7)
7. See, for example, Alvin W. Gouldner, *Patterns of Industrial Bureaucracy* (Glencoe, Ill., The Free Press, 1954), p. 160. Michel Crozier, *The Bureaucratic Phenomenon* (Chicago, Phoenix Books, The University of Chicago Press, 1964), pp. 187-94.

6

Reform and Adaptation Policies : Experiences from Europe

I

Introduction

There is no systematic and comprehensive, international report on the failures and successes of the larger administrative reforms in government which have been launched during the post-war period. The general impression from existing reports on the subject is that the failure rate is high, and that even the more successful efforts have only partly met their goals. This seems to be true for both industrialised and developing countries.

One explanation of the failure or limited success may be a lack of appropriate implementation strategies. In most cases the reform effort has not been considered and conducted as a dynamic change process. The time factor and other factors crucial for implementation have been underrated or not taken into account.

The strategies for change in the public administration have to be chosen with regard to the societal situation and cultural factors (environmental factors), the internal situation within the public administration (structure and processes), and the ideology and objectives chosen for future development.

It is not possible to give a normative recipe of a universal strategy for the management of change, even if some fundamental factors always should be taken into account. The strategies and main policies presented in this paper are chosen on the basis of conditions and experiences in Norway. Further information on the situation in Norway is available in the National Paper prepared for this symposium.

The expression "administrative development and improvement" used in the present paper is meant to cover the process of administrative and organisational change in a wide sense, including terms like administrative reform, reorganisation and organisation development. The general objectives of an administrative development and improvement process or programme may be stated as :

Changes in the services from the public administration to society, *e.g.* changes in quality or volume of services, creating new or abolishing outdated services.

- Better quality of and better internal work conditions in the public administration itself.
- Improved utilization of available resources.

These objectives or principal goals may be more or less in conflict, and should, therefore, be considered carefully in the planning of a change programme.

Some Basic Views on Change and Development in the Public Administration—Strategies and Main Policies

Administrative Development Regarded as an Induced and Directed Process of Change

This view implies that administrative development in government should be considered as a change process based on objectives and strategies that have been agreed upon, not only as isolated or incoherent adjustments and changes which are not planned and co-ordinated. The whole development of society and the corresponding changes in objectives and tasks of the public administration demand a systematic and co-ordinated approach to administrative change.

The change process should be induced and directed in view of the public administration as a whole, its different parts being inter-related and inter-dependent, as subsystems of a government system.

The basic concept of administrative development and improvement as a change process does not mean that formalization and legitimation of changes through laws and regulations is disregarded. It is, however, an open question how far new laws and regulations can and should be used as tools in the change process. Abolition or revision of laws and regulations may in some cases be more important. Very often, new laws will only give a frame which must be filled by other tools and measures, and they may also have negative effects in the process.

How the inducement and direction is going to be performed raises a series of important questions, including such issues as centralization/decentralization, participation, democratization and the roles of politicians and bureaucrats in the change process. We shall later return to some of these questions.

A Continuous Change Process, Which May Include Both Fundamental, Major and Incremental Changes (Macro, Meso and Micro Changes)

In many cases administrative reform has been conceived and planned as a special, time-limited effort for fundamental or large changes in the public administration. This approach has often led to problems and failures in the implementation phase. My assumption is that the administrative development needed in government cannot be achieved through a one-time, special reform effort of limited duration. Under given circumstances there may certainly be a need for special, fundamental reform efforts, but at all times changes for adaptation and development of some kind are needed. Connected with the more fundamental changes, there will always be a need for related major or minor changes, and always a need for later adaptation and follow-up. This means a continuous process covering different types of objectives and using a mix of instruments or means. Beside the changes which have been formally decided on, there will also be informal changes which result from the human and organisational development.

Responsibility for Administrative Development Formally and Effectively Placed with the Authority and Leadership at the Different Levels of the Organisational Structure

A primary condition in managing the needed administrative development is recognition and acceptance by politicians and bureaucrats of the fact that administrative and organisational matters are of high importance and must be attended to. Perception of the needs for change and management of change is part of general management. Unfortunately, an advanced, effective internal administration has generally not been a characteristic of the machinery of government. It is also unrealistic to believe that every high-level bureaucrat is going to fill his managerial responsibilities in administrative development. But even so, there should be no doubt about his formal responsibility, and this should be followed up by appropriate measures for management development at the different levels of the hierarchy.

The individual, managerial ability and performance of even a small number of outstanding civil servants may be a most important asset in implementing change. In our long practical experience, we have often been amazed at the influence and effect a single person can have in implementing and backstopping administrative change in a large organisation—or impeding the change.

The question of effective responsibility and commitment is also a question of decentralization and participation, which is taken up in section 6.

A Programme for Administrative Development should be Planned, Organised and Controlled as an Integrated Part of the General Planning, Programming-, Budgeting-, Reporting System of Government, at a Longer Term and Short Term Basis

The government planning activities have until now mostly been concentrated on technological, economic and social aspects, without much regard to the administrative and organisational needs and prerequisites. Administrative structures and processes should provide an appropriate framework for policy-making and implementation in the various policy sectors. Consequently, the planning should also provide for effective administrative structures and processes, that is administrative development and improvement. Organisational structures and processes is also an important component of the policy-making itself. A planning programming process for change in the public administration may be considered as a natural and necessary development of the existing planning-programming-budgeting system in government.

In the same way, the general reporting-controlling system

should also include reports on the implementation and results of the administrative development programme for the different organisational units and levels of government.

Implementation is Closely Related to the Other Phases of the Change Process, and should not be Considered as an Isolated Phase

The process of change starts with the human perception of a problem or an idea, may be long before any clear conception of what the change should be has emerged. From this first embryo of change, the process will develop through different phases and iterative steps. All these phases or steps may influence the implementation of change in the organisation, positively or negatively. It is, therefore, a useful approach and strategy to consider all phases of the change process as inter-related steps that will influence the organisation and effect the possibilities of imple-mentation. The whole process of change should be geared towards the problem-solving itself, through the implementation of change.

Main Phases of the Change Process

If we accept the view that implementation is closely related to the preceding phases of the change process, we also have to consider the whole process in discussing implementation strategies.

The main phases of a directed, problem-solving or change process may be described in different ways, *e.g.*, as :

- *Initiation,* with the personal initiative to take up a problem or a question of change, and the decision to start the process.
- *Information gathering.* Communication and information gathering is the ground-work for problem solving, the final decision or solution is never better than the information it is built on. Adequate information is very much a question of relevant information and not the volume of information, of quality more than quantity. It is easy to spend a lot of time and resources in detailed information collection and processing which does not help the problem solving and implementation.
- *Analysis and diagnosis* must be based on information. What are the real problems and what are the symptoms?

Not all problems can be solved at the same time. Which are the critical ones? What type of analysis methods should be used? These questions and others have to be answered.

- *Main design of possible solutions (alternative), cost-benefit analysis.* This phase should give an adequate basis for choice of solutions, taking into account the objectives, the possible means and tools, and the consequences in terms of costs, benefits and negative effects.
- *Decision on solution.* This is often a critical phase, with disagreements, conflicts, postponements and demands of further information, analysis and alternatives, and with bargaining and compromises. The lack of a decision or agreement may turn out to be the main obstacle for implementation. Endless delays make one think that any decision, even a rejection of the alternatives presented, would be better than no decision.
- *Detailed design of chosen solution.* This may be a productive and progressive phase, if the main decision problems really have been solved, not only formally.
- *Implementation* itself, which we shall take up in the next section.

In real life the change process will, of course, often be quite different from this logical step-by-step procedure. The sequence may vary, and a total or partial iteration of the steps may be needed. The design and discussion of alternatives may be weak or non-existent. The decision on a major solution may in reality be made at a very early stage, based on the exiting power structure and prior attitudes and conceptions of the decision-makers. All the same, a logical model of this type is very helpful in systematic management of change as a planning tool, a checklist and a managerial 'conscience.'

Work Tasks (Sub-Phases) of the Implementation Phase

When the change has been decided on and the solution elaborated, there may be a number of work tasks which have to be done before it is time to start the execution itself.

Preparation work will usually be needed, as the first sub-phase of implementation. Lack of careful preparation has often grounded or delayed a sound administrative change. Generally, the preparations will cover tasks like :

- Further information to and training of personnel that are involved in the change, development of human resources.
- Recruitment, transfer, etc. connected with reorganisation.
- Detailed review of and changes in related systems and regulations.
- Detailed set-up of work arrangements, locations, etc.
- Acquisition of technical equipment and materials.

Clear responsibility for the management of these different tasks (*e.g.* designation of a project manager) is necessary.

The *execution* itself is also very much a question of planning and organisation and good management. In implementing larger changes, unforeseen problems are liable to create difficulties. The management must be prepared for and capable of tackling and solving these difficulties rapidly.

Feed-back and evaluation, both of the results or actual consequences of the change and of the execution of change is most important in a continuous process of administrative development and improvement. Nevertheless, it is often neglected. For larger changes there should be systematic, written reports, comparing the goals and estimated consequences of the change with the actual results. A reporting of this type is also needed for the last sub-phase of implementation, namely *follow-up, adaptation of solution.* In some cases, it is not only a question of adaptation but a larger revision, or even a new solution. This last sub-phase of implementation may, therefore, also be considered as a link to new changes in a continuous change process.

Use of Experiments, Tests, etc.

Implementation of administrative change is often a question of the possibility and opportunity to try out new solutions before a final decision is taken to accept the solutions generally. The willingness of the interested party to try out new ideas and solutions and to allocate resources for this purpose may be decisive for a possible implementation.

But also the experiment or test has to be evaluated in terms of costs, time, benefits and risks of failure. It may be a use of valuable time and resources in order to do things that have been done before, or that have small chances of success.

The need for experiments or tests is also dependent on the type of change involved, e.g. :

- *Innovations,* which give new solutions that have not been tried before, and often are most difficult to evaluate because there is no prior experience.
- *New applications of solutions* or methodology that have been used in other areas, where there is experience.
- *Solutions which are known* and have been used within the same application area, with documented experiences.

It is surprising how often time and resources are used to reinvent former inventions, partially or totally, through larger research and development projects or smaller administrative change projects. The justification and primary goal for most of these projects should not be to invent or design new models or application systems, but to train and develop the people that are involved in the change.

Utilizing experiments and tests for implementing change, there is also a choice between different types, *e.g.* :

- *Experiments,* conducted apart from the operational application, *e.g.* as part of a research project.
- *Feasibility studies,* which often are more limited studies using theoretical models and simulation, consequence analysis, etc., as main tools.
- *Pilot projects,* with the purpose of trying out a solution at a limited, but operational basis, in order to get some practical experience before the solution is evaluated and accepted.
- *Partial implementation,* for example by executing the change in a few out of a larger number of organisational units involved.
- *Parallel implementation,* by keeping up the old solution for an initial period, which may be used for some types of administrative change, like new information systems.

The research institutions working in the field of public administration or in fields of general administrative interest like organisational psychology, sociology, systems theory and informatics, have in most countries not been much involved in the practical, administrative development and improvement in government. This situation is now changing in some countries, and I believe that the co-operation between the public administration and the universities and research institutes could and should be much stronger in the future. Needed support for experiments and tests could also be included in this co-operation.

Main Conditions or Factors for Implementation

Critical Implementation Factors—Different Types of Implementation Situations

The road to administrative change is often paved with good intentions and wishful thinking, which do not give a good base for implementation. The objectives may be unrealistic. The measures and tools may not be adequate or consistent with the objectives. The level of ambition is often too high, and not geared to the possibilities of the existing organisation. Tensions and conflicts within the organisation may obstruct change. All these and other problems should in principle be solved by the "management of change," which in itself often is inadequate and may be the most difficult problem.

We shall shortly consider some of these factors. But first we shall look at some different types of changes and see how they give different implementation situations. From the point of view of the organisation or institution effected, the change may lead to :

- an increase,
- continuation of the status quo, or
- a reduction

in its work tasks and/or resources, primarily personnel resources.

A significant increase in resources, with or without new work tasks, will usually mean good possibilities for implementation. Establishment of a new organisational unit with completely new tasks is perhaps the easiest type of change. A continuation of the status quo in personnel resources and changes in work tasks may also be made without large problems, if the change in tasks are accepted by those affected in the organisation. A reduction in personnel resources, with or without changes in work tasks, will very often create problems and strong opposition, even if there are exceptions. The total elimination of an organisational unit may be more feasible than a strong reduction of the same unit.

In general, these observations only confirm the fact that administrative change will influence the human situation and behaviour, and that these factors, therefore, must be taken into account before implementation takes place.

For the same reason, changes in organisational structures and in the corresponding personal status of civil servants are often problematic and sensitive. In my own experiences, I have often heard discussions on formal changes in organisational structures going on endlessly, without any results. A main reason for this is in my opinion that the discussion is limited to the formal structure and does not include all the other important (and total) aspects of administrative change in the organisation.

Clarification and Acceptance of Objectives

The objectives of administrative development and improvement (see Section I, Introduction) should be discussed and cleared out at the political level in government, and included in the longer term development planning documents. This is not only a question of general or ultimate objectives, but also of operational, down-to-earth objectives which can be used as a basis for selection of means and tools and for setting priorities in the development programme.

The objectives may change over time, *e.g.* with political changes, and they may often be conflicting. The objective of a reduction in the total, public spending may be in conflict with the objective of giving more and better services to the public. The objective of equal rights before the law may be in conflict with the objective of simplifying laws or regulations and decentralizing decisions. A better utilization of personnel resources in government may be in conflict with the objective of better work conditions for civil servants.

There is also the question of how far the objectives decided on are accepted within the public administration. The implementation possibilities of changes are directly related to the agreement or disagreement of the interest groups affected, on the objectives behind the change. In other words, the motivation for change has to be considered in managing the change process.

Motivation, Participation, Bargaining

In selecting strategies for change, one of the most important and difficult questions is how far the change process can or should be built on participation, collaboration and consensus. The opposite choice would be to use a conflict, or confrontation model. It may be argued that in spite of the wide acceptance of particiapative management, it is still uncertain how far it stimulates administrative change. However, some type of motivation, incentives or influence will always be part of the change process. Direct coercion may prove to be more damaging than useful. If there are genuine differences of interest between the parties affected, some type of bargaining (negotiations) may be a solution. In some countries, participation has developed into formalized bargaining between the government as employer and the civil servant unions representing the employees.

Participation of the public (users, clients) on one hand, *e.g.* as part of a democratic, political system, built on representation, and participation of the civil servants affected by the change on the other hand, is also a question of balancing the general, public interests against the special interests of civil servants.

The effects of participation will depend on the different forms it takes, *e.g.* :

- opportunities to get information, take part in discussions and present opinions, *e.g.* through hearings;
- consultations, discussing alternatives and giving advice;
- direct participation in the change process, *e.g.* as member of a project organisation;
- participation in the final decision-making, *e.g.* through board membership or through bargaining.

In some Scandinavian countries, including my own, internal participation has developed during the whole post-war period. Starting with joint information and consultation councils in each institution, internal participation has developed gradually, also with direct participation in the administrative development projects. The participation has been formalized partly through general agreements between the civil servant unions and the government, giving a basis for bargaining in administrative matters, partly through new laws giving rights to civil servants to take part in the decision-making process and to elect members to boards and governing councils.

Resource Availability—Human Development

We shall here consider mainly human resources, and not go into the aspects of time as a resource, the importance of technical/physical resources and the often complex allocation systems of financial resources.

The need for human resources may be divided into the need for resources to cover the change process work itself, and the need for resources in the operational situation after the change has been implemented.

The first and fundamental question of human resources in the administrative change process is to find people for the management of change, the "change-agents" in a wide sense. There is usually also a need for specialists in different administrative fields, like information systems, planning-budgeting-accounting, general management, personnel management, etc.

Then comes the need for a strong participation from those who work in the organisation and should be involved in the change process, which means that these civil servants for a certain period have to be partially or totally released from their former work tasks.

The development work has to be given priority before other administrative or operational work, to an extent which fills the needs of the development projects. This is often not only a question of formally allocating resources, but also of follow-up and withstanding the pressure to use the allocated persons to fill their former tasks.

The administrative change process should very much be a human development process. Citing from Crozier-Friedberg's book : *The Actor and the System* (page 338) : "The change is also the discovery and the acquisition of new capacities." Usually, the human resources wanted in order to manage the change process, are not fully available in terms of qualifications and quantity. The solution is to make use of and to develop the available people in the best possible way. This also includes the persons who are going to be in-charge of operations after the change has been implemented.

Instruments for Change—Choice of Means and Tools, Planning and Organising Methods

In evaluating and selecting means and tools for change, there is often a tendency to consider the means and tools separately and not in combination. Changes in organisational structures are discussed without proper regard to changes in the processes and type of management. New information and EDP systems are implemented without considering the consequences for the work situation, the need for training and personnel development, and for changes in the decision-making process and the organisational structure. In a planned process of administrative change built on a choice of objectives, a mix of means and tools are generally needed.

There is also a two-way relationship between the objectives and the instruments for change. The instruments should be chosen in order to fill the objectives, but it may also be necessary to modify the operational objectives because the instruments and resources for change are limited. Feasibility considerations, also taking account of the time factor, are important.

A primary instrument for change is the variety of techniques and methods to be used in planning-organising-executing the change process itself. This instrument may play a large role in the whole management of change, also in the implementation. It is often neglected or given very little attention. In my own experience, I have found the principles and techniques of modern project planning and management to be very applicable and useful in the administrative change process.

Norwegian Experience in Planning and Implementing an Administrative Development and Improvement Programme

The situation and experiences in Norway are described in the National Paper for this symposium. I shall here only give a short summary and some personal views on the future development. Let me add that in my opinion we have a long way to go before the situation and the development efforts can be considered as satisfactory.

Since 1970, there have been regulations stating that each government department at least once a year shall consider administrative development and improvement measures, *e.g.* in connection with the preparation of its yearly budget proposal, and set up a plan for such measures. The department also has an obligation to take initiatives regarding such measures and plans for its subordinate institutions/agencies.

In the yearly budget proposal, each department shall give a summary of implemented and on-going development and improvement measures within its sector, and of future plans.

There regulations have had some effect, and the budget proposals have given a summary of the development and improvement measures, but with greatly varying quality from one sector/institution to the other. This, of course, might be expected.

In 1975, an initiative was taken to prepare an overall review in Central Government of plans and existing major projects for development and improvement. The purpose was mainly to stimulate these activities, further better planning and organising and clarify objectives stated and instruments used.

Based on written reports from the departments and larger institutions, discussion meetings were held with each department. After these discussions, the plans for future work were revised, and the whole review, including the discussions, was documented by a report which contains a description of all projects, a total of around 340.

A second review, structured in the same way, was conducted in 1977. A main reason for this was to compare the information gathered for the 2 periods. This time, the total number of projects was around 325.

These reviews indicated that the departments and larger institutions should be made capable of contributing more actively in planning and organising administrative development projects. The allocation of sufficient resources to the development projects is a serious problem. A better planning-programming and a better management of planned projects is much needed in many departments and institutions. However, there were cases showing that some larger institutions had a systematic planning-programming-implementing process for administrative development.

In the further work of establishing and developing a process for planning, programming and implementing administrative change as a total programme for the government, with decentralized responsibility, the following may provide a main approach :

1. The longer term development plan (in our case the 4 year-programme) should include objectives and major policies to be followed in the management of change in the public administration.
2. Each year, there should be a planning and review of the administrative change work, at the institutional, sectoral and central level in government, establishing a total development programme with specification of larger projects in terms of objectives, work tasks and instruments, resources and time schedules.
3. A summary of the administrative development programme should be presented in the yearly budget proposals.
4. Once a year, a central meeting with participation from the departments of Finance and Administration, change agencies and other interested parties should be held. This central meeting should discuss selected subjects of special importance and main issues of the administrative development programme.
5. Occasionally, as needed, *e.g.* once in a two year period, there should be sectoral planning and review meetings with participation from the sectoral department (represented by the minister), institutions under the department, the departments of finance and administration and the change agencies.

This outline would mean a further development of the present procedure and organisation. It is based on the special situation of the country, and it is open for discussion how far it is suitable for other countries.

Some Conclusions

Implementation cannot be regarded as an isolated phase in the change process. All the former phases may affect the implementation, and in principle the whole process of change should be geared towards the implementation of change.

As a basis for administrative change, the recognition of organisational structures and processes as very important factors in society generally, and especially in the public administration, is necessary. This applies equally to both politicians and bureaucrats.

The strategies and main policies for administrative development have to be chosen with regard to the societal situation and cultural factors in the country, the internal situation within the public administration, and the ideology and objectives for future development. In this paper some main views are presented. Administrative development in government should be considered as a continuous, induced and directed process of change. The responsibility for change should formally and effectively be placed with the authority and leadership at the different levels of the organisational structure. A programme for administrative development should be planned, organised and controlled as an integrated part of the general planning—, programming—, budgeting—, reporting system of government.

The objectives of administrative development and improvement should be discussed and cleared out at the political level in government, both general objectives, and operational objectives based on available instruments and resources and feasibility considerations.

In selecting implementation strategies for change, the question of participation, collaboration and consensus have to be cleared out. Strategies for the use of experiments or tests should also be considered.

Implementation includes much more than the direct execution of the change decided upon. Preparation work before the execution is usually very important, and after the execution, feedback and evaluation, follow-up and adaptation should be considered as part of the implementation.

Among the critical conditions or factors for implementation are :

- the content of change in tasks and resources in the implementation situation;
- the motivation for accepting objectives and the choice of instruments;
- resource availability and development; and
- the quality of the management of change itself. The management is also a question of techniques and methods to be used in planning—organising—executing the change.

II

Outline of the Situation

In today's society, characterized by important changes which frequently occur in a rapid and tumultuous way, unforeseen and impossible to forecast, there is an imperative need for bright, effective and flexible management.

The increasing social complexity emphasizes the necessity of a responsible decision-making process. So many people are now concerned with this process that one can no longer be sure that it will develop appropriately. The responsibility for the decision will increasingly depend upon a small number of persons. The growing size of administrative units and the multiplication of the links of social interdependence in which these people have to move, make it such that it often becomes impossible to appreciate the significance and the scope of their action.[1]

Facts and Concepts

Any effective reform of the public services requires an adaptation strategy. Such a strategy is made of a plan, a method and objectives. Its implementation must take place within a given context, *i.e.* that action and change are necessary : action in the field of the adaptation of structures; action in the sense of changing individuals, or the actors, concerned.

- It is sometimes assumed that "structure" refer to an environment in which certain things are inconceivable or in which constraints exist which make achievement difficult or impossible.
- It is sometimes assumed that "individual," or actors, refers to knowledge and experience, learning and motivation, resistance and control of the action.

This means that the action process, the organisational functioning process would be easy to carry out if it were only a question of objective method. But one must also take into account the subjective values, as well as the unpredictable variables or constraints.

Relations between the Systems

For a long time, it has been thought that change and reform

were to be achieved while making use of the knowledge, the means and the methods of a given system to try to influence other systems. The idea of such a relationship follows from the natural tendency of social systems to isolate themselves, generating a life of their own. Consequently, the necessary technological knowledge, methodological approach and the capacity for innovation begins to diminish, so that the systems can no longer adapt to a changed environment. This inbreeding process, generating isolation and bureaucracy often negates the educational effect of experience. This has led to systems being submitted to the influence of other systems with a view to change. The principle is right in essence, but the way it is put into practice is too traditional, using methods such as teaching, seminars, courses, etc. Each system remains caught in its own bureaucratic environment, accusing the other of insufficient understanding for its specific situation.

The core of this is what I call "feudalisation" of modern societies.

> "Just as in the Middle Ages when counts and barons struggled for power and predominance, rather than serving their monarch, today large bureaucracies fight for their position and expansion, regardless of the service which they were supposed to render to the public. As Dean Donaldson, of Yale School of Management puts it : large organisations become to an increasing degree unmanageable.
>
> In the permanent war between organisatons, the arms are not, like they were in the Middle Ages, swords, but they are rules, procedures and more recently—and this is the real paradox—modern management techniques. This is why we are in a Babelonic language situation when we speak of management training for large organisations. Because, if all we do is to better equip, in this case public agencies, to avoid content and substance so as to better fight other organisations, we do the contrary of optimizing goals and resources. We are encouraging, enhancing anti-management in the fullest sense of the word."[2]

Susman and Evered say : "There is a crisis in the field of organisational science. The principal symptom of this crisis is that as our research methods and techniques have become more sophisticated, they have also become increasingly less useful for solving the practical problems that members of organisations face. The methods of organisational science have generated knowledge that has led to improvements in the effectiveness and efficiency of organisations, but often at the expense of the quality of working life of their members."[3]

These questions led me to develop some reflections upon our education system, especially in its relation to our current economic needs.

> "For, when change comes, we may have to pose new questions; the old familiar institutions may no longer be doing what we set them up to do. Perhaps (some) hospitals are making (some) patients more ill? Perhaps (some) prisons are making (some) convicts more criminal? What then of (some) management schools and (some) managers? These questions have been thrown up by the very speed of contemporary change; we can no longer be so confident about our experts as once we were, since their worlds have become so complex that they cannot always know where they are being taken. However emphatically they claim to be masters of their arts and sciences, the evidence is that iatrogenesis has come to stay; the *iatrogenic malaise* is created by the healer himself, but only of late has our vigilance against it been aroused."[4]

Is it, therefore, entirely unlikely that the obstinate problems of public service training agencies or systems whose ultimate function is to improve the managerial potential in a given environment, are not, to some extent, also iatrogenic? May it not be, too, that the persistent anxiety within its education movement about evaluating its own efforts is a subconscious expression of the same dread by the experts themselves?

The "Original Sin" : Standardization

By all this, I mean that there are, in the type of activity in which all systems are involved, a number of characteristics which make it very difficult to talk about reform, change and real adaptation. Like in the case of the original sin, these characteristics can never be completely eliminated. But if we can be constantly and actively aware of their existence, we go a long way in mastering excessive inconvenience stemming from them. What are they then? I can think of four, which are :

- *Unclear objectives,* with, as a consequence, the impossibility to evaluate results.
- *Mixing essentials with details.* Management training is not just a matter of courses.
- *Poor Communications.* If it is true that the success of training initiatives somehow results from the joint efforts of public organisations, individuals and schools, then good communications should be essential.
- Management development and training cannot be "canned" or "deepfrozen." Management training is directly linked to conditions which are constantly changing in time, and are different in space.[5]

Taking all these characteristics into consideration, we can easily conclude that all activities which are momentarily undertaken by one system to influence or to change another system, became a broad variety of traditional, similar standardized products, which are determined very often by ineffective production and market oriented aspects.

Unconscious, standardisation has become the ultimate compromise between experts and academic producers, political buyers and administrative consumers. The circle is closed, the economic system works.

Preparation for Change[6]

As we have seen, people in organisations always wish to learn and to adapt to new situations; to say it briefly, they feel the need to learn in order to improve their position. This need, this master-pupil relationship has always existed, whatever the form. In the field of training for civil servants in central agencies and in local government, we can distinguish between three kinds of education :

Technical Training

If we take the example of the training of policemen, we see that it implements the principle of "learning by doing;" this is the filed of skills, *e.g.* the skill to handle a gun. We notice that aptitude is important, although not sufficient. For example, one swims better than the other, but both must have the knowledge of how to move and how to breathe correctly.

Intellectual Training

This is a basic preparation which aims at providing the theoretical and intellectual knowledge necessary to practice a discipline or a profession, *e.g.* engineer, lawyer, treasurer. Usually, this preparation does not focus on practical life, the operational approach in the organisation : one learns what to do, but not how to do it. This preparation gradually tends to get closer to the reality : one could speak of a kind of post-training, *e.g.*, post-graduate or specialized courses, in-service or complementary education.

Post-experience Training

This is training for people without university education, or for people who are preparing themselves for a career promotion, or in other words a sort of "higher education of the second chance."

Management Development

Management : A Specific Function

All these kinds of training are undoubtedly useful, but they are hardly, if at all, preparation for a management function. Such training is not sufficient. We have certainly talked about skills, training, knowledge, behaviour, but not about management as such. The reasons for this are various :

- we used to live in a simple world, made of small entities, which made management superfluous;
- the idea was that leadership is an inborn skill : you have it or you don't;
- there was no accurate knowledge of the specific function of management responsibilities. This is why the Institut Administration-Université has decided that the promotion of management training was indispensable. The question is : can we train people in that sense? My answer is : yes; the more complex the world becomes the more necessary is a methodological approach. And every method can be learned.

The Objective of Education is Learning

My conclusion is that experience alone is not enough; experience trains but mistrains too. There is a need for theoretical knowledge in the field of the approach to real problems. Theory and practice may not be separated. Management education must also obey particular pedagogical principles. The adult *learning process* should :

- complement or revise theoretical and conceptual background;
- include real problems to be solved (objectives, motivation);
- include awareness of behaviour in a learning context;
- adapt the action according to critical discussions.

What to Know—How to Do and Why

The seminars led by our Institute combine all aspects of training systems applied to real problems, change and innovation. The skills ("how") and the attitudes ("why") of people play a decisive part. This type of approach, linking theory to practice, demands actual knowledge ("what") of the problems and of the situation. Therefore, it must rest on study and research work. Where else better than in research communities can we pursue such research? I suggest, in the universities, with the help of the public servants, as knowledge of social environment variables is relevant to these concerns.

Learning from Experiments

From Traditional Training to Internal Programmes

The Belgian Institut Administration-Université has gained a lot during the first years of its existence. Generally speaking, the Belgian civil service has been persuaded of the utility and the necessity of the training action initiated for their managers. In five years time, the seminars I mentioned before have attracted more than a thousand participants. However, if the system in itself seems to have been widely accepted, its practical implementation has been less frequent.

The progress accomplished in gaining knowledge of training methods obviously showed that the education of managers in the public service would remain a limited action if not carried out within the organisation itself, dealing with situations specific to the public agencies.

"The purpose of the Institute was to help the public bodies define their own problems as far as human development was concerned, and elaborate a type of organisation and management able to allow people to fulfil their aspirations. We had to promote new ways of education and training, designed for people belonging to similar structural communities, expressing identical needs and motivations. In order to develop such training policies within the public services, we would have to switch to direct, structurally suitable interventions. Such internal programmes could not rest on the study of artificial cases, but had to deal with real precise needs. These operations would demand narrow relationships between the training of the individual and the everyday reality of his function in the organisation, as well as the involvement of all hierarchical levels in the training process."[7]

We started from Rapoport's definition of Action Research which aims to contribute both :

- to practical concerns of people in an immediate problematic situation; and
- to the goals of social science by collaboration within a mutually acceptable ethical framework.

While Rapoports definition focuses on the aim, action research can also be viewed as a cyclical process with five phases :

- *diagnosis—action planning—action taking—evaluating—specifying learning.*

The infrastructure within the client system maintains and regulates some or all of these five phases jointly.[8]

Practical Examples

I have briefly described the way we have switched from traditional programmes to internal operations. Let us talk now of practical examples, their evolution and the results we obtained.

A first achievement was the creation of an *analysis group* in the Department of National Education, the purpose of which was to analyse and describe the problems of the agency, as well as to derive lessons from this process at a personal level. The public officers were enthusiastic with this kind of "anatomical vivisection" an they decided to go on with it. Two years long, the "Hawthorne-effect" played its role : the participants were glad to be at the centre of attention. But a major problem was that the operation did not focus on real problems.

As a conclusion, we may say that two important steps of the learning process were skipped : there was no trial of their theory in the real world, and no review of this trial action.

The Institute then had the opportunity to launch a first research and development programme in the budgetary field to be conducted in two pilot-agencies. The objective was to prepare—technically as well as psychologically—the introduction of the PPB system in the *Belgian Public Services.* As a matter of fact, this was a first attempt to approach the big problems of the Public Services from the point of view of both methodology and training. The method rested on the desire to exploit the ability of the individual to profit from the analysis and solution of problems existing in his organisation.[9]

It must be recognized that the operation—and this is true not only for the Belgian Pubic Services—was not a complete success. Why not?

- we saw it as an integrated management system to be built in the Public Services, whereas the politicians merely thought of the introduction of a new technique, a new instrument, the ultimate purpose of which was to save money;
- we did not give enough weight to the necessary political consensus and to the powers present in the administrative system.

And we may draw the following conclusion from the experiment :

- the action must grow and develop from within the agency itself;
- the results could have been more positive if we had better defined the objectives in relation to the analysis of the situation—at political, as well as at administrative and budgetary level;
- but the experiment was worthwhile, because the by-products proved to be more interesting than the achievement of the original objective itself.

Perhaps we should have tried to save the project from a premature formalization and from a bureaucratic implementation following from a generalized political decision.

Conclusions and Results

These and many more of our examples illustrate the need to reinterpret common experiences, and to learn from everyday tasks. There exist many theories of learning; we do not intend to review them here. There is learning by "nature," learning by association, learning by imitation, learning by insight, learning by trial. In our view, these are all variations of the same paradigm. This may be expressed in the five following steps :

- *the assembly of information.* This may be called the stage of *"survey"* or input;
- *the rearrangement of this input to suggest new ideas* or new patterns or new relationships relevant to the curiosity or need to learn; this may be called the *"theory"* stage;
- *the try-out of this "theory" in the real world;* this may be called the stage of *"action"* or trial;
- *the review of the results of this trial action;* did the *"theory"* fit? We may call this fourth stage that of *"review;"*
- *the confirmation, modification or rejection of the "theory,"* in the light of this "review." It is assumed that if the results are much what they were predicted to be, the idea behind the results is to be accepted. This we may call the stage of *"consolidation."*[10]

Implementation and Involvement of the Participants[11]

Learning by Doing

The Fondation Industrie-UniversitÈ, the Institut Administration-UniversitÈ and their associated university centres have made major efforts to develop management training by action. But what exactly is the meaning of this concept?

In 1960, our Managing Board decided to start a range of enquiries with the objective of defining the training needs of organisations. In 1962, eight agencies accepted to delegate, for a full-time three month period, a high level civil servant whose judgement they respected. The team interviewed the civil servants in the participating agencies, analysed the results and prepared conclusions.

During the following years, nine teams of six or seven managers each proceeded in the same way. In all experiments, the evaluation made after three months of enquiry showed the cardinal training effect of the work on the interviewers, although no particular teaching had taken place, except for a short introduction in the techniques of interviewing and outcome analysis.

A Methodological Approach

This, together with Professor Revans's studies on action learning in Great Britain, let our Institute to imagine a methodology centred on the conduct of a project as a training method. The fundamental idea consists of conducting studies "in situ" of a strategic problem and the negotiation lined to the implementation of the solutions, as opposed to the traditional process of lectures followed by debates.

One can wonder whether there is a difference between such a method and the current activity of leaders and executives in the organisations, and why the training impact is greater in the first case. Let us begin by saying that every managing action, as well as every other action, contains a training by-product—or a mistraining one. The action-process modifies the knowledge, the attitudes and the behaviours. However, and this has been shown in various studies, the training by-product is generally not valorized.

What should be remembered from all this is the following :

- Action trains . . . and mistrains as well. It may inculcate knowledge, attitudes and behaviours which are obsolete, outdated and inappropriate. It is said that "practice makes perfect," but practice may well make worse!
- The positive and dynamic aspects of the action, carried along in the flow of urgent and everyday decisions, do not retain attention and, consequently, are not considered worthwhile.

The Inter-University Programme for Management Education[12]

A programme such as that set up for business and public executives tends to eliminate these shortcomings. The experience of several sessions organised for private companies has proved the importance of the following aspects :

- It is essential to withdraw the participants from the pressure of the everyday decisions, *i.e.* from their management responsibilities in their organisations. This allows them to concentrate entirely on the "educational by-product" of their projects.
- The project may not be any expert problem preoccupying the top management of the host organisation, but rather a problem to be solved, the training impact of which is as thorough as possible. Therefore, the choice must fall on an unstructured, complex problem requiring the collection of information at various levels, where it is more important to pose questions than to answer them, where no technical solution is at hand, and which demands time to listen, to understand, and allow the judgement to mature; which implies tactful negotiations, etc.
- The critical examination of the knowledge, attitudes and behaviour supposes a permanent confrontation of the outcome of the action between the participants, the managers of the host organisations and the scientific staff of the university training centres. Diagnoses and recommendations for action are constantly submitted to criticism by managers on the one hand and by university experts on the other hand.
- Experience has shown that it is essential for the participants to conduct a project in an organisation unlike their own. The participant escapes the "power system" of the organisation which is paying him; his liberty is greater for judgement, proposals and conclusions. As he is an outsider in the host organisation, it is easier for him to gather information from its management, he is more independent and his judgement is less biased.

Such confrontation between the filed study and the results of scientific research is able to complement the theories of management. The conditions are similar to the ones existing in the "university hospitals."

The top managers of the organisations who have delegated

staff members to the Programme think that the latter offers two fundamental advantages :

- It allows for the opportunity to considerably broaden the approach to management problems, highlighting the long-term aspect, which provides everyday management with more coherence.
- It develops the aptitude to listen to the partner, to negotiate, to "manage the conflict," which is moreover a sign of greater emotional stability in the face of change.

Evolution and New Orientations

Need for a Distinctive Competence

All this has taught us that it was high time to promote a "New Deal," a new "entrepreneurial management," a new "open systems approach" in the management schools and institutions as well as in the public organisations. To make the interaction between both systems' useful, and to give it a social utility, there was an imperative need for a distinctive competence.

Need for Social Utility and Usefulness

Achieving social utility and usefulness means involving all parties concerned in the process. This is the way we see the new and broadened structure of our Institute; all people responsible for the social system must collaborate : the elected members and the representatives of the trade unions, the heads of the administrative "laboratories" and the "practitioners" of the universities.

A "New Look" Implementation

This distinctive competence should not only reconcile theory and practice, universities and public services, the sociological science and the myth of action. Its main purpose will be to show people in the system how to tackle their own problems with the help of the methodological experience we have gained from the practical experiments which were conducted and the lessons we have derived from the sociological organisational research.

The enquiries made on "implementation" have shown us that :

- to evade responsibility can have worse effects than to manage with excessive authority;

- the organisations are more determined by hierarchical structures than by direct decisions or management techniques;
- the differences at the human level persist and provide every organisation with a specific pattern of relationships;
- a better knowledge of the partner's standpoint does not develop conflicts, but, on the contrary, creates new opportunities for the introduction of strategies.[13]

We would like to translate all this into new "projects" to be conducted in :

- the Belgian Post Office (55,000 employees);
- the New City of Ghent (250,000 employees);
- the parastatal or semi-public organisations (250,000 employees).

In a simple way, with modest means (money and human resources), these will be an attempt to create a change situation by providing the conditions in which people in the organisations can learn from each other.

To encourage people working within complex systems to develop their ability to communicate better, we need to observe the following conditions :

- those in-charge must be actively concerned to improve communications, they should not merely talk about the need for doing so;
- the desire to learn how to communicate better, among those where the work is done and where the quality of work depends upon the felicity of the communications, must be genuine;
- the subjects trying to improve their communications must be given the chance to *try out* what they feel might be better methods.

Conclusion—Synthesis

Looking back over the plan of my communication, I may state there is a *malaise* in the field of management development and its implementation. It is perhaps not amazing, but it could be a bad omen. I warn you today : we rely too heavily on standardized conventional weapons in order to keep existing structures alive. The arsenal of the training sessions and methods probably do exercise an impact on the participants. But undoubtedly they also serve to dishearten them when they discover how seldom opportunities arise to implement in their organisations what they have learned in the training.

The weapons of yesterday have become obsolete. We must now initiate a new development strategy, and this will prove difficult to achieve, and demand long and continuous efforts on our part. Remember the story of the young man newly arrived in New York. Strolling about the city, he accosts an elderly man and asks him : "Excuse me Sir, how do I get to Carnegie Hall?" And he hears the answers : "Practice, young man, continuous practice!"

All this is the proof that "il n'y a de richesse que d'hommes" (the only richness is man). Only humans can experiment with conflict situations, and only they are capable of resolving them and benefiting in the process. "The manager's intervention is essential only in the arbitration, in the conflict and in the mobilization of the new resources involved in this process; in the direct and rational commond, it is less important than one might imagine" says M. Crozier.

This is why the report of the European Foundation for Management Development on the situation of management in Europe calls itself : *"Towards a New Deal."* The hint at the famous slogan of President Roosevelt is made intentionally. The unsteady and confusing situation which has emerged from the study makes it necessary to completely revise the role of each of the parties concerned—thus a true "New Deal." This, and this only, will make it possible to develop something new, but something proceeding from within. The action will succeed only if it releases an evolutionary process in the system, instead of forcing it to conform to an *a priori* model.

> "Without going into details, this certainly means to a certain extent dismantling the present large bureaucracies. But it also means a completely different manager—much more of an *entrepreneur* : one who will set out to perform certain functions, reach some objectives by some combination of human and other resources within the framework of an existing information and reference system. The old myth of

the "civil servant' preparing and executing decisions taken by some political authority external to him is as dead as is the fiction of private managers executing the decision of the shareholders in the company. Technical and political processes are now mixed inside the organisation as well as in its relation to the overall society and we need a completely different look as to how it is that the best combinations of goals and resources can be achieved."[2]

It is impossible to treat reform, change, implementation, action learning, etc., independently from the culture from which they must emerge.

References

1. Van Beylen A., *Present Situation and Problems of the Public Administration in Belgium,* Study Group of European Public Service Training Agencies, Annual Meeting, Helsinki, 1976.
2. Talpaert, R., *How Can Public Training Agencies Approach the Concept of Their Management Programs.* Study Group of European Public Service Training Agencies, Annual Meeting, Madrid, 1978.
3. Susman, G., Evered R., *An Assessment of the Scientific Merits of Action Research,* Administrative Science. Quarterly, December, 1978.
4. Revans, R.W., *Preface,* unedited book on Action Learning, Altrincham, 1978.
5. Talpaert, R., *L'Arroseur arrosé,* Final Report on *Management of Management Centres,* European Foundation for Management Development (EFMD), Brussels, 1978.
6. Van Beylen, A., *T.V. Series on Management in Local Government,* Brussels, 1977.
7. Van Beylen, A., *Introduction,* Report on Activities Institut Administration-Université, Brussels, 1968.
8. Susman, G., Evered, R., *An Assessment of the Scientific Merits of Action Research,* Administrative Science Quarterly, December, 1978.
9. Van Beylen, A., *La programmation des dépenses publiques : une exigence de l'Etat moderne,* Brussels, 1969.
10. Revans, R.W., *Theory of Staff Development,* The Hospital Centre, Manchester, 1972.
11. Deurinck, G., *Introduction,* Report on Activities Foundation Industrie-Université, Brussels, 1973.
12. *Programme Interuniversitaire de Formation á la Direction,* Fondation Industrie-Université, 6ème session, 1978-1979.
13. Crozier, M., *La Formation des cadres et la sociologie des organisations,* Paris, 1975.

7

"Steel Frame" : Structure and Orientation

Administrations of all countries are essentially alike. Cultural, political, historical, but also juridical aspects only define the outward side. Organisations have their own laws and rules which are in force throughout the world.

People, whether in capitalist, communist, developed or less developed countries, all react similarly. Therefore, this statement does not specifically concern the developed world, although it will certainly contain some typical elements.

Is Our Society Actually as Much in Motion as We Think ?

Behind the theme "Steel Frame : Structure and Orientation" is the theory that today's society is in a swift current. It is commonly stated that everything is moving, nothing remains, we have to continuously adapt ourselves and to revise our opinions.

This theory, however, is seldom substantiated. I hesitate to conclude that it is correct in every respect. Aren't we too often comparing the past to the present, using anachronistic standards? Does the flow of information permit us to have a clear view of the changes that really matter? Aren't we human beings? Have we changed that much, after all?

Information is often badly handled. Many reports have been written and studies made, but many of these have ended up in people's drawers. Not because they are getting out of date so fast, but because we often don't know what to do with them. Often, information is not divided into what is important and what is not. On the other hand, we often know very little about the issues that really do matter. Information processing in administration is still an undeveloped area. It should consist of much more than knowledge concerning the processing of administrative information (with or without the use of computers).

But even if the supposition that everything is in motion is true, there is still the question : should the administration react to all these changes—either immediately or later on? In my opinion, the essence of governing is to discover and to follow the main lines of developments and to adapt one's policy thereto. Government is not concerned with *ad hoc* reactions to daily facts, but with keeping an eye on facts of strategic value. Even waiting or doing nothing can be an action. Too often, we adopt an attitude towards a new development, while we have inadequate understanding of what exactly is going on. The ability to acquire that understanding is not being stimulated enough.

In this way, certain developments are taken as something new, while, actually, they represent an evolution of something started elsewhere. Instead of building on existing activities, the policy is often to create new institutions.

A complete survey of the activities of the administration and the structure connected with it is often absent. I think that such a survey would produce very important conclusions. It will appear that one could speak of a collection of incoherent activities and involuntary results.

What Should be Reformed in the Administration?

Has it been sufficiently analysed if and how the administration should be reformed? Is it not a fact that the increasing restrictions imposed by the administration are arousing only feelings of discontent? Could we not say that these feelings result from the idea that we have of what an administration should do and what should be its place in society? Is this conception clear and universally accepted? Is it realistic?

It is not difficult to theorize about changes in structure, *e.g.* of the ministerial organisation. In practice, however, experience of changing organisations, certainly large scale or macro change, is not favourable. Change involves an intricate process; it takes a long time and it causes various counter-effects. Afterwards one wonders whether the situation has improved.

Issues of less importance are hardly discussed. A closer look reveals many shortcomings in the small-scale or micro-structure, or in human functioning.

Procedures, decision-making, advisory systems and regulatory systems laid down in laws, appear not to operate well in practice. In the initial stage, too little attention is paid to system construction. Later, alterations may make things worse, because one may lose sight of the original plan.

It is striking to find that little use is made of the experience which exists within the organisation. Ministers or top civil servants are rarely asked for their experience with the organisation during their term of office. I think they could produce valuable practical information about the situation within the organisation and on the surrounding bodies or organisations. Information of this nature is of vital importance and is relatively easy to obtain.

Innovations and new methods are also discussed freely, as well as techniques and strategies which should enable us to improve the administration. However, we should guard against the illusion that we can find solutions there. There are not many new ideas that one can think of—much of what we have now is based on what we had. Besides, consideration of new possibilities easily distracts attention from the faults of the present. The fact that evaluations are hardly ever made can be significant here. When simple systems are not functioning well, what about the more complicated systems? Take planning for instance. Simple planning appears difficult to realize in practice, yet we keep striving at more refined and all-embracing planning systems. Successful results are still very rare.

Much more attention should be paid to the people working in the administration, flexibility and productivity should be encouraged. A point, rarely mentioned in this respect, is that, while it is seen as normal that captains of industry should meet very high demands, the function of a minister is largely underestimated, both the candidate himself and by the political organisations. The task of a minister concerns functions that have changed in the course of the years and which have gained a dimension and significance that is seldom equalled in industry. There is poor insight as to the capacities candidates must have in order to be able to occupy such a post—especially in our day and age. For example, is a minister the highest decision maker, or has he become a manager?

Even when there are defects in the structure or the functioning, and even when adaptions are made, these changes do not always lead to a better policy.[1] This, we believe is the main problem. Often there is no clear idea about the objectives and the limitations especially with respect to finance, personnel and organisation. Such considerations should enter into the initial stages of policy formulation. Much thought should be given to this point.

Structure and the functioning depend on the policy pursued. However, within the present structure much more can be done and we, therefore, at the same time, urge that effort be put into finding ways to improve the present system. Certainly, in what we would call the 'dark corners of the organisation,' much human and financial capacity is being wasted. I think that what we may call 'small efficiency' improvement is more important than big and, seemingly, better renovation. Too often a deterioration of the financial and economic situation is the first motive to start thinking about improvement. Most of the time, the only answers are : tax increases, slowing down of activities or a cutting back of personnel.

Are We Speaking Too Much in Magical Terms ?

There is a clear cohesion between the above and the way in which we started to speak of administration. We use words like 'the government,' 'parliament,' and 'democracy.' But these have become vague, meaningless notions, and are often just based on (juridical) fictions, not indicating institutions or systems. We have forgotten that the administration concerns organisations and systems which are subject to, mostly, very simple rules.

Precisely because we have forgotten this, we now have the impression that we live with magical institutions with unlimited power and possibilities. I think this is also the very reason why it is taboo to speak of these things. What for instance is known of the true relation between the government and the parliament, the tasks and the demands of politicians and ministers, the decision making within ministries and between the various ministries, the position of government officers? Rarely, are such subjects investigated, although this could help significantly to improve the functioning of those institutions and the persons working in them.

Distorted views are formed in this way. One would think ministries possess a great deal of information. If parliament wants to perform its task well—according to popular judgement—it should have at its disposal information obtained through its own efforts. To provide this, sometimes even shadow ministries are created. Yet, the question arises whether information is not being confused with assessment. For it is remarkable how little relevant information the administration has at hand.

To mention another example. Important, powerful positions are allocated to government officers. The expression "the fourth power" has even been introduced to describe the situation. However, it is not made sufficiently clear whether this power really exists or whether it is really essential. The relationship between officers and ministers—an issue which needs more study—is not fully understood.

Only recently did people become aware that even government bodies consist of human beings. Why do we use the expression 'government officers' or 'civil servants' instead of employees or workers? Symptoms of stress such as taking more sick leave and opting for early retirement have been brushed aside for a long time.

Involving government officers in changes and re-organisations, and the rise of interest groups of government officers manifesting in various ways and who want to be engaged in the policy-making, are other ways of treating them as human beings and areas that should be reconsidered. For example what is the role of the government officer?

We must find a way to a genuine public administration. The citizens have a right to this, for it is 'their' organisation. Things like public participation, decentralization and the existence of an ombudsman are actually only marginal phenomena. Many problems, caused by the uncommunicative attitude and taboos against discussing things, are caused by inability and lack of information and insight more than by anything else. But bringing the public closer to the administration can give the opposite impression. The population should have an understanding of what government administration can and cannot do. Politicians, trade union leaders and others who represent the people in one way or another are inclined to underestimate the commonsense of the people that they represent. Often they are (too) distant from the people. This has become a phenomenon in itself.

Should the Position and the Role of the Government be Revised?

For many reasons we speak in favour of a re-organisation of the role of the administration and the government and their place in today's society. The former law-and-order-government has become a welfare-government.[2] The administration has grown into a sort of shelter to perform all sorts of activities which cannot be done by other groups. The cohesion of all those activities and that of the government has long been lost. Yet we see the administration in traditional (juridical) ways. The fact that the government is an organisation which is subject to various, almost legal organisational demands, has also been forgotten.

In my opinion, we should aim at another kind of administration, built more on a basis of a clear concept, while observing the constraints of finance, personnel, and organisation, and not merely on a basis of the sum of wishes and desires of what the people want the administration to do.

It will have to be a government that stimulates and that exploits the possibilities of others. The administration should not always do things itself, but it should delegate certain responsibilities to others—groups or individuals. This does not diminish its power, as is often thought, but makes better use of its power. The government can become more flexible this way and less vulnerable to growing rigid.[3]

Final Remarks

What I said before was not intended to be a concrete solution to problems which undoubtedly exist in many administrations. I have only suggested another way of looking and thinking and tried to take a more realistic view of the many utterances calling for change, new strategies, methods, etc. In particular, I wanted to indicate a number of self-evident things, which are forgotten so often because of our hurry to make things even more beautiful and bigger.

In this respect, more use should be made of the management science. Parallels can be drawn constantly. Almost every problem within the administration can be traced back to organisational origins.

People often are envious of industry. Also part of the magic. Big firms especially suffer from the same bureaucratic symptoms, only one does not realize it. Lack of management appears to be the main reason why many firms do not function well—the economic problems come after that. Administration and industry can learn a lot from each other.

In the increasing internationalization of the government's task, it has become important to look at the international organisations too. Although these are presented with specific problems, I think they face and will face more and more the same kind of problems as those I tried to indicate above. Also on that level, people do not sufficiently recognize the fact that an organisation has its own laws, and that, here also, there is lack of cohesion between policy, structure and functioning. Here also, too little attention is given to the need, especially for an organisation that is growing in size—for continuous evaluation.

Finally, the attempts to gain the interest of the politicians, and even to get their help on changing the governmental organisation, have not been successful. This can be explained, I believe. It is not primarily the task of a politician to occupy himself intensively making organisational changes. He has responsibilities of his own. First of all his task involves policy making and maintaining control on policy implementation. So the politician should be included in the process of defining the role of the government and administration within the wider sense of these terms. He cannot be involved in defining and modifying the resulting organisation.

Ministry Department and Political Planning

Definition of planning—All activities serving the preparation and implementation of political-administrative decisions may be subsumed under the term 'political planning.' Political planning will, however, have to satisfy the requirements of a qualified type of governmental and administrative action, in other words : it will have to find expression in an improvement of governmental procedures for the solution of problems, and in an increased leadership capacity of governmental institutions.

Increased demand for planning—during recent years the demands on the government to influence the form of agricultural policy have increased considerably. The international and national interlacement of agricultural policy has increased.

Since the Common Market became reality, the formerly national competence in the field of market and price policy has passed over to the supranational bodies of the EEC. Therefore, it is necessary to take into consideration when developing new concepts and reform projects not only the special interests of one state, but also the interests of presently nine, and in the foreseeable future twelve, member states.

Due to regulations relating to constitutional law, the agricultural structure policy has to be jointly planned and financed by the Federal Government and the eleven Federal Laender. Although a change in the distribution of funds among the Federal Laender presents difficulties due to a distinct desire to maintain the *status quo*, there is, nevertheless, a great demand for planning with regard to the elaboration and further development of support directives and the appraisal of individual measures in the field of structure policy.

Owing to the fact that since the early seventies the spectrum of objectives and tasks which are relevant from an agricultural policy point of view has broadened considerably, larger planning efforts have become necessary. Rural social policy has developed into a comprehensive social security system of the rural population. The requirements for adequate protection of the environment have had to be taken into account in the agricultural sector, too. In order not to endanger the ecological balance, adequate initiatives are necessary in the field of regulatory and structure policy.

The quantitative augmentation of tasks is accompanied by a qualitative change with regard to the structure of tasks. Individual actions have been replaced by systematically conceived promotional programmes. Since, for example, agricultural structure policy is being considered today to be an integral development policy for rural areas, aspects of regional, employment, traffic and city planning policy have to be taken into account to a greater extent than in the past.

Planning System of the Federal Ministry of Food, Agriculture and Forestry

In view of the increased demand for planning, in 1973 the Federal Ministry of Food, Agriculture and Forestry introduced, on the basis of preliminary work done by a project group for governmental and administrative reform of the Federal Ministry of the Interior, an integrated planning scheme of tasks and finance. It comprises the following elements :

- Structure of objectives and programmes
- Organisation oriented along programmes
- Systematical analysis of priorities in the field of agricultural policy
- Annual elaboration and extrapolation of a medium-term plan of tasks and finance

The main objectives of this system of planning consist of :

- achieving improved co-ordination of policy;
- identifying, at an early stage, future developments and problems;
- developing proposals for solutions and appraising them in the light of political objectives; and
- studying current measures and programmes with respect to their economic and social benefits.

Improved Co-ordination of Policy

(1) Structure of objectives and programmes–A comprehensive structure of objectives was elaborated for the entire field of activities of the Ministry. The system comprises 4 main objectives, approximately 30 sub-objectives and approximately 85 partial objectives. It shall serve as a guide for the disclosure of conflicts with regard to objectives, for the identification of gaps with regard to measures and for the appraisal of measures.

Eleven programmes have been set up to obtain potential planning measures, to group together those measures which have related technical contents and to define boundaries. In this way the Ministry's field of activity is clarified, and the establishment of a programme budget is facilitated. The programmes are described in the annual agricultural reports of the Federal Government.

So far, funds have been allocated for the programmes only to the extent that the measures had 'external' financial effects. However, for administrative expenditures, *i.e.* personnel expenditure and non-personnel costs, no funds have been allocated.

It has not proved practicable to develop further the structure of objectives and programmes as the decisive instrument for orienting all planning decisions. So far, it has not been possible to solve satisfactorily certain methodological problems concerning : *(i)* the weighing of objectives, and *(ii)* the exact assessment of the manifold relations between the objectives and the funds, on the one hand, and the reduction of the political risks of quantitied statements with regard to objectives, on the other hand.

(2) Organisation—An adequately adapted organisation is a prerequisite for the integrated planning of tasks and finance. For this reason, the tasks and competences have been centralized within one division or sub-division whenever possible. Technical planning is done in principle by the technical sections (where specialist knowledge is particularly concentrated) or by small interdivisional *ad hoc* working parties. A co-ordinating section has been established for each division to deal with the co-ordination of planning work done by the technical divisions (programmes).

The planning group is an important organisational unit for the preparation of decisions. It is composed of the heads of the sections for co-ordination of planning (management), for budget matters and long-term EEC matters, as well as of the heads of co-ordinating sections. The planning group is chaired by the head of the sub-division for the co-ordination of planning. The group of division heads (conference heads of divisions), chaired by the State Secretary, ranks above the planning group. This conference of heads of divisions discusses, in final form, the proposals elaborated by the planning group for the Federal Minister and the State Secretaries. As the conference of heads of divisions has the function of a decision-taking body with overall responsibility, its decision have a binding character for the subsequent implementation phase. However, they are subject to a vote by the Federal Minister.

The co-ordination of total planning activities with regard to time, objectives and contents is done by the sub-division for the co-ordination of planning, by the respective co-ordinating sections, by the planning group and the conference of heads of divisions.

Systematic Analysis of Interdivisional Task-related Priorities

Interdivisional task-related priorities generally refers to task having considerable political weight, often requiring further development of essential sections of the concept of agricultural policy. Such tasks often are identical with problems emerging above all when conflicts, discord and deviations from hitherto existing objectives become apparent in the course of future developments.

The selection of the main priorities of work is being undertaken through identification by the technical sections, and establishment of priorities by the planning group. The conference of heads of divisions decides on which problems shall be treated with priority. In this way, the political interests of the Federal Minister and the State Secretaries are also taken into account, even when these interests hamper a rational and economic solution. A consideration of political priorities prevents technical planning based on economic data from becoming an academic planning game.

The technical section responsible in the specific case jointly elaborates, with an *ad hoc* working party, a so-called basic paper relating to the priority of work. This paper is submitted to the members of the planning group for consideration and discussion. Later on the conference of heads of divisions takes a preliminary decision on the alternative solutions suggested by the planning group which will be submitted to the Federal Minister for final decision.

The sub-division for the co-ordination of planning, i.e. responsible for long-term analyses, cost-benefit analyses and research planning, also takes up problems relevant from an agricultural policy point of view and submits its proposals for a solution to the planning group.

The planning results relating to priorities of work may find their expression either in legislative initiatives, in new or amended directives on support or in a modification, extension or restriction of hitherto existing programmes and measures. The resulting financial consequences are taken into consideration when the annual plan of tasks and finance is set up.

Excursus : the research sector dependent on the Federal Ministry of Food, Agriculture and Forestry is also included in the planning of tasks. This is done, on the one hand by means of a short- or medium-term general research plan within which the research projects of the scientific institutes have been adapted to the research requirements of the Ministry. On the other hand, the Ministry and the research institutes have set up a list of long-term tasks resulting from the analysis and appraisal of future problems. Jointly elaborated hypotheses on changes with regard to the general, social and economic conditions for the Ministry's policy represent the basis for identifying problems.

The inclusion of research planning in the Ministry's political task planning is facilitated by the fact that the Minister's sub-division for the co-ordination of planning is responsible for overall co-ordination.

Annual Elaboration of a Medium-term Plan of Tasks and Finance

The majority of political tasks and governmental support measures are reflected in the financial plan and budget. As funds are always limited, any planning of tasks will necessarily also have to be a planning of resource expenditures.

As a general rule, the medium-term plan of tasks and finance is set up during the period from the end of October to the end of February. The process of planning begins with the request made by the head of the division for budgetary, organisational and personnel matters and the head of the division for the co-ordination of planning and observation of the economy. This request is addressed to all technical divisions :

- to note all relevant financial measures for the budget and financial plan; and
- to justify the major ones in view of the objectives pursued.

In the framework of this task, certain measures are carefully appraised, on a selective basis, with regard to their effects and results. These include above all new measures, measures whose concept is to be changed, and measures exposed to particular criticism. Furthermore, an exact explanation and a statement of the basic elements of calculation are necessary. The competent technical and co-ordinating sections are responsible for these activities. Furthermore, the co-ordinating sections elaborate an outline in which the tasks and finance are summarized (partly in tables) and classified according to programmes. This outline is completed by the information necessary for the further process of decision-taking (i.e. priorities, demand for basic decisions in the field of agricultural policy).

Subsequently, the proposals of the technical divisions are reviewed, in a general way, by the budget section and the section for the co-ordination of planning. The sections for long-term analyses and for cost-benefit analyses participate in this revision.

The comment elaborated in the form of a joint memorandum is discussed, together with the planning results, within the planning group and then channelled to the conference of heads of divisions for discussion and preliminary decision. The final decision is taken by the Federal Minister.

During this procedure an annual, comprehensive analysis of all programme fields is deliberately dispensed with. Nevertheless, this procedure shall ensure that all particularly urgent, as well as all problematic, measures will be analysed in detail.

In the past, the budget and the financial plan have been set up in bilateral negotiations between the technical and the budget sections. The draft budget consisted, in the main, of extrapolations of earlier estimates which were not oriented along cost-benefit considerations and priorities.

Resume

1. Owing to the integrated planning of tasks and finance, policy co-ordination has improved within the Ministry.

2. The major problems are taken up quickly, alternative solutions are considered without delay, if possible and the necessary decisions are prepared in a timely fashion.

3. The decentralized implementation of planning tasks by the technical sections and their centralized co-ordination by the planning group and the conference of heads of divisions has stood the test.

4. A system of management for the rationalization of administrative work, oriented along internal work cycles offered advantages, *e.g.* the work plans and the time schedules decided upon by the Federal Minister and the State Secretaries, designed for the analysis of work priorities and the implementation of the planning of tasks and finance, had very positive effects.

5. During the gradual completion of the planning process, the argumentative weighing of the 'pros' and 'cons' among the participants (technical sections, planning group, conference of heads of divisions) is intentionally used as an aid for the preparation of the Ministry's decisions. Formalized procedures (*e.g.* benefit analyses) on the basis of quantitative models have proved to be useful only to a very limited extent.

6. In the framework of political planning attention has to be directed towards political analysis and the development of

strategies for the realization of objectives. In this way, the different political interests and socio-political ideals, as well as general, social and political conditions, will have to be taken into particular account. Reaching agreement and settling conflicts in the real political arena very often prove to be the real testing ground for rational concepts and attempts at reform.

References

1. A political turn or change, or a new constitution are often used as an argument to change the organisation of the administration. In my opinion changes in the political or the constitutional situation are less elementary than people are inclined to think—or rather : hope? A large part of the government's activities is not altered by such changes. They don't always evoke a new policy, so such changes do not necessarily imply immediate consequences for the organisation. Besides, in such a situation, one would prefer continuity of the organisation rather than relying on an organisation which still has to establish and consolidate itself.
2. I have already mentioned the need for a clear survey of the activities of the government. The government has all sorts or responsibilities, but is unable to give these responsibilities organisational form.
3. The less developed countries often claim that they cannot yet afford such a 'new' administration, because they think that, first they have to go through the same stages until 'development' is obtained.

   I think people accept this view too easily. Besides, one should not forget that changing organisations, and that's what we are talking about, is much more difficult than creating them. They should learn from the bad experiences of government institutions in the developed countries.

8

Administrative Options and Development : A Behavioural Analysis

Since bureaucracy as a system of government has come to stay in almost all countries and certainly in India, it is only to be expected that the bureaucratic phenomenon will grow in the coming years. More and more state activities which are on the anvil, will inevitably see the burgeoning of the bureaucracy in fields which have traditionally been outside the purview of the governmental system. From all evidence of the recent history of India every new state activity seems inexorably to lead to greater bureaucratic growth and consequently bureaucratization.

Is this process as inevitable as it seems? The question could take different forms in different countries. In the Third World non-Socialist countries, the question gets linked with fundamental problems of development. Is development a process of social evolution through environmental interaction in which scope for human intervention is limited? Or can development be engineered to suit the needs and tastes of man and the society in which he lives.

The experience of the post-planning period in India clearly demonstrates that the developmental process can be greatly accelerated through state action. Compared to the first two quarters of the twentieth century, the pace of development in the third quarter has decidedly been superior and faster. In other words, development is not merely an outgrowth of history but can be engineered and compressed in time.

The problem of development seems ultimately to hinge upon management, especially how the process of development is conceived, handled and administered. In other words, this means management in the broader sense. Evidence suggests that developmental activities are broadly of two types. Discrete activities such as building of roads, bridges, communications, transport, dams etc., and diffused activities like education, health, family welfare etc. The former are amenable to discrete organisational treatment. The latter are not. The diffused sector needs different forms of organisation. Evidence also suggests that where the process is more people-based it is qualitatively different; that with all their limitations, in the people-based programme, to the extent that they succeed in involving the people closely into the programme, the success level in the diffused sector seems to be much greater.

This poses basic problems to development management. On the one hand development in countries like India sees the almost inevitable growth of bureaucracy as the sole instrument of state policy. On the other hand, bureaucracy also develops a stranglehold on the developmental process and it adjusts this process to suit its own pace and liking whether it meets the needs of a country like India which is primarily interested in accelerating development or not.

Even more fundamental, as studies by Robert Michels, Peter Blau and others have pointed out are certain inherent contradictions between bureaucracy and democracy. The essential values of bureaucracy are hierarchy, status, secrecy, specialisation, rules and an unflinching obedience to authority. In contrast, democracy is built around almost diametrically opposite values of egalitarianism, non-hierarchism, open discussion and above all dissent. The guiding principle of bureaucracy is rationality which, in essence, means efficiency. The guiding principle of democracy is popular will.

At the same time there are almost no examples to show democratic institutions as instruments of implementation or actual day-to-day management. All democracies have, therefore, had to fall back upon bureaucracies as their principal instruments for getting things done. This is what Peter Blau calls a paradox, that is, the necessary co-existence of democratic and bureaucratic institutions.

The question, therefore, is not whether or not we need bureaucracy but what kind of bureaucracy or bureaucracies. Can we afford the classical Weberian type of bureaucracy which is essentially static in its values and orientations? Or do we need the types of modifications which many scholars and also practitioners, have seen the need for. To an extent changes have indeed been made from time to time in the bureaucratic apparatus even in India. But these changes have been within the existing framework and at least Indian bureaucracy basically wears the looks of the classical Weberian model both structurally and behaviourally, with excessive emphasis on hierarchy, status, secrecy and authority, not to speak of rule-orientation and impersonality.

From these perspectives the findings of the present study are important. While we did find a significant level of incompatibility between bureaucratic values and developmental values, the results were far more complex. As bureaucracy came face to face with developmental tasks—especially tasks requiring people's participation and involvement—bureaucratic norms and values began to undergo a metamorphosis. There was a marked and percentile trend towards lessening the rigours of the structural and behavioural patterns of bureaucracy. The structure of bureaucracy began to get adapted. The hierarchies became less rigid the system of rules lost their deadly strangehold, they began to be more responsive albeit in limited terms. More importantly, behavioural values began to get radically affected. Impersonality became less rigorous and the needs of the citizen became a little more important. This was more so in respect of the field agencies, especially in the agricultural sector where people's involvement and participation are essential for the successful implementation of the programme of development. In other words the bureaucracy showed signs of dynamic institution.

It was perhaps a crucial finding that developmental bureaucracies which are more at the 'receiving end' *i.e.*, those requiring citizen co-operation for bureaucratic performance rather than at the 'giving end' *i.e.* the civil service dishing out favours, permits etc., tend to get structurally less rigid and behaviourally more responsive. The whole 'gestalt' of the bureaucracy gets altered and the concerns begin to shift, undoubtedly through necessity to meet the needs of the people rather than of the bureaucracy itself. This holds out the prospect that even the traditional bureaucratic organisations such as the ones in India are not beyond hope. More so since the kind of transformation that has taken place thus far in different bureaucratic organisations is entirely accidental and not by design—accidental in the sense that the occurrence is a consequence of something not planned in a systematic manner. A well-planned adaptation could, therefore, yield far greater results, an issue that will be dealt in some more detail later.

The incompatibility which we found between the traditional, bureaucratic, structural, and behavioural values and the values of development, therefore, is not entirely a negative conclusion. It only means that while the classical model may be irrelevant for India, bureaucracy *per se* is not necessarily so. As an organisational instrument it can be modified, altered and adapted to meet, at least to some extent the needs of development.

Determinants of Policy

In other words, the findings of the study have profound policy implications. As noted earlier, during the entire era of planned developments the administrative policy of the state in India barring a few exceptions has been based on the assumption that the state would use the bureaucracy as its key instrument of development management. In other words, the administrative policy of the country has been essentially predicated upon the bureaucracy. There have, of course, been several attempts at reforming the administative system. But all these attempts have been within the existing framework. And what is more, they have been unsuccessful in bringing about any significant change in the workings of Indian bureaucracy.

It is not conceivable that in the near future the administrative policy of the state in India will undergo any basic change. Bureaucracy is exceedingly resistant to reform and the political system lacks either the will or the capability to force a change. If this be so the findings of the study pose some fundamental problems. Above all, if there are some inherent contradictions between bureaucratic values and developmental values, how far would bureaucracy be able to deliver the goods? To what extent would it be able to meet the challenges of the future especially in the complicated and of rural development? If the study has to be believed, bureaucracy would not be able to deliver the goods so long as it continues to retain its present character.

What then are the options? One important but perhaps a rather difficult way would be to transform the existing bureaucratic system, at least at the higher levels, by integrating it with the political system. That is to say, that the higher bureaucracy would be politicized and key bureaucratic positions would be manned by the cadres of the ruling party so that there is an active and direct involvement of the political system in the actual implementation of development programmes. To some extent there is a parallel to this in some Western countries not to speak of the socialist countries. This is by no means an easy solution and goes against the grain of the 'neutral' bureaucratic system which has been built in India since Independence. There is also no guarantee that such a system will necessarily be able to perform better. But to the extent that the ruling party at any given point of time is interested in its political future in a free and democratic system, it is likely that the party will seek to ensure better performance at the grass-roots. This alternative, therefore, deserves to be experimented upon in a limited way and in selective fields.

A variant of this approach would be to design a bureaucratic system which seeks a greater involvement of the people in its work programme. In other words, to design the system in such a way that people's institutions are given more and more say in developmental functions. One way to do this would be to develop the Panchayat institutions especially at the grass-roots level and help them to develop as instruments of administration rather than as merely local political institutions.

We have at least two States which have extensive experience in this field, namely Gujarat and Maharashtra. In Gujarat the Taluka Panchayat is a pivotal institution with an elected President who directs the entire Taluka development office with a senior officer called the Taluka Development Officer to assist him in his function. In Maharashtra the principal institution is the Zilla Parishad with an elected President and a Chief Executive Officer as the administrative head. Even here the experiment has stopped short of giving full powers in local developmental matters to the Panchayat institutions.

The institutional base, however, already exists and it would not be difficult to build these people's representative institutions into full scale instruments both of development and local self-government. Despite many limitations in terms of availability of necessary levels of skills and capabilities, it would be possible to give these representative institutions a much greater say and role in matters of local importance and those having a direct bearing on the life of the immediate community. Admittedly not the entire country would be ready for such an experiment in decentralization and devolution of development administration. At least an immediate beginning can be made where the base already exists while preparatory work could be started in other cases.

A third alternative would be to identify whatever people's organisations exist at various levels and strengthen and support them with a view to enabling them to play a greater and expanded role in development administration. Several voluntary organisations, sometimes affiliated to political parties, but quite often independent of partisan involvement exist with excellent record of development services to the local community. These exist extensively in fields like education, health, agriculture and sometimes even in the small-scale industrial fields. These are precisely the areas where people's institutions are ideal vehicles of development effort. However limited it may be, voluntary effort has repeatedly been found to be more efficacious than bureaucratic effort imposed from the top. This type of effort from within needs to be encouraged, nurtured and supported as a matter of deliberate administrative policy.

While on this alternative special mention should be made of the co-operative system. Amul, the milk co-operative in Gujarat, has amply demonstrated in most effective terms, what a well organised co-operative system can do for the development of a whole and crucial sector even against natural odds. Many parts of India especially Gujarat, Maharashtra, Tamil Nadu, etc., have long traditions of effective and sound co-operatives. In recent years political factors have eroded their strength. Even so a conscious policy to utilise the co-operatives, along with voluntary organisations, as instruments of development administration, will not only infuse new life into this sector, but provide the state with a less expensive and more efficacious instrument of implementation and development.

A fourth alternative could be the direct association of the citizen clientele with the official agencies at the key performance levels so that the people have a say in programmes directly affecting them. This may involve setting up of people's committees either functionally or in aggregate areas. This would ensure a greater dovetailing of the people's expectations and aspirations into the administrative apparatus and enable an easier and speedier adaptation of both the citizen and the administration to the needs of the development programme. Admittedly there are not many successful illustrations of this approach with possible exceptions in the socialist countries. But it is a method that could be selectively used in programmes of a developmental character, such as in agriculture.

Experiment with these various alternatives should and need to be tested and tried out. From a theoretical standpoint if the people's direct involvement is a greater guarantee of performance, then the developmental pay-off of these policies would be much greater and, therefore, deserve serious administrative policy consideration. There are thus crucial macro-policy implications of the study.

These alternative, do not, however, imply that bureaucracy will have no role in development administration. Many discrete sectors such as transport, roads, medium and large irrigation, public sector enterprises etc. will continue to be and need to be organised on bureaucratic lines. These sectors will be large and important enough for the bureaucracy to be fully occupied and perhaps with benefit to the nation.

What, however, if such alternatives do not get the support they deserve? Is it possible to conceive of more limited options within the existing administrative framework? That is to say, if bureaucracy remains the only or at least the principal instrument of development administration, can changes and modification be made within the existing organisational parameters to adapt it more effectively for performance of these tasks?

Even from such a narrower or intra-bureaucratic perspective, the study has indicated several policy suggestions. Not all of these deserve to be repeated here and suffice it to highlight the most crucial ones, especially those relevant to development administration.

First of all, since the study reveals a certain degree of

dysfunctionality between hierarchy and development orientation, it is necessary that the steeply hierarchical propensities and traditions of Indian bureaucracy be curbed or modified. These propensities and traditions have posed every conceivable barrier within the bureaucracy and have been inimical to the development of effective working relationship between the civil service and the citizen especially in the developmental context. The task of de-hierarchization will be undoubtedly difficult since it is a deeply ingrained value in the Indian governmental system. Even so, it will be beneficial to the system to organise somewhat more flat organisations, insist less on superior-subordinate status relationship and generally encourage a greater degree of informality and flow within the bureaucratic system and with the people at large, especially with the citizen clientele.

The negative relationship of division of labour with change, result-orientation and citizen-orientation is also suggestive of necessary prescriptive action. Excessive division of labour tends to diffuse creative response of the bureaucracy in essential terms. Here too some modification should be designed to give the people more integrated service. High differentiation appears to lessen bureaucratic concern with social aspects of the change process and responsiveness to the people's needs. This implies that the government needs to take greater care in designing jobs and in organising the departmental systems than has been done so far. Considerable literature already exists on job enrichment and work design which need not be elaborated here.

The behavioural characteristic of impersonality which is so strongly ingrained in the Indian bureaucracy generally, though not so strongly in the developmental one, also poses problems. Impersonality and change-orientation are negatively related. Similar relationship extends to commitment, though no such conflict is demonstrated between impersonality and result-orientation.

Modifications would, therefore, be necessary to make the Indian bureaucratic system less impersonal. This poses problems because a personalized bureaucratic system could also create several difficulties in programme implementation. As the study indicates the nature of the tasks itself in certain developmental areas like agriculture, ensures to an extent that the bureaucracy would be less impersonal. Ideally, therefore, what needs to be done is to design administrative tasks and functions in which the citizen is at the 'giving end' and the bureaucracy at the 'receiving end.' This will compel the latter to be more understanding and accommodating of the people's needs than in a system where the civil servant is at the giving end. Designing administrative systems of this type is no easy task and will take some ingenuity. Fortunately, in the developmental sector, the effort would be relatively easy and meaningful. Tools like training which have an effect of reducing 'impersonality' could be more effectively used.

Lastly, on rule-orientation, similar corrective action is necessary. Rule-orientation is the normal and oft-decried propensity of bureaucracies all over—no less in India. Its negative relationship with key developmental variables has similar policy consequences. How to develop a culture in which rule-orientation gets diluted and bureaucracy becomes more responsive to the tasks to be performed is the basic problem of administrative policy. As the findings of the study show, higher education can help in reducing the rigid rule-orientation of the bureaucrats. The tool could be used to a greater degree so that end-goals and not the rules can once again become the central foci in bureaucratic operation.

In broader perspective, therefore, hierarchy, impersonality and rule-orientation are the three critical characteristics of bureaucratic organisation and behaviour which appear to run counter to the administrative policy needs of development administration. There is almost a certain level of contradiction between these three characteristics and development-orientation. Each of them, therefore, suggests policy measures to obviate avoidable adverse impact. Such measures are obviously available to a lesser or greater extent and they need to be adopted. Without such a conscious effort, there would be many hurdles in the performance of developmental functions in the country. More detailed conclusions are available in the individual chapters.

Concerns and Issues

The study has thrown up issues in theory building both on bureaucracy and development administration. Bureaucratic theory is, of course, of a much older vintage and despite several recent criticisms, still remains useful especially in developing countries like India where the bureaucratic organisation is the principal instrument of public administration. However, the study shows, the structural and behavioural characteristics are not necessarily related and that the actual behavioural propensities begin to alter the structural characteristics to an important extent. A static theory of bureaucracy, therefore, does not adequately reflect the actual modifications that come in or the true character of bureaucracy which emerges. Hence, a single bureaucratic model appears to be difficult to sustain, though a broadly generalisable framework perhaps can still be built. From the practical point of view it would be far better to develop a range of models in which many factors which have been widely discussed could be provided for.

The various constructs presented in the study perhaps need to be examined in greater detail both in relation to traditional bureaucracy as well as the developmental one. This will throw up more data on the hypotheses suggested by the present study and help us build better theoretical frameworks.

The building of further bureaucratic theory is indeed very crucial especially to the developing countries where bureaucracy of one hue or another will remain important for quite some time to come. Even in the developed world this would be no less important. Experience has shown that bureaucracies tend to proliferate in both the capitalist and socialist countries of the West. In the developing countries, even if some of the alternatives suggested above are tried, there will still be a large and important bureaucratic sector. Hence appropriate theory building will be an important challenge which the academia and the professional bureaucracy will have to face.

On the other hand, the theory of development administration used here is more beset with problems. Neither national nor international literature covers adequately these theoretical issues. To the extent that change-orientation, result-orientation and citizen participative-orientation are significantly related to each other, they do suggest a theoretically useful model for building further frameworks as well as testing them in other situations. Perhaps other attempts at conceptualization will bring out other constructs which will help build the theory of development administration further. Special efforts need to be promoted in this direction.

These issues are stressed here because they are important to both academic and policy purposes. To an extent the first step has been taken to relate bureaucratic theory directly to development administration and to test their neutral congruity or otherwise. That there is a theoretical incongruity which is borne out by the present study is an important milestone for theory building and for policy purposes. This should spur future work in new directions.

Finally the study of bureaucracy as an administrative institution needs to be further examined in relationship to bureaucracy as a political institution. What is its political role especially in developing countries like India with a bureaucracy of imperial traditions? Is it possible ordinarily to have democracy at the Central or State levels and bureaucracy elsewhere? Both theoretically and in policy terms this does not look like a feasible proposition. The present paper does not warrant any conclusion on this topic. It only urges attention to this crucial issue.

Institutions and Work Culture

All institutional arrangements, designed though they are to facilitate attainment of certain goals, are finally mediated through the actions of individuals. This is true as much in relation to the system of public administration as others. The behaviour of civil servants is an important determiner of the outputs which any public administration system is expected to yield.

In India, wide gaps between the expected and the actual behaviour or performance of the civil service have driven home the realization that real life bureaucracy cannot be understood solely on the basis of the formal organisational system; that the behviour of civil servants in their job roles is determined by a host of factors related to the personality of the civil servants themselves and the conditions in which they join the civil service and serve in it. However, although knowledge about the conditions in which civil servants do their work is important to both academicians and politicians, systematic studies in this area are few. In the present study we felt that the study of development bureaucracy would be rather incomplete without a certain amount of attention paid to the working climate experienced by the civil servants.

The Developing Milieu

A formal organisation with a certain division of work among its members and a system of relationships among them, is essentially a purposeful creation. It is supposed to justify its existence by performing predetermined functions. Towards this objective the members of the organisation are engaged in various activities and tasks. Studies in this subject have amply demonstrated that the behaviour of employees is governed mainly by the individual's characteristics and their perceptions of the various factors in the setting or environment in which they discharge their functions from day-to-day. These factors include practices relating, among others, to superior-subordinate relationships, entrustment of responsibility and authority, utilization of the capabilities of personnel, development of personnel, styles of management and of control and treatment of citizen clientele. In the literature on organisational behaviour, these kinds of factors are often described as constituting the working climate of an organisation, office or agency.

To the extent the working climate is an important determinant of the behaviour of organisational personnel, the importance of it in development administration also cannot be overemphasized. Any efforts to improve the chances of the developmental civil servants performing their functions efficiently must also include steps to ensure the existence of the working climate that is most conducive to such a performance. In the present study, we have attempted to diagnose the working climate of developmental agencies in the sample in terms of certain key characteristics. We believe that a systematic diagnosis of the present is the first necessary step towards further improvements in it.

Coping with Responsibility

One of the key variables in the efficient operations of the administrative machinery is the willingness of the civil servants to accept increasing responsibility for handling their work. The problems facing public servants working in development programmes are often complex and demand dynamism of approach. The success in dealing with these problems, therefore, depends in an important way on the self-starting ability of the civil servants reflected in such attitudes as the readiness to assume larger responsibilities.

In the present study we ascertained the attitude of civil servants towards responsibility by asking them the following question :

> In terms of the quality of work how much responsibility would you like to take in your present position?

As Table 8.1 shows, a large majority of the respondents of the study reported a favourable attitude towards accepting more responsibility in their present work. Thus nearly 73 per cent of the respondents are disposed to assume much more or somewhat more responsibility for quality work in their present position.

Table 8.1
Results of Responsibility Factor

In terms of the quality of work, how much more responsibility would you like to take	*Number Reporting*	*Per cent*
Very much more	271	37.5
Somewhat more	256	35.4
Keep things as they are	149	20.7
Somewhat less	21	2.9
Very much less	14	1.8
Not replied	12	1.7
Total	723	100.0%

It is noteworthy that the emphasis in the above question was not so much on the volume of work transacted by the respondents as on the qualitative aspects of it like the scope for decision-making permitted in one's job role, the difficulty level that is comparable with the capabilities of job incumbents, etc. The results, therefore, suggest relative downgrading of jobs at least in the Governmental agencies studied. These agencies, as reported earlier, deal with

Table 8.2
Results of Responsibility by Class

Willing to have responsibility for quality of work	*Number Reporting*		
	Class I (%)	*Class II (%)*	*Class III (%)*
Very much more	29.9	35.3	40.5
Somewhat more	44.5	39.7	32.9
Keep things as they are	22.7	21.3	20.8
Somewhat less	2.9	3.7	5.8
Very much less	—	—	—
Total	100.0% (N = 137)	100.0% (N = 136)	100.0% (N = 449)

important developmental programmes. It was expected that the work content of the jobs of civil servants serving in them would be more varied and challenging.

The study also found similar attitudes towards responsibility among Class I, II and III respondents (Table 8.2). Little over 80 per cent of the respondents from each class would like to have 'very much more' or 'somewhat more' responsibility in terms of the quality of their work. On the other hand only about one-quarter of the respondents from each of the three classes would like either to keep things as they are or have somewhat less responsibility than they presently have.

A corollary of the above finding of the study about responsible work assigned to the respondents was their feeling that they do into get maximal opportunities for utilizing their training and education in their present positions. The reference here was intended to be to the capabilities of the respondents acquired through formal education and institutional and on the job training during service and their utilization in their present positions. The data show that only about 30 per cent of the respondents feel that their present positions give them opportunities to use their capabilities to the full, whereas a good 40 per cent feel their capabilities utilized only moderately. The balance of 30 per cent respondents have reported that the work currently assigned to them draws little upon their talents. The feelings of the respondents about the utilization of their capabilities in their current assignments are broken down in Table 8.3 according to the class of service.

Table 8.3
Utilization of Capabilities by Class

Extent of Utilization Reported	*Number Reporting*		
	Class I (%)	*Class II (%)*	*Class III (%)*
Fully	27.7	19.8	33.4
Moderately	54.7	40.2	37.9
Little	17.6	40.0	28.7
Total	100.0% (N = 137)	100.0% (N = 136)	100.0% (N = 449)

We expected that with longer service and upward mobility, the value of the civil servants would increase and that it would be reflected in the employing agencies drawing more and more on the pool of experience and abilities that such a civil servant represented. The above results, however, show not only sub-optimal manpower utilization in the agencies studied but also the limited opportunities available to the civil servants for growth and development through their day-to-day routine.

Delegation by Superiors

Besides enriching civil service jobs, delegation of authority to the subordinates is generally accepted as one of the most desirable means of training administrators. Such delegation improves administrative competence of the civil servants and stimulates their growth potential. Delegation also expedites disposal of work. The need for adequate delegation down the hierarchy is even greater in development administration so that delays in decision-making and achievement of programmatic goals are minimized. Table 8.4 shows how the respondents of the present study felt about the delegation of authority by their superior officers.

As the results show, 35 per cent of the civil servant respondents have superiors delegating to them as much authority as they desire to take on and even more, while for the remaining 65 per cent there was not enough or there was little or no delegation of authority. To the extent readiness of the subordinates to assume increasing responsibilities is an important variable of the delegation of authority by their superiors, the study shows that there is considerably more scope for it than the present practices seem to make.

Table 8.4
Perceived Delegation of Authority by Superiors

Extent of Delegation by Superiors	*Number Reporting*	*Per cent*
Great deal	77	10.7
Enough	175	24.2
Some, but not enough	214	29.6
Little	73	23.9
None	84	11.6
Total	723	100.0%

Do difference in class of service cause differences in the delegation of authority by superiors? The data in this regard are presented in Table 8.5.

Table 8.5
Perceived Delegation by Superiors According to the Class of Respondents

Extent of Delegation Reported	*Number Reporting*		
	Class I (%)	*Class II (%)*	*Class III (%)*
Great deal	8.8	7.6	12.4
Enough	44.8	25.9	17.5
Some, but not enough	28.6	27.4	30.2
Little	12.5	28.8	26.2
None	5.3	10.3	13.7
Total	100.0% (N = 137)	100.0% (N = 136)	100.0% (N = 449)

The above table shows that respondents from Class I experience greater delegation of authority from their superiors than those from Class II and III. Thus about 54 per cent of them reported 'good deal' or 'enough of delegation' compared to 33 per cent from Class II and 30 per cent from Class III. Similarly only 18 per cent of Class I respondents reported 'little' or 'nil' delegation by their superiors, while the same extent of delegation was reported by about 40 per cent of the Class II and III respondents. These results suggest that the sharing of responsibilities between superiors and their subordinates is prevalent to a greater extent among Class I civil servants than among lower class civil servants. Indeed, the experience of Class II and III civil servants in this regard is highly comparable.

Images About Assuming Responsibility

The respondents of this study clearly indicated that they would like to be entrusted with more responsibility than at present. We also sought to find out the organisational climate relating to assumption of responsibility in which the respondents are functioning. In particular, they reported their perceptions about the attitude towards responsibility among their superior and subordinate officers. As regards the former, the following perceptions were reported.

Table 8.6
Image of Superiors Undertaking Responsibility

In your opinion, do your superior officers	*Number Reporting*	*Per cent*
Like to take great deal of responsibility	99	13.7
Like to take little more than enough responsibility	78	10.8
Like to take just enough responsibility	203	28.7
Like to take very little responsibility	240	33.2
Do not like to take any responsibility	103	14.2
Total	723	100.0%

It is noteworthy that as many as 47 per cent of the respondents reported that their superior officers took very little or no responsibility. On the other hand one-fourth of the respondents perceived their superiors willing to assume appreciable amount of responsibility, while 28 per cent of the superiors are reported to be taking on themselves just enough responsibility. A positive orientation of the superior officers towards responsibility not only indicates their high degree of involvement in the official activities but also serves as a stimulant for a similar attitude among the subordinates. The foregoing results show that at least as their subordinates perceive, the superior officers are not highly involved in their work.

When we further analyzed the respondents' image about the attitude of their superiors towards responsibility, according to the class of service to which they currently belonged, the following distributional pattern emerged.

As Table 8.7 shows, the proportion of the superiors reported to be taking great deal or more than enough responsibility is on the decline with about 40 per cent according to Class III respondents, 19 per cent according to Class II respondents and only 12.5 per cent according to Class I respondents. However, Class II and Class III respondents also report 48.51 per cent of their superiors to be taking little or less responsibility in their work, compared to 42 per cent of the superiors of Class I respondents reported to be taking responsibility to the similar extent. On the whole, therefore, there does not appear to be significant difference in the pattern of the superiors' attitude to responsibility reported by the respondents in the three classes. Nevertheless, to the extent the decidedly positive attitude to responsibility on the part of a

Table 8.7
Image of Superiors Undertaking Responsibility According to Class of Respondents

In your opinion do your superiors	*Number Reporting*		
	Class I (%)	*Class II (%)*	*Class III (%)*
Like to take great deal of responsibility	5.9	13.1	16.2
Like to take little more than enough responsibility	6.6	5.8	13.6
Like to take just enough responsibility	45.6	29.9	22.0
Like to take just very little responsibility	34.6	38.7	31.3
Do not like to take any responsibility	7.3	12.5	16.9
Total	100.0% (N = 137)	100.0% (N = 136)	100.0% (N = 449)

superior has a wholesome influence on the behaviour of the subordinates we imagine it to be present less and less at the higher echelons of bureaucracy.

We also ascertained the perceptions of the superior civil servants themselves about the attitude of their subordinates towards responsibility, as shown in Table 8.8 below. As the Class III respondents in the sample were not likely to have any subordinates working under them we have reported the perceptions of Class I and Class II respondents only (N= 273).

Table 8.8 shows that, if the subordinate civil servants generally have a poor opinion about their superiors' readiness to accept responsibility in work, the superiors themselves do not have any

Table 8.8
Image of Subordinates Undertaking Responsibility

In your opinion, are your subordinate officers	*Number Reporting*	*Per cent*
Willing to take great deal of responsibility	5	1.8
Willing to take just enough responsibility	65	23.8
Willing to take some, but not enough responsibility	97	35.6
Willing to take very little responsibility	69	25.3
Not willing to take any responsibility	23	8.4
Not reported	14	5.1
Total	273	100.0%

better or different image about their subordinates' attitude to responsibility. Thus little over one-third of the respondents in Class I and II together have reported that their subordinates are willing to take very little or no responsibility. In contrast, one in every four of the superior respondents have to say that his subordinates are willing to take just enough or a great deal of responsibility in work. Again for nearly 36 per cent of the supervisory respondents, their subordinates do take responsibility in work but it is not enough.

The foregoing findings show that the superior and the subordinate officials at least in the agencies studied do not entertain a positive image of each other as far as shouldering the developmental responsibilities is concerned. Overall, it indicates concern for just enough or minimal involvement in the developmental process. Earlier, we have seen that the respondents themselves would like more responsibility to be entrusted to them. We have thus the phenomenon of the civil servants whose superiors are not quite enthusiastic about fulfilling organisational responsibilities and whose subordinates too have a passive attitude towards responsibilities and finally who are themselves experiencing low level of responsibility being assigned to them. The resulting confusion about accountability for performance is bound to be dysfunctional to the achievement of programmatic goals of development administration.

Styles in Employee Supervision

Research in the field of organisational behaviour has amply demonstrated that the styles of employee supervision have a significant influence upon the morale of employees and in consequence upon their efficiency of job performance. In this study we have examined certain aspects of the pattern of supervision in the four developmental agencies on the basis of the perceptions reported by the respondents.

For the purpose of the present study, we considered overwhelmingly 'task-centred' style of supervision and overwhelmingly employee-centred style of supervision to be two extreme polar positions on the continuum of employee supervision. Our basic premise was that the complexities of the tasks facing the civil servants today, especially in the development spheres, require *(i)* that they handle their work with great initiative and enthusiasm, and *(ii)* that they enjoy opportunities to grow professionally in the service. As these considerations are tapped in the concept of employee-centered style of supervision, we tried to find out to what extent this style is being experienced by our respondents.

As described, we defined employee-orientation of superiors in terms of the efforts they make to adequately explain and teach their subordinates how to perform difficult tasks, their accessibility to all the subordinates without discrimination, the friendliness of their relationship with the subordinates, and the openness of inter-personal relations wherein the subordinate feels free to discuss his personal and work problems with his superior. Since the behavioural response of the employees is determined significantly by their own perceptions about employee-orientedness of their superiors, despite how subjective this can be, we asked the respondents to rate their superiors on this scale of employee-orientedness. The results are reported below in Table 8.9.

Table 8.9
Employee-Orientation of Superiors

Degree of Employee-orientation of Superiors	*Number Reporting*	*Per cent*
High*	184	25.5
Moderate	395	54.7
Low	143	19.8
Total	722	100.0

* For classification into high, moderate and low degree of employee-orientation, see chapter on methodology.

The table shows only 20 per cent of the respondents perceiving their superiors as poorly oriented to them in the sense in which we have defined such orientation here. On the other hand, one-fourth of the respondents have the superiors who are very positively oriented towards them. The modal employee-orientation of the superiors is, however, reported to be of moderate degree. When we further examined this issue in relation to the class, the following distributional pattern emerged (Table 8.10).

It is found in the table that Class II and III respondents experience a similar pattern of supervisory behaviour towards their person. As regards Class I respondents, they have a smaller proportion reporting both highly and poorly employee-oriented superiors; about two-third of this group is however reported to have moderately employee-oriented superiors.

Table 8.10
Employee-Orientation of Superiors By Class

Degree of Employee-orientation	*Number Reporting*		
	Class I (%)	*Class II (%)*	*Class III (%)*
High	18.2	27.9	26.3
Moderate	64.2	50.0	51.4
Low	13.8	17.6	21.8
N.R.	3.8	4.5	0.5
Total	100.0% (N = 137)	100.0% (N = 136)	100.0% (N = 449)

The employee *vs.* task-orientation of superiors has attracted the attention of social scientists because of its influence on the motivation of employees and the sharing of organisational responsibilities. To explore this relationship further in the context of development administration, we analyzed the employee orientation of their superiors reported by our respondents, on the one hand, and the amount of authority delegated to them by their superiors. The results are presented in Table 8.11 below.

Table 8.11
Employee-Orientation and Delegation of Authority

Degree of Employee-orientation of Superiors	*Amount of Delegation of Authority Reported*			*Total*
	Great deal and enough per cent	*Some but not enough per cent*	*Little/none per cent*	
High	50.2	24.9	24.9	100.0% (N = 184)
Moderate	31.2	34.8	34.0	100.0% (N = 395)
Low	23.9	21.2	54.9	100.0% (N = 143)

The foregoing table shows that the respondents in the sample who find their superiors quite positively ('high' in the table) oriented towards them are more often delegated much authority and less often little authority by these superiors. In contrast, respondents who perceive their superiors to be poorly ('low' in the table) oriented towards them are reported to be more often enjoying little delegated authority and less often as much of delegated authority as they would like to have. Implicit in the employee-orientation of the superiors considered in the study is the relationship of trust and interest between the superior and his subordinates which is reflected in the former sharing his responsibilities with the latter to a large extent.

How do the civil servants who are having employee-oriented superiors respond when the superiors are prepared to delegate more authority to them? Our data in this regard reported below does not, however, show that the respondents with employee-oriented superiors have a particularly positive attitude to responsibility. It will be recalled that the latter was ascertained through the question : In terms of the quality of work, how much more or less responsibility would you like to have than at present? As reported above, a great majority of the respondents have asked for more responsibility than is presently given to them. Possibly because of this skewness in the replies, the study could not discover the relationship between employee-orientation of superiors and the subordinates' attitude to responsibility in work.

Table 8.12
Employee-Orientation and Attitude to Responsibility

	Amount of Responsibility Desired			
Degree of Employee-orientation of Superiors	*Much more/more (%)*	*Status quo (%)*	*Much less/less (%)*	*Total*
High	78.1	20.8	1.1	100.0% (N = 184)
Moderate	72.4	21.5	6.1	100.0% (N = 395)
Low	61.7	22.0	16.3	100.0% (N = 143)

Attitudes in Personnel Development

In this study it was found that as many as 68 per cent of the respondents have not received any formal in-service training throughout their career so far. Most of the remaining 32 per cent trained respondents appear to have been given formal training to meet the needs of their immediate job assignments. Since formal training is insufficiently used, it follows that the major development of the civil servants takes place through their day-to-day work. We noticed earlier that by and large the respondents of this study felt that their jobs did not prove to be an adequate challenge to their abilities. Apart from this, development of the civil servants also depends upon the interest taken by their superiors to help them to learn more to assume higher responsibilities. In the present study the respondents of Class I, II and III reported the following attitudes of their superiors in this regard.

Table 8.13
Attitudes in Personnel Development by Class of Respondents

	Number Reporting			
Does your superior help you to learn to assume higher responsibilities	*Class I (%)*	*Class II (%)*	*Class III (%)*	*Total (%)*
Always	15.0	14.0	22.0	19.4
Usually	33.0	24.0	25.0	27.0
Sometimes	22.0	25.0	26.0	24.3
Rarely	22.0	27.0	17.0	20.2
Never	8.0	10.0	10.0	9.1
	100.0% (N = 137)	100.0% (N = 136)	100.0% (N = 449)	100.0% (N = 723)*

* One respondent did not report his class of service

Table 8.13 shows that in the view of about 48 per cent of Class I, 38 per cent of Class II respondents and 47 per cent of Class III respondents, their superiors are taking 'high' interest in helping their professional growth and thereby preparing them for positions of greater responsibility. It is also important to note that one-fourth of Class III respondents and little over one-third of Class I and II respondents report little or no interest taken by their superiors in their development. With limited formal training facilities and equally limited interest taken by their superiors, these civil servants are bound to require an inordinately long time to acquire higher capabilities.

Perception of Criteria of Promotions

It is the stated policy of the government to promote civil servants on the basis of seniority and merit (merit being most commonly assessed through confidential reports). At the same time, other considerations are also believed to influence decisions about promotions. In the final analysis, the behaviour of the civil servants in their job roles is governed by their own experience and understanding of the factors that go into decisions about promotions in government service, whatever be the declared policy relating to it.

The urgency of civil servants in the developmental programmes turning out the desired level of output in their work, both in terms of quality and quantity cannot be overemphasized. It is widely recognized that one of the long-term incentives for high standards of performance in work is the system of promotions that is understood to be based on competence. In the present study, therefore, we attempted to ascertain the perceived importance of merit for promotions in government service in relation to that of other criteria, according to our respondents. In other words, the respondents indicated their understanding of the weight of several factors in promotional matters in the civil service. The factors we considered are : seniority, hard work, superior quality of work, being a good politician in the sense of the ability to manipulate the things to one's own benefit, being a friend or relation of higher officials, and getting along well with one's superior. Of these, seniority consideration is determined by the length of service in a particular position or grade. Hard work and superior quality of work represent merit considerations, while the last three factors are essentially in the nature of social considerations. In the questionnaire the listing of these factors was preceded by the following instructional set :

> "Speaking about your own personal impressions, which of the following things do you believe help the person most to advance in government service? Please put 1 against what you consider to be the most important factor, 2 against the next important and so on until you have put 6 against the least important factor."

The perceptions reported by the respondents are described in Table 8.14.

Table 8.14
Perceived Relative Importance of Criteria of Promotions

Criteria of Promotions	*Rank order of Importance Reported*						
	Rank I per cent	*Rank II per cent*	*Rank III per cent*	*Rank IV per cent*	*Rank V per cent*	*Rank VI per cent*	*Total*
Seniority	31.9	17.3	21.6	19.1	4.7	5.4	100.0% (N = 716)
Hard work	13.7	18.5	17.4	9.3	23.6	17.5	100.0% (N = 715)
Superior quality of work	14.7	18.8	20.6	13.8	14.8	17.3	100% (N = 711)
Being a good politician	10.4	13.5	10.4	13.5	17.6	34.6	100.0% (N = 711)
Being a friend/ relation of higher officials	23.7	16.7	6.6	8.4	26.7	17.9	100.0% (N = 711)
Getting along well with one's superior	4.8	14.5	23.1	34.6	10.1	12.9	100.0% (N = 714)

Notes : *(a)* Higher rank = more importance
Lower rank = less importance
(b) In the last column 'N' is different for different criteria because all the respondents did not check all criteria.

The table shows that seniority is clearly perceived by the respondent civil servants as the relatively most important factor responsible for promotion in government service. The average ranking of this factor has been 2.6th.[1] On the other hand, the factor of superior quality of work is given the second highest average rank (3.3rd). However, the proportion of respondents giving first to sixth rank of importance to this factor is about equal indicating thereby considerable ambivalence with regard to the place of quality work in promotional decisions in government service. In contrast, the clear importance of seniority is evident from the fact that there is a sharp decline in the per cent of respondents assigning lower rank to this factor. The ambivalence towards being a politician for getting ahead in the service is shown by the data; nevertheless, it does not indicate that the civil servants have discounted this factor as of no consequence in earning promotions (average rank = 4.1 st). On the other hand hard work as an element in decision-making in promotions is found to be at 3.5th rank, suggesting that it is just of average importance.

Similar average ranking is given by the respondents to 'being a friend/relation of higher officials.' It is noted that as many as 40 per cent of the respondents have assigned the first two rank orders of importance to this factor, while about the same proportion have assigned it the last two ranks. The implication is that friendship and familial considerations are either of crucial importance or not at all. Lastly, nearly 60 per cent of the respondents have indicated 3rd and 4th rank order of importance of getting along well with one's superior in promotional matters. This may mean that although this factor is neither insignificant nor all that important for promotions in the service, it does 'help.' In as much as the confidential reports of the superior officer are an input for deciding about promotions, the working relationship between the superior and his subordinate is unlikely to be perceived as unimportant.

Are there any differences in the rankings of promotional criteria according to different groups the respondents may belong to? As regards the class of the respondents the findings of the study are as in Table 8.15.

Table 8.15
Importance of Promotions Criteria By Class

Criteria of Promotion	*Average Rank Order of Importance**		
	Class I (N = 137)	*Class II (N = 136)*	*Class III (N = 449)*
Seniority	2.9	2.7	2.5
Hard work	4.1	3.7	3.3
Superior quality of work	3.9	3.3	3.3
Being a Politician	3.2	4.2	4.2
Being a friend/relation of higher officials	3.0	3.0	3.6
Getting along well with superiors	3.1	3.3	3.9

* Lower the average score, the higher the rank order of importance.

In the table the average rank order of importance for each criterion of promotion ranged between 1 and 6 with the lower score denoting higher perceived importance of a criterion, and the higher score indicating lower perceived importance of it. Any score below 3.5 could, therefore, be regarded as indicative of relatively higher importance.

The table clearly brings out that according to the respondents from all classes, seniority is still the most important basis of promotion in government service. None of the other factors of promotion is given lower than 3rd average rank by the respondents. Next to seniority, being a friend/relation of the immediate superior is ranked as an important consideration by the Class I respondents. We are rather surprised to find the sample of civil servants perceiving quality of work and hard work as a relatively less important requirement of promotion, less important than 'being a politician.'

On the other hand manoeuvring activities are considered to be least necessary by the Class I and III respondents. In fact, Class III respondents have reported hard work and superior quality of work as the important consideration in promotional decisions, next only to seniority. This class of civil servants also believe that superior officers are less useful than Class I and II civil servants think them to be. The study thus brings out two features of present practice in the government for granting promotions as significant in the view of our respondents. First and foremost, the seniority of the civil servant has the maximum weightage in these decisions. Secondly, that the higher the level of the civil servant, the lower the perceived importance of merit (consisting of hard work and quality work that he is able to put in) for promotions. Admittedly we have assessed the relative importance of different criteria of promotions at the level of perceptions of our respondents. It cannot, however, be gainsaid that perceptions of people are one of the important determinants of their behaviour.

We also considered the respondents who have been promoted once or more times and those who have not so far received any promotion in terms of their perceptions of promotional factors.

Table 8.16 shows that both the groups of promoted and non-promoted respondents perceive seniority as the most important basis of promotions in government service. The relative importance ascribed by the two groups to other criteria are similar except in the matter of working relationship with the superior officer and hard work. Surprisingly, the promoted civil servants consider the place of hard work in promotion less important than do the civil servants who have not received any promotion so far. On the other

Table 8.16
Perceived Importance of Promotion Criteria by Promotions Received

Criteria of Promotion	*Average Rank Order of Importance**	
	Promoters (N = 463)	*Non-promoters (N = 256)*
Seniority	2.6	2.1
Hard work	3.9	3.5
Superior quality of work	3.4	3.5
Being a politician	4.2	4.0
Being a friend/relation of higher officials	3.5	3.3
Getting along well with one's superior	3.5	4.0

* The lower the average rank importance of a factor, the higher the perceived importance of it for promotions.

hand, the former perceive good working relations with their superiors to be of greater help. On the whole, the experience of having received promotions does not seem to make for material differences in the perceived importance of different criteria of promotions in civil service.

Need Fulfilment in Civil Service

Civil servants have various needs and they legitimately expect to have them fulfilled in their service in government. In fact, the match between their expectations of several things from the service and the extent to which they are able to actually enjoy them indicates the level of job satisfaction or dissatisfaction. The latter is an important stimulant for the civil servants to perform well. In the present study, therefore, we also tried to find out how much the development agencies studied are providing for the fulfilment of the needs of their employees.

The needs considered by us are listed in Table 8.17. Admittedly, an important need of the civil servants, namely their emoluments, is missing in our list. Two major considerations were before us when we decided on this omission. In the first place, there are many components of the earnings of the civil servants like the basic pay, dearness allowance, house rent allowance, other allowances, provision for pension etc. This dimension of the civil servants' need, therefore, requires an elaborate treatment which

Table 8.17
Perceived Need Fulfilment by Class

	*Mean Fulfilment Reported**		
Needs Considered	*Class I*	*Class II*	*Class III*
Social prestige of job	3.7	3.2	3.2
Helping relationship among co-workers	3.3	3.4	2.8
Recognition of good work	3.0	2.5	3.4
Growth in one's work	3.8	2.8	3.7
Feeling of accomplishment	3.7	3.6	3.8
Interesting work	3.7	3.5	3.6
Variety in work	3.5	4.1	3.2
Working relationship with superiors	4.3	3.4	4.1
Work suited to capabilities	3.9	3.5	3.7
Opportunities for further promotions	2.8	2.2	2.5
Feeling of job security	3.6	3.6	3.2

* The minimum and the maximum possible score on each need/job factor ranged from 1 to 5, so that higher mean score denotes higher fulfilment of the need and lower mean-score, the lower fulfilment of the need.

was somewhat beyond the nature of the present study. Secondly, even if we had confined ourselves to the take-home pay, nothing new would probably have been added to the study by its inclusion since the lack of enthusiasm on this score among civil servants is quite well-known. On the other hand, not much empirical data were available on the job factors that we considered.

It is true that certain needs of, say, two different civil servants may have been fulfilled to the same extent and yet the levels of satisfaction derived may not be comparable because the relative importance of different needs may differ among these civil servants. For instance, employees A and B may report that their jobs provide a 'good amount of challenge.' However, if A has pitched his expectation at a higher level he would be relatively less satisfied with his job than B whose expectations are as much as the job provides. Realising this we conducted a pilot survey among the sub-sample of the respondents of this study to find out the relative importance ascribed by them to the job factors studied (ranging from the least important to the most important) towards making them satisfied with their jobs. The analysis of these responses showed these job factors to be of comparable importance. Hence, in the final study, we only ascertained the degree to which different needs of the respondents from their present jobs are reported to be fulfilled. In a sense, the reported degrees of fulfilment represent the levels of job satisfaction experienced by the respondents.

As Table 8.17 shows, respondents coming from Class I, II and III differ appreciably in respect of the level of fulfilment of these job factors, namely, recognition of good work done by them, professional growth in their work, variety in work, working relationship with their superiors and opportunities for upward mobility in the service. On the other hand, a somewhat comparable degree of need-fulfilment is reported by all the respondents with reference to the feeling of accomplishing something towards the success of the agencies in which they served, the feeling of job security, having to do the work that is suited to their capabilities, interesting character of work, and the social prestige of their job among the outside people.

In terms of the level of fulfilment the data show that 'opportunities for promotions' is the least fulfilled need of the respondents generally, implying that the chances of rapid promotions in government service are perceived to be poor. Similarly, the respondents, need for recognition of even a particularly good piece of work done by them is also not being fulfilled at a higher than just tolerable level.

The needs of the respondents as a whole which appear to be particularly fulfilled are : having working relationship with their superiors, getting a feeling of having accomplished something worthwhile in their work, having variety in work, having interesting work, and the feeling of job security.

The expectations of the employees working in organisations are sometimes broadly classified into those that are external or extrinsic to the job or tasks performed by the employees and those that are intrinsic to them. It is noted in many a research that the latter group of expectations often spur the employees to work harder on their jobs and thus contribute directly to orgnisational performance. For the purpose of the present study we picked out the following task/job-related expectations from the above list to find out the extent to which they are being fulfilled by the agencies studied. We have considered the level of fulfilment as equivalent to the level of satisfaction reported by the respondents.

(a) Need to accomplish something worthwhile in one's work
(b) Interesting nature of work
(c) Variety in work
(d) Work that is suited to one's capabilities
(e) Opportunities for learning for higher jobs

Based on the above factors, we constructed an index of intrinsic job satisfaction as explained in the methodological literature. The performance of the respondents on this index is described in Table 8.18.

Table 8.18
Levels of Intrinsic Job Satisfaction by Class of Respondents

Levels of Intrinsic Job Satisfaction	*Number Reporting*			
	Class I (%)	*Class II (%)*	*Class III (%)*	*Overall (%)*
High	32.9	21.9	33.5	31.1
Moderate	54.1	48.0	43.3	45.9
Low	13.0	30.1	23.2	23.0
Total	100.0% (N = 137)	100.0% (N = 136)	100.0% (N = 449)	100.0% (N = 723)*

* The class of one respondent was not reported.

As the table shows, about one third of Class I and II respondents are reported to enjoy a high degree of intrinsic job satisfaction in their present work. The proportion of Class II respondents reporting similar experience is, however, less being about 22 per cent. A good proportion of 30 per cent of these respondents are also getting low intrinsic job satisfaction. On the other hand, only 13 per cent of Class I respondents find their job yielding low intrinsic satisfaction. The fact remains that a larger proportion of the respondents from each class perceive their jobs as giving them a moderate degree of intrinsic satisfaction. Overall, it is interesting that 77 per cent of the 723 development personnel in the sample studied have reported as high or moderate the satisfaction they get from their work itself.

Attitudes in Citizen Administrator Relationships

All democracies place considerable emphasis upon co-operation rather than coercion of citizens in the fulfilment of development programmes. The readiness of the citizens to co-operate with public servants in carrying out public policies and programmes depends significantly upon the treatment which citizens receive at the hands of public servants. In this study, we obtained the perceptions of the civil servants themselves about the kind of treatment meted out to the citizen clientele. These perceptions were obtained along three dimensions :

(*a*) attitude towards citizen contacts;
(*b*) image of citizens and
(*c*) treatment of citizens.

Attitude Towards Citizen Contacts

We asked the respondents whether they liked to meet the people who visit their office on business. The replies are tabulated in the following frequency distribution (Table 8.19).

Table 8.19
Attitude Towards Citizen Contacts

Attitude towards Citizen Contacts	*Number Reporting*	*Per cent*
Like very much to meet citizens	118	16.3
Like to meet them	140	19.4
Do not mind meeting them	328	45.4
Do not like to meet them	80	11.0
Strongly dislike to meet them	39	5.4
Not replied	18	2.5
Total	723	100.0

The significant proportion of 45 per cent of the respondents who did not mind meeting the citizens was in keeping with the high degree of impersonal approach to work reported by these respondents and discussed in the earlier paper of the book. We do not know if having to meet citizens is necessary for the performance of the job roles of the respondents. Nevertheless, when we juxtaposed the above results with the frequency of contacts of the respondents with citizen clientele, we found as shown in Table 8.20 that these contacts do have a positive associationship with civil servants' attitudes to citizen contacts.

Table 8.20
Citizen Contacts and Attitude Towards Them

Frequency of Citizen Contacts Reported	*Attitude to Citizen Contacts*			
	Positive	*Neutral*	*Negative*	*Total*
High	53.8%	43.3%	2.9%	100.0% (N = 288)
Moderate	36.0%	54.0%	10.0%	100.0% (N = 161)
Low	17.5%	45.3%	37.2%	100.0% (N = 256)

We cannot conclude that having to meet the public more frequently generates a positive feeling towards them in the civil servants. Nor can we say that pro-client civil servants tend to welcome contacts more often with the public. Nonetheless, it is interesting to note that at least in development administration, contacts with citizen clients have the support of a positive attitude on the part of the civil servants towards them. The basic neutral attitude of a large proportion of the civil servants in this regard, however, continues to stay. This has also emerged in the following table which examines this problem in relation to the class of the respondents.

Table 8.21
Attitude to Citizen Contact by Class of Respondents

Attitude to Citizen Contacts	*Number Reporting*		
	Class I (%)	*Class II (%)*	*Class III (%)*
Positive	35.0	13.2	42.7
Neutral	58.4	55.9	38.1
Negative	4.4	27.2	16.8
Not reported	2.2	3.7	2.4
	100.0% (N = 137)	100.0% (N = 136)	100.0% (N = 449)

As regards the development agencies we found the following pattern of attitude to citizen contacts among their employees.

Table 8.22
Attitude to Citizen Contacts by Agencies Studied

Attitude to Citizen Contacts	*Number Reporting*			
	Agency A (%)	*Agency B* (%)	*Agency C* (%)	*Agency D* (%)
Positive	16.0	27.5	27.0	61.0
Neutral	53.4	61.4	54.8	26.9
Negative	30.6	11.1	18.2	12.1
Total	100.0% (N = 215)	100.0% (N = 109)	100.0% (N = 137)	100.0% (N = 262)

The foregoing table strikingly demonstrates that the civil servants serving in agency D which handles agricultural development programmes and community development schemes are significantly most often positively oriented to their clientele; that the tradition of neutrality is breaking down fast among them. On the other hand, this tradition continues among the members of agency B which, in our sample, handles development programmes in industry at the field level. The secretariat/central agencies A and C dealing with industrial and agricultural programmes respectively of course have the traditional neutral attitude.

Image of Citizen Attitudes

When we tried to assess the perceptions of the respondents about the behaviour of citizen clientele towards them, we found that about 70 per cent of the respondents felt that the citizens generally are 'very much' or 'quite respectful' to the civil servants. In reply to another question 78 per cent of the respondents reported that the citizens were not at all or only slightly afraid of the civil servants. These results suggest that the mental barriers of the citizens towards the civil servants are breaking down at least in the development administration.

Treatment of Citizens

There is a widespread feeling among the public that the civil servants are generally not helpful in their dealings with them. What do the civil servants themselves have to say about this matter? The respondents of this study held the following perceptions about the behaviour of officials of their department towards people who came to them for work.

Table 8.23
Reported Treatment of Citizens

Behaviour Towards Citizens	*Number Reporting*	*Per cent*
Very often helpful	176	24.3
Often helpful	321	44.4
Sometimes helpful	164	22.7
Rarely helpful	51	7.1
Never helpful	7	1.0
Not reported	4	0.5
Total	723	100.0

The foregoing findings of the study are in sharp contrast to the public feeling mentioned above. Obviously, there is a woeful mismatch between the help sought by the public and the concept of it according to the civil servants. In other words, the role of the civil servants in respect of citizen problems is being viewed differently by the citizens themselves and the civil servants on their part, indicating a gap in the communication between the two.

Summary and Conclusions

In this chapter, we were concerned with some aspects of the working climate in development administration. We were especially interested in finding out the working climate in which our respondents performed their functions or tasks because of its importance as one of the determiners of human behaviour in organizations. The aspects we considered were : the attitudes towards responsibility, attitude to delegation, attitudes in employee supervision and development, perceptions about criteria of promotions in government service, and attitudes in citizen-administrator relationships.

We hypothesized that the working climate conducive to efficiency of developmental functions should have the following prominent features :

1. The developmental personnel at all hierarchical levels

should have a high degree of positive attitude towards responsibility in work : they should be prepared to take on more and not less responsibility;

2. there should be a vigorous programme of delegation of authority to the personnel at subordinate levels not only to expedite work but also to provide for their individual growth;
3. the style of supervision should be predominantly employee-centred because such a style is known to enhance the possibilities of better employee performance in the long-run. Besides, it is the corollary of the pro-citizen attitude required of developmental personnel which we have emphasized separately;
4. as the number of opportunities for institutional training of developmental personnel are bound to be limited, planned and deliberate efforts should be made to develop these personnel on their jobs or through their work-day experience;
5. promotions should be perceived to be based primarily on merit so as to provide a direct and continuing incentive to the civil servants to perform better. Merit-based promotions also enhance the chances of fulfilment of organisational goals which in the context of development administration is of crucial significance;
6. the developmental personnel should experience a fairly good level of intrinsic job satisfaction since it is directly related to better performance in their assignments; and
7. the developmental personnel should feel positively obliged to help the clientele that come to them for work and with their problems.

On the basis of the findings of the study presented in the foregoing pages, can we conclude that the working climate in development administration represented by the civil servants in our sample is distinguished by the above seven features? Our conclusions in this regard are based on modal findings.

As regards the attitude towards responsibility the study found a vast majority (over 70 per cent) of the respondents in all the three classes willing to undertake very much more or somewhat more responsibility in their work in terms of quality. To the extent the positive attitude to responsibility on the part of civil servants is a necessary pre-condition for success of developmental efforts, the study shows that such a condition does exist in a substantial measure. At the same time, the results could imply that the civil service jobs are not sufficiently well structured to suit the capabilities of their incumbents. That these jobs are more routinized than the civil servants care for is also indicated by the feeling of a large proportion of the respondents of this study that their training and experience are only partially used up in the work of their present positions. It is significant that the higher level positions are found as 'little' or 'poorly' challenging as the lower level positions.

The lack of sufficient challenge in the task contents of their jobs is bound to retard the personal growth of civil servants. Apart from this, other opportunities available to the civil servants for personal growth also appear to be limited. Thus nearly two-thirds of the respondents have the superiors delegating to them less than enough authority. This is, however, less true of the higher level than of the lower civil servants.

Both the perceived mismatch between the capabilities of the civil servants and the work performed by them and the restricted delegation of authority by their superiors indicate the limited intrinsic worth of civil service jobs. This is further corroborated by our data on intrinsic job satisfaction experienced by the respondents—almost half of the respondents reported to have a moderate degree of it while twenty-three per cent expressed a low level of intrinsic job satisfaction. It may be recalled that we have defined intrinsic job satisfaction in terms of certain factors like interesting nature of work, variety in the work, opportunities for gaining experience useful for higher jobs etc., which are inherent in the work performed by the civil servants. That is, the chances of fulfilment of these factors are built into the work itself. On the whole, therefore, on the basis of the data of the present study, it is difficult to conclude that the structure of the jobs in development administration is presently such as to enable civil servants to feel both psychologically and intellectually involved in doing them. To the extent such a feeling of involvement is an important ingredient of better performance, we are not likely to see much of the latter in the existing situation.

The study has thrown up gratifying findings about employee-orientation of superiors inasmuch as 80 per cent of the respondents have reported their immediate superiors to be highly or at least moderately positively oriented towards them. The resulting climate of interpersonal trust and regard is not without a payoff. The study shows that there is a positive association between employee-orientation of superiors on the one hand, and the attitude to responsibility among the subordinates and the delegation of authority to the subordinates on the other. That is, the more the respondents find their superiors to be employee-oriented, the more willing they are to take responsibility for quality work and the more delegation of authority by their superiors. (These results are found to be statistically significant.)

It cannot be gainsaid that institutional rules may be responsible for superiors in the civil service not having a positive attitude towards using delegation as an aggressive instrument both to expedite disposal of work and to develop lower level employees. These rules may give a feeling to the superiors that they alone are responsible for anything that happens under their charge, and hence it is better that they themselves do as many things as possible. This notion of accountability is clearly dysfunctional to the complexities of developmental tasks and the need to involve different personnel in performing them. While, therefore, it would be necessary to dispel it, the present study shows that greater delegation does in fact take place informally, depending on the egalitarian relationship between the superior and his subordinates. The fact however remains that the long-term solution to this problem has to come from organisation planners in the government.

The problems arising from the poor marriage between the intrinsic aspects of civil service jobs and the needs and capabilities of the civil servants manning them can be tackled either *(a)* by scaling down the man specifications associated with different positions, or *(b)* by upgrading the jobs in terms of quality of work expected from job incumbents. The needs of development administration are likely to be met by the latter course of action.

Besides formal training and challenging job designs, the direct interest taken by the superior officers is an important aid to the development of subordinates. As regards the civil servants in the sample, their superiors are reported to be making varying efforts to help them to assume higher responsibilities. Thus the superiors do not seem to be able presently to devote sufficient attention to the development of their subordinates. This circumstance leads to different civil servants being prepared for higher positions at different paces. In this process those fortunate civil servants having superiors who give high priority to personnel development would have an edge over their colleagues whose superiors are not able to carry out this responsibility as much as expected, for one reason or the other. The latter group of civil servants are bound to feel frustrated by this experience. To afford comparable opportunities for professional growth, it is necessary to build this responsibility into the role definition of the superior officers and assess them periodically for it along with their other responsibilities.

From the foregoing analysis, we did not get the impression that the agencies studied are making clear, conscious efforts to develop their personnel professionally, although we do not deny that some such efforts are being made. On their own initiative also the respondents are not likely to exert much to develop themselves. One of the long-term incentives in this regard is the system of promotions based primarily on merit, by which is meant the ability to work hard and turn out superior quality work. However, the relative importance of different factors in promoitional decisions in the civil service as perceived by the respondents is not likely to spur them to put in their best. According to the respondents of all classes, seniority continues to weigh maximally. While merit is at best assigned a second order of importance, other considerations too are reported to play some part in promotion decisions. It is indeed unfortunate that the higher the level of the civil servants, the lower is the importance of merit as a promotional factor.

It is maintained that promotions in government service are based at least as much, if not more, on merit as upon seniority. On the basis of the present study, it cannot be said that the civil servants perceive it to be so. Moreover, their behaviour in job roles is likely to be determined more by their own perceptions rather than by the assertions made by others. It is thus not enough to claim that promotions are based on merit, but they must also appear to be so determined to the civil servants. To this end government need to lay down merit criteria for promotions to different positions more explicitly and take active steps to ensure that civil servants understand these criteria and the manner of their assessment. Civil servants are then more likely to make positive efforts to improve their capabilities and consequently their job performance.

Lastly, the relatively cold attitude of the civil servants towards the public as revealed in the present study poses a serious problem for their changed role. It may be recalled that the governmental agencies covered in the study are engaged in key development activities. By its very key premise, development administration requires a client-oriented approach with public administrators actively seeking to meet the needs of their clientele. The problem of the pro-citizen attitude of civil servants is indeed complex and has no roots in the civil service traditions of this country. Exhortations apart, more studies are needed to explore its dimensions and nature before beginning to make prescriptions in this important area.

We have no comparative data to conclude if the working climate in the agencies studied is better or different to that prevailing in other segments of the civil service. Nonetheless, it is distinguished, as in many other government agencies, by a lack of high premium either on performance or on the development of their human resources. In view of this we imagine that the civil servants serving in these agencies are fulfilling their developmental role rather routinely.

References

1. To arrive at average ranking, 1st to 6th ranks were assigned 1 to 6 numbers so that the lower the average numerical rank of a factor, the greater its perceived importance for promotions.

9

Administration and Development Strategies : Issues in Decision-Making

I

POLICY PARAMETERS

'Development' indicates an urge for a desirable change in the existing state of affairs and it is supposed traditionally to consist of—

(i) building up of economic infrastructure and extension services for rapid economic growth.
(ii) ensuring equitable distribution of opportunities.

Thus, development administration has been traditionally expected to mobilize the necessary resources both human and material, put them to proper use, monitor production of goods and services and to ensure their equitable distribution.

Non-provision of adequate arrangements to ensure sustainability of maintenance of assets created, has been one of the major shortcomings of development administration, not only in India but also in all developing countries.

Development is the act or process of developing. It is a gradual unfolding or growth which is an evolution rather than any sudden change or revolution. Development means one or all of the following :

1. to lay open by degrees,
2. free from that which envelopes or hides,
3. to bring out or to work out what is latent or beneficial in a thing,
4. to bring to a more advanced or more organised state.
5. to advance through successive stages to a higher, more complex or more fully grown stage.

Thus, development can never be taken to be a magic wand. It has to be a very gradual process by its very meaning. It is the opposite of the word 'envelope' as per its origin, though this meaning is no longer much in use. Whereas to envelope means to cover or hide, to develop means to free from that which envelopes. Thus, development by definition is a process which lays bare and opens up rather than hides. That which is secretive or restrictive or exclusive to a sect or caste cannot be called development.

Decision is the act of or product of deciding. To decide means, any one or all of the following :

(i) to determine,
(ii) to put terms or bounds to a thing,
(iii) to end,
(iv) to settle,
(v) to resolve, and
(vi) to make up one's mind.

The decision means a finality, whether an intermediate or ultimate one. It is antithetical to the process of development because development is a continuous process of unfolding, growth or advancement. Development is a process rather than an end product. It cannot be settled or finalized once and for all.

The work 'administration' comes from the word 'administer' which means "to minister." From the concept of the work 'minister' we may think that it involves something of higher decision-making and enjoyment of power. But it is not the appropriate meaning of the word 'minister.' To minister does not mean to rule or to govern. It means one or all of the following :

(i) to give attention and service,
(ii) to perform duties,

(iii) to supply or do things needful, and
(iv) to attend and serve.

That is why the king had ministers who were attending on him and serving him and were performing duties allotted to them. They were not governing or ruling.

Development administration should, therefore, be meant to provide attentive services and perform duties in different fields effectively in relation to development. Administration should not dictate development but it should act as a catalytic agent to the process of development, the urge for which has to come from the clientele. The nomenclatures Block Development Officers, Sub-divisional Development Officers, District Development Officers, Deputy Development Commissioners, Development Commissioners, Chief Development Commissioners, are, therefore, out of place and so much archaic. Just like a Revenue Officer, Judicial Officer, Commercial Tax Officer, we talk of the post of a Development Officer or a Development Commissioner. Development is not a tax or fees to be collected or a law to be enforced. But our bureaucracy has put it into that mould ever since it started. Development should neither on the one hand mean construction or distribution activities nor it should mean enjoyment of powers in matters of development.

Growth is different from development as—

(i) growth means a gradual increase in size,
(ii) to become enlarged by a natural process, and
(iii) to become greater in any way.

Very often it is confused with development, but every one knows that every growth is not advancement or development. For example population growth, cancerous growth, etc. are not development.

Similarly 'progress' also is not same thing as development. Progress only stands for forward movement or as advancement to something. It cannot be equated with development. Very often when we talk of development administration, we confuse it with growth or progress meaning thereby, taking up steps to achieve economic growth which means higher production, higher productivity, higher income generation, etc. Something can progress without developing what is latent or beneficial in it. It can progress without getting more organized or advanced.

'Bureaucracy' is a system of government by officials who are responsible only to the departmental chief. 'Cracy' is the suffix used to indicate rule or government by a particular group, just as democracy or mobocracy. In this sense there can actually be nothing called 'bureaucracy' because government officials always serve under and are responsible to either a democratic or a dictatorial government, a republican or monarchic government. They never rule by themselves.

To sum up, therefore, we should understand as to what development administration does or not imply.

(i) No decision in development administration can have any finality to call it properly a decision because development is a continuous process. If one takes any item to be a decision in the process of development and tries to stick to it, then it would retard the development process.

(ii) Development does not mean economic growth or progress.

(iii) Administration is neither government nor rule. It only means attending to any service. It does not connote power or authority.

The traditional textbooks on development administration have prescribed the essential pre-requisites of administrative behaviour in development as

(i) fixation of responsibilities,

(ii) valuation of performance with a system of reward and punishment,

(iii) eradication of corruption and lethargy,

(iv) democratization of decision-making.

The steps required to make development a sustainable movement and not a government, programmes are very rarely mentioned. Popular participation at all levels of decision-making and implementation, emotional commitment of all the participants and beneficiaries which can only come out of a sense of ownership, are factors which are missing from traditional textbooks on development administration, because of basically two factors :

(i) The feudal and semi-feudal classes and the enlightened middle class elite always thought that they had a devinely ordained duty and responsibility to develop

the common man who is poor and down-trodden. It is from these two classes that the human resource material was mostly taken to politics and development administration. Just as the imperialist European powers thought that all the blacks and browns in the colonies were the "Whiteman's burden," the politicians and bureaucrats thought and most of them still think that the clientele is their 'burden,' who do not know what is best for them.

(ii) For the politicians it became also an issue of *quid pro quo*. They must give something in return of having got votes. Either way, the relationship has become one of giver and receiver, ward and warden, ruler and subject but not of citizen and administration.

Administration in India could not change to adjust and readjust itself to the changing needs of the country and, therefore, failed to respond adequately to the developmental programme. It emphasized on creation of infrastructure for about two decades. It got lost in individual beneficiary oriented programmes of loans and subsidies. Creation of assets has now become a byproduct of providing employment in rural development programmes. Durability aspect of the assets created has been thoroughly neglected.

The usual reviews and criticisms of development administration in India contained items like concentration of administrative powers, non-delegation, red-tapism, corruption, buck-passing, nepotism, political interference and a climate of disbelief. But nobody appreciated that even with the most efficient delivery system and technology, another critical input was missing. It was a sense of belonging of the pay masters who are also the clientele namely the citizenry. Somewhere in the jungle of development administration the pay masters and the clientele were both lost sight of. The attendants in service to the pay masters became the principal characters. Development became a cake to be shared between the people's representatives, the bureaucracy, the technocracy and the middlemen. Very little of the cake reached those for whom it was baked, and what is more important, with whose funds it was baked. That the people themselves could bake the cake has been kept hidden from them for nearly half a century of the development administration, better termed as "envelope administration."

The need for adequate administrative decentralization and effective popular participation in formulation and execution of rural development programmes cannot be over-emphasized. Administrative decentralization brings the State machinery in all development administrations at the door steps of the people and makes them responsible to the letter's needs and aspirations. This decentralization was expected to arouse enthusiasm of the people so that development was to become a self-propelling process. Local Self-Government at the level of Gram Panchayat, Panchayati Raj and Zila Parishad and involvement of MLAs and MPs in decision-making at District Rural Development : Agency level have not generated the required enthusiasm to make development sustainable, and the assets durable.

Development administration should envisage achievement of the development goals in a particular area of development by making the system more efficient rather than by short-term solutions and arrangements. It has to re-enforce a system by imparting it an element of stability. The requirement of future developmental challenges have got to be met by any system established. Organisations set up in the development processes should not become dead wood with the passage of time and change of environment. It is here that many of our plan schemes and projects fall short of expectations.

There have to be the following pre-requisites for a sound system of development administration :

(i) Security has to be ensured against external aggression and internal disorder;

(ii) Development goals have to be clearly pronounced and organically linked for inter-sectoral consistencies;

(iii) Organisational logistics and personnel required to implement the developmental policies should be adequate;

(iv) Programmes commensurate with the goals have to be framed and implemented within a specific time frame for each programme and project;

(v) An effective strategy of implementation has to be designed and priorities between different departmental goals and objectives have to be firmly fixed.

Modern welfare stands for welfare of weaker and backward

sections of the society. Development administration, therefore, has to be positively responsive, increasingly sensitive and emotionally attached to the needs of the down-trodden. But development is neither welfare nor relief. It has been taken for both at different times and even now. This confusion has landed us in the present position. The point at which welfare should end and development should take over, has not yet been agreed to in India and as a result, for the weaker sections and backward areas it is relief and welfare which are served as development and infinitum. We make beggars out of the weaker sections, backward classes and even backward regions by putting them on permanent relief.

It is not enough that only the implementing side takes care of the commitment to development. The tax payers, elected representatives, the bureaucracy, the judiciary and the clientele all must have the involvement and commitment. It is not also enough that the rural poor have to be encouraged and enthused to come forward and participate in the local decision-making process but they should stay on in the development process, pay for it and maintain the assets. They should be taught specifically to give up the mentality of seeking relief and bask under the welfare umbrella for another century. It is here that the politician and the traditional bureaucrat will not allow you a free hand. How ego satisfying it is to distribute *pattas* of land, loans and subsidies, put up a college, provide a pipe water supply scheme to a village, distribute clothes and utensils in drought affected tribal pockets? But how difficult it is to ask the same people and make them pay for maintenance of the water supply system or motivate them to give up paddy cultivation and go for dryland cultivation? How easy it is to construct a minor irrigation project to irrigate two hundred acres, but how challenging it is to motivate the water users to form a Committee and take over the management of the project?

India went for one window approach of the community development blocks. Then she went for rapid departmentalization and neglected the Blocks. She went again for the programme agencies like ITDAs, DRDAs Micro Projects and FFDAs, etc., for achieving specific goals and reaching specific target groups. She went for achieving physical and financial targets like inseminating 'X' number of cows, covering 'Y' number of families with loan and subsidy and spending 'R' amount of money during a particular time frame. She confused achievement of targets with development. The present tendency is again going back either to departmentalization or to the Gram Panchayats which are the two extremes. The autonomous programme agencies and the departmental heads have become MLA and politician oriented in decision-making. When you go whole hog to Gram Panchayats without the necessary psychological and sociological preparation for sustainable development, you only end up in providing periodic and uncertain rural employment and multiplying non-productive assets.

The following components have direct impact on the functional operation of an organisation, dealing with development administration :

(i) Attitude to work;
(ii) Degree of professionalisation;
(iii) Attitude towards superiors;
(iv) Attitude towards subordinates;
(v) Attitude towards delegation of authority;
(vi) Attitude towards acceptance of responsibility;
(vii) Attitude towards corruption;
(viii) Attitude towards and acceptance of innovation;
(ix) Attitude towards risk taking.

Development administration has to be a carrier of innovative values. Establishment of a machinery alone for planned economical growth and mobilization, allocation or utilization of resources for various growth needs is not sufficient. We have departments and agencies in large numbers, but each of them ends up in being an "end" in itself.

The present system of election is not conducive to the growth of healthy democratic participation at the local level. The elections divide the people rather than unite them. Groups are appeased and short-term needs and comforts are taken care of rather than long-term goals and objectives. Healthy survival of development administration could be achieved if it is made totally election neutral. A political system which puts the highest premium on maximization of votes in the coming elections can only give you welfare administration and relief administration, but it would not be development. These would achieve just the opposite objectives. Instead of freeing the society from the 'envelopes' of ignorance dependence, lack of self-esteem and a beggar mentality, vote politics will take us back by centuries. In such a system the MLA or the MP or the bureaucrat decides what is good for the people. What he gives whom, where and when and in what measure in his discretion. Substituting the MLA by Sarpanch or Chairman Panchayat Samiti or Chairman Zila Parishad is not development per se. Similarly substituting any or all of these by the Collector or the BDO is equally worse. What is required is to free man from servitude to nature, to ignorance, to other man, to an institute, etc. which are considered oppressive so as to initiate them for positive self-actualization through the development process. This jargon of 'positive self actualization' is neither a metaphysical nor a Yogic expression. In the context of development administration it means realizing of development in action on the part of a citizen, not as merely a voter or a wage earner in the digging of a canal, but as the "doer" himself.

So far, the academic and bureaucratic presumptions about development administration, have been mainly the following :

(i) The role of government will continue to expand to direct overall process of development;

(ii) Policy-making and implementation will be within two sets of functionaries, political and bureaucratic respectively;

(iii) Government activities will become increasingly complex and specialized and the benefits accruing to the people would be so great that people would welcome more of government than resist it;

(iv) The need for planning, co-ordination, control and regulation will be great because the welfare State will affect all walks of life;

(v) Administrative attempt at influencing the political process as in earlier days of planned development would continue;

(vi) Managerial orientations and techniques will play a crucial role in speeding up the process of development;

(vii) Training and personnel management are crucial to the whole process of development administration;

(viii) Part of the additional resources generated out of planned development would be mopped up by tax and would

be available for maintenance of assets created by the process; and

(ix) maintenance of assets created would be done by the same staff who would continue to be engaged in other planned projects as well.

Development administration in the Indian context has so far not been very successful in delivering the goods as most of the assumptions enumerated above, have either proved to be false or have materialized in just the opposite direction.

(i) There has not developed a working partnership between the people and their elected representatives. Therefore, political leadership very often does not represent the real interest of the people. The leaders have misconceived their role as doners and doers much as the kings of princely States and bureaucrat of the fifties and sixties—with a devinely ordained task to give salvation to the masses.

(ii) The services rendered by the delivery systems of development administration at the grass-root have not been efficient in spite of increase in the strength and comforts of the government personnel, both legitimate and otherwise. There has not been adequate delegation in decision-making to the grass-root level to take care of the local needs and variations.

(iii) The filed staff have not devoted themselves to the development process. They have willy nilly either worked for or against the rural masses but not with the rural masses and they have not been able to carry them along in the development process.

(iv) There has been little knowledge of local needs and aspirations at the level where budgeting and planning has been done and feedback from the field has not been incorporated into the projects and schemes in the right time.

(v) After the Independence struggle there has not been a sense of sacrifice, service and spirit of dedication on the part of leaders at the social, political and administrative levels. Development, therefore, has been confined to and confused with plan documents, budget,

reappropriations, reports and returns, expenditure, achievement reports of physical targets and utilization certificates.

(vi) It has been realized that government activities and programmes cannot continue to expand indefinitely and the more it would expand the more it would bungle. But every plan and budget has continued to expand these activities and programmes without taking care of logistics and administrative means.

(vii) There is need to simplify government procedures and programmes so that it is within the comprehension of the pay masters (voters) and their representatives. But there has been no attempt to make the decision-making process comprehensible to the common man.

(viii) Planning has got to be decentralized and there is greater need for co-ordination at the grass-root level between the functionaries of different departments than at the Secretariat or Heads of Department level.

(ix) There is need to reduce control at all levels and eliminate control at many levels. This realization in the Centre has not percolated to the grass-roots.

(x) Political attempt at influencing administrative process at all levels have succeeded and administrative attempt to influence political decision-making have failed and are being generally given up. The MLA or the Chairman Zila Parishad or the MP hopes to gradually take over the job of Chief Executive, now that decision-making at the Block, the subdivision and District has become collective in nature in different committees, Samitis and Governing Bodies. Very rarely now, critical investment decisions in the district are left to the individual decisions of Sub-Collector, Project Director, DRDA or Collector.

(xi) In many States decision-making at Head of Deptt. level and in the Secretariat has also become MLA oriented because Ministers have wanted it that way. Every plan and non-plan provision is attempted to be split up constituency-wise and distributed on items selected by MLAs.

(xii) Instead of more and more managerial orientation and technical inputs for sustainable development easier

option of populistic appeasement, has been accepted by the people's representatives almost at all levels.

(xiii) Training and personnel management generally have been relegated to the back seat. Whenever there has been any training and management input in development administration, it has meant training of officials and improving the management skill of officials. Training of people's representatives and non-officials so as to cultivate in them a sense of belonging to the development process is missing.

(xiv) The official-people intertace has been nowhere in picture except through the political representatives and there is a general apathy in people's representatives towards empowering people themselves in maintenance of assets and in deciding which project should be taken up where. People's representatives would much rather dole out development infrastructure and service points as government gifts so that in return they would get votes. Thus, what is a national asset has been taken as a government property.

(xv) Plan investments and improvements in economic infrastructure have generated some surplus, but additional resource mobilization out of that to finance plan and non-plan expenditure has not been adequate to take care of physical maintenance of assets after meeting the needs of salary, wages, pension and dearness allowance. There is a great reluctance to adequately tax the surplus may be because part of the surplus is also used in black to enrich party coffers. But temptation to announce concessions, subsidies, rebates, unproductive rural employment schemes is ever on the increase. The politicians and bureaucrats have a common interest in the continuance of this soft-option anarchy. Instead of tightening of belt, the would take loan after loan to pay salary and for repayment of earlier loans. Politicians would throw crumbs to the people and get votes. O'Bureaucrat, you say 'yes' to the political dictates so that your salary and perks continue irrespective of whether any number of external loans are taken for the purpose or not. The nation, thus has been thrust with a

> one point programme of supporting the massive state machinery both political and administrative.

It is in the above context that the need for rationality in decision-making assumes importance. To quote Tarlok Singh on the "Speed and Efficiency in Development Administration," "in every important field the quality of execution can be gradually improved if the government policy directives, while being based on a proper study of facts, are set out in bold and specific terms so that they provide a definite perspective for positive and sustained implementation." .... "Within defined limits, each individual should be given full responsibility and with it the necessary measures of support and trust. If he fails in the discharge of his responsibilities he should be replaced. But so long as he holds an office he should accept all its obligations and equally he should then be in a position effectively to discharge them. With responsibility thus specified it should be open to him to seek such advice and consultation as he may require, but these should not become necessary ingredients of the executive process itself." The above ideal conditions very seldom have been allowed to the development administrators in India. No wonder, therefore, that results have not been achieved. Where ideal conditions have existed or have been created, results have been wonderful.

To quote B.K. Dey on the subject of "Bureaucracy and Development Some Reflections," "but much more significant from the angle of model making for a developmental bureaucracy, is the man, the bureaucrat, the raw material. Unless this man is made to look different or asked to think differently or motivated to function more purposively, no amount of investment in structural sophistication or modernization in machine procedure will be in a position to hit the jack-pot by way of raising the level of developmental productivity. The critical ingredient, the bureaucrat himself, must, therefore, be freed from the existing conceptual orthodoxies age old affiliations and narrow mental grooves so as to be the fitting torch bearer of a new and bright developmental order." It is a question that should be asked now if not anytime earlier. How much has the politico-bureaucrat nexus in the system of so called "development" administration tolerated or appreciated any unorthodoxy? How much have "different outlook" and "different thinking" been tolerated, not to speak "appreciated" or "encouraged?" How much have the financial rules and treasury code, audit code and rules of inspection, rules and guidelines for different programmes kept a scope for innovative thinking and experimentation?

The Tokyo Conference on Implementation held in October, 1973 suggested some broad guidelines which have been briefly summarized by Ram K. Vepa in his article on "Implementation—Problems of Achieving Results" (Development Administration—IIPA)

(i) Implementation is but one aspect of a larger process of society and is, therefore, affected decisively by the environment in which a particular programme is implemented;

(ii) An important facet of the environment is the political mileu at the national, regional and field levels which can be either beneficial or counter-productive;

(iii) Programme administrators need to develop skills for playing the political game so as to optimize political support for the programme. This can be done through frequent consultation and helps to sustain the programme through timely budget releases;

(iv) Suitable organisational framework is essential for effective implementation; this involves allocation of resources, both material and human, recruitment of suitable personnel and allocation of meaningful responsibilities to them;

(v) Consultation with, and involvement of the beneficiaries of the programme is essential and needs to the built consciously into the implementation machinery;

(vi) Accurate data and timely information must be compiled and fed back to appropriate levels for effective monitoring of the programme during implementation. Field reports should be simple and direct and should be acted upon at the headquarters;

(vii) Programme leadership is an important criterion for the success of a programme, but mere charismatic leadership of a single individual is likely to be transient and ephemeral. What is needed is competence and commitment at all levels of the implementation hierarchy.

> This implies not merely technical skills relevant to the programme but also managerial expertise in implementation, human skills in personal management and motivating people to achieve results and lastly, political skills to obtain and sustain co-operation and support from leaders of public opinion in the community and country.

The above guidelines still hold good today after twenty years and will hold good for many years more. They cannot be improved upon for the time being.

Herbert A. Simon summarises the position regarding decision-making process in administrative organisation in his book "Administrative Behaviour." According to him administrative theory is peculiarly the theory of intended and bounded rationality —of the behaviour of human beings who satisfy because they have not the wits to maximise. Whereas the economic man maximises selects the best alternative from many of those available to him, the administrative man, satisfices—looks for course of action that is satisfactory or good enough. The administrative man, is content to leave out of account those aspects of reality that appear irrelevant at a given time. Administrative men could make their choice without first examining all possible behaviour alternatives and without ascertaining that these are in fact all the alternatives. The administrative man, because he 'satisfices' rather than maximises, can makes his decisions without relatively simple rules of thumb that generally make impossible demands upon his capacity for thought. He ignores the interrelatedness of all things.

The task of decision-making according to Herbert A. Simon involves three stages, *viz.* *(i)* listing of alternative strategies, *(ii)* determination of all the consequences without following on each of these strategies and the comparative valuation of these consequences, and *(iii)* actual decision-making. It is obviously impossible for the individual to know all his alternatives or all their consequences and this impossibility is a very important departure for the actual behaviour from the model of objective rationality.

According to H. Simon—

(i) Complete rationality in decision-making requires complete knowledge and indication of the consequences

that will follow on each choice but knowledge of consequences is always fragmentary;

(ii) Imagination must supplement the lack of experience in attaching a value to the consequence;

(iii) Where data is inadequate and consequences cannot be forecast "Common Sense" should step in.

Herbert Simon has established clearly that the pattern of human choice is even more crucial and a "stimulous-response pattern" is more common than a "choice amongst alternatives." Human rationality operates within the limits of actual environment and not the 'real' or ideal environment. Ten years ago 'A' distributed the highest acreage of ceiling surplus land and government wasteland in his district. Miss 'B' constructed in her district the largest number of housing schemes for the economically weaker sections of people under Integrated Housing Scheme and Indira Awas Yojana. Mrs 'C' released three hundred bonded labourers and gave them rehabilitation assistance in her district. Ten years ago, 'X' could achieve a record number of energization of pumpsets in his district. Miss 'Y' stood first in the state in number of biogas plants installed, Mrs. 'Z' exceeded the target by one hundred per cent in distribution of IRD loans and subsidy. Let us go to these districts now. How many beneficiaries assisted with ceiling surplus land and government wasteland and financial assistance are actually in cultivating possession of the lands and how many of them crossed the poverty line with this assistance? What percentage of houses under the rural housing schemes for the weaker sections are under occupation and use and how many colonies set up continue to be inhabited? What is the economic condition of the freed and rehabilitated bonded labourers? Are the energized dugwells still irrigating the fields around them? Could the small and marginal farmers repay the loans taken for the pumpsets out of the sale proceeds of crops raised around the well? Are they getting supply of power regularly? Are the biogas plants still functioning and in use or given up as bad investments? How many IRD beneficiaries who were below the poverty line at the time of getting IRD assistance over ten years back have crossed the poverty line by now even with the second dose of assistance?

Every Indian now carries a loan burden of Rs. 5,000 on his head. In 1985-86 the debt was Rs. 40,311 crores. In 1986-87 it became

Rs. 1,21,869 crores. In 1991-92 the debt burden was Rs. 2,09,698 crores, per capita income has increased 1.7 per cent in 45 years. The vicious circle of unproductive expenditure, higher imports, lower exports, trade deficit, loan, deficit financing more taxes to repay with interest, inflation increase in the dearness allowance, more inflation goes on and on. It is clear that the Indian bureaucrat has been able to 'maximize' anything desirable. What has been maximised all these years is perhaps 'corruption' from the bottom to the top. Has the Indian bureaucrat been able then to 'satisfice'? Is the common man satisfied with his decision and performance? Is the poorest of the poor satisfied with him? Does he look to him for his deliverance? Is the politician satisfied with him? If so, what variety of politician is satisfied with him and for what reasons? Is the average politician of India today satisfied with the honest, upright and law abiding bureaucrat? With what species of bureaucrat is the average Indian politician satisfied then? If neither maximization nor satisfaction has been achieved, then what else is achieved besides self-survival? Unhindered self perpetuation is no longer possible for the bureaucracy with the present state of the nation's economy. How long will sheer self-survival last is anybody's guess.

We have seen enough models and experimented with many of them. But in running after the ideal solution bureaucracy has always run after mirages. The "ideal" is with the people themselves. It is not in World Bank project reports or in Planning Commission documents. It cannot be found in Assembly debates or Book Circulars. It cannot be traced in reports, returns or utilization certificates. It has not been found in Treasury Codes or grading given to states in the performance of Twenty Point Programme. Decision-making in a bureaucracy should, therefore, first realise that there cannot be a decision in development administration because administration is not the same as ruling or governing and development is not the samething as growth or progress. By binding us down with all rules, codes, regulations, policy circulars, audits, etc. we are more and more "enveloping" what is good fiom the people rather than developing. Very often we come across expressions like "explaining" the development programmes of the government to the people. We maintain specialized information and public relations departments for the purpose. This conveys that the imperialistic mode of development administration still continues and this is most unsuitable for achievement of any sustainability of development. Unless this mode changes into a truly democratic mode, development administration itself would be a wasteful effort. Bureaucracy and political participants would be convinced that they are doing great things but in terms of sustainability and long-term results it would come to nothing. Let the 'Bureaucracy' take the leadership in 'debureaucratizing' development administration. The resistance from politicians and politician dominated unions will be tremendous but they would also see reasons sooner or later. A political philosophy called Marxism based on sound historical logic and economics failed miserably because of bureaucratization of development administration and of the Communist Party. The "red tape" killed the Red Flag, emasculated the Red Army and finished the political party which was once the most powerful in the world. Indian democracy is too feeble to resist the decay and degeneration caused by criminalization of politics and bureaucratization of development administration. The masses have already alienated the 'elite.' Before they disown and overthrow the system, let us get into the job of debureaucratizing. The death knell for the nation would be much less pleasant to hear than the death knell for the bureaucracy.

It is not too late now to make a gradual but steady withdrawal from the grass-root delivery system of development welfare and relief administration and hand them over lock stock and barrel to the people's and users' organizations who would own and maintain them. Once the decision is taken at the national level as a national programme irrespective of which political party is in power, decision-making and the lower levels would become simpler and easier. Let us resolve to move from 'envelopment' to development from governing to administering, from working for the people to working with the people and move to the twenty-first century. Let us decide here and now, not to decide for the people, but to assist them in taking their own decisions and maintaining their own assets. It is a challenge that has to be accepted today. Tomorrow may be too late.

II

PARTNERSHIP WITH PRIVATE SECTOR

Policy Liberalisation in the Eighties : Issues and Evidence

The dismal performance of the manufacturing sector during the interregnum (1966-69, average yearly growth rate 2.1 per cent) and the Fourth Plan period (1969-74, average yearly growth at 3.7 per cent) had brought home the point to the policy makers that it was essential to concentrate on production efficiency aspects of the industrial system and to phase out the other objectives of industrial policy and delineate the objective of each policy instrument. There was by now a consensus on the futility of using licensing as an instrument to achieve multiple objectives and about it's adverse effect in terms of delay, cost escalation and allocative inefficiency. It was realised that the policy instruments like the MRTP Act and FERA could perhaps be made more effective in achieving these objectives and, therefore, should replace lincensing policy in many respects. It also became inevitable to re-state in clear terms the policy towards public sector, small scale sector, large houses and foreign companies. Outside the exclusive areas, it was felt, there was no need for any control except for monitoring purposes.

In view of this thought process, several measures were announced in the mid-seventies aiming at more liberal policy stance towards capacity expansion, simplification of procedures and reduction in time delays and more liberal access to imported technology and capital goods. Consequently, manufacturing production increased modestly by 5.7 per cent per annum during the Fifth Plan, 1974-79 and by 5.3 per cent during the Sixth Plan, 1980-85.

However, the first major attempt towards policy reforms in the industrial sector was made in March 1985 when twenty-five industries were delicensed subject to the restrictions concerning MRTPA or FERA, reservations for the small scale sector and policy concerning location within urban areas. In June, 1985 delicensing was extended to 82 bulk drugs and related drug formulations. In December, 1985 delicensing was extended to MRTPA and FERA companies. In addition, the schemes of broad banding and re-endorsement of capacity were permitted on a liberal basis. Far reaching policy reforms were also announced for the textiles and electronics sectors.

After these policy measures were announced, the performance of the Indian economy surpassed the targets set in the Seventh Plan. Thus real GDP increased by around 5.7 per cent per annum as against the target of 5 per cent. Similarly, GDP of the agriculture sector increased at a rate of 3.6 per cent against the target of 2.5 per cent; industry GDP increased by 7.1 per cent against the target of 6.9 per cent and services sector GDP increased by 6.7 per cent against the target of 6.1 per cent. Also actual export volume growth rate of 8 per cent per annum exceeded the target of 7 per cent per annum. These achievements look even more impressive if one keeps in view the facts that average actual investment/GDP ratio of 22.8 per cent fell short of the target of 25.3 per cent, mainly because of shortfall in the domestic rate of savings by as much as 3.2 per cent (actual rate being 20.5 per cent against the target of 23.7 per cent).

In the industrial sector, the general index of industrial production accelerated gradually from 3.2 per cent in 1982-83 to 6.7 per cent in 1983-84, 8.6 per cent in 1984-85, 8.7 per cent in 1985-86 and 9.1 per cent in 1986-87. Excepting in 1987-88, when the growth rate dipped to 7.3 per cent, it hovered around 8.7 per cent. On an annual average basis, the industrial production increased by 8.5 per cent per annum during 1985-90 against 7 per cent during 1981-85. Electricity recorded acceleration from 8.9 per cent to 9.4 per cent and manufacturing from 5.8 per cent to 8.8 per cent. Major deceleration was recorded in the mining sector where rate of growth declined from 12.7 per cent to 5.7 per cent. The performance in 1990-91 broadly indicated the continuance of the trends in the Seventh Plan with the general index of industrial production increasing by 8.5 per cent, manufacturing by 9.1 per cent and electricity and mining by 9.4 per cent and 5.7 per cent respectively.

So far it looks as if the speeding up of liberalisation in the mid-eighties had a definite positive impact on the growth rate which quite clearly had by now become the single major objective of industrial policy. However, at the same time several dissenting voices were raised questioning the wisdom of these policy changes. These mainly related to :

(*a*) the rate of growth itself, argument being that the growth rate in net value added was much lower than the gross value added;

(*b*) the growth process, argument being that there was greater wastage of resources to sustain the same rate of growth;

(*c*) pattern of growth, argument being that faster growth of chemicals based industries as compared with the metal based industries, in which India 'has' comparative advantage, was undesirable from both development and equity point of view; and

(*d*) import intensity of production and exports increased sharply deepening the fiscal and payments imbalances notwithstanding the acceleration in gross value of industrial production and export earnings.

In the light to these observations, an attempt was made in the present exercise to analyse in some greater details the trends in industrial production during the eighties using the available empirical evidence. Following observations are warranted :

(*i*) The acceleration in industrial production was led by the capital goods sector, rate of growth being 14.8 per cent in the Seventh Plan as against 6.3 per cent during 1981-85; acceleration was also recorded in the consumer goods sector, from 5.3 per cent to 7.3 per cent per annum. With in this group, consumer durables showed recessionary tendencies as the rate of growth declined from the peak of 21.6 per cent in 1984-85 to 7.8 per cent in 1987-88 and just 1.7 per cent in 1989-90. The year 1990-91, however, indicated revival in consumer durables but deceleration in capital goods sector.

(*ii*) Analysing by the index at two digit level of classification, the major industries where significant acceleration in the rate of growth occurred included textile products (weight in IIP being 0.82 per cent), chemicals and allied products (weight 12.5 per cent), basic metals and alloys (weight 9.8 per cent), machinery and machine tools (weight 6.2 per cent) and electric machinery and appliances (weight 5.8). Cotton textiles with weight of 12.3 per cent registered marginal increase in growth rate whereas food products, beverages, jute products, wood products, paper and paper products, leather and fur products, rubber and plastic goods, non-metallic mineral products and transport equipment registered sharp deceleration in the rate of growth.

(iii) Analysis of detailed data on production and capacity installed given in Planning Commission's Annual Plan for various years does not provide any unequivocal evidence to show that capacity utilisation improved across the sectors after the industrial policy changes announced in 1985. Thus 40 industries out of 95 reported average capacity utilisation in 1985-90 less than the same realised in 1984-85. Among these were consumer durables, two wheelers, several chemicals and synthetic fibres, tractors and jute manufactures, etc.

(iv) Similarly, the same data does not lead to any unambiguous conclusion that the measures led to significant accretion to installed capacity across the sectors in the aftermath of 1985. Thus the rate of accretion to capacity accelerated in 33 industries during 1985-88 over the rate during 1983-85. During the same period, however, 46 industries reported deceleration. Again during 1987-90, 37 industries reported acceleration in the rate of accretion to capacity over the period 1985-88 whereas 42 industries reported deceleration. There were only a handful of industries which reported sustained accretion to capacity after 1985-86. These included steel ingots, saleable steel, sponge iron, vanaspati, paper, diesel and electric locomotives and domestic refrigerators.

(v) Considered over a longer time period, say the entire eighties when compared with the seventies, there does not appear to have occurred any radical change in the pattern of growth of industrial production. The Spearman's rank correlation between trend growth rates of industrial production of 42 items during the seventies and eighties turns out at 34.1 per cent indicating that in totality the pattern of growth was similar among these industries during the two decades. At the same time some industries recorded higher than average growth rates during the eighties. These included electronics

items, automobiles, steel castings, cement, aluminium and POL products.

(vi) Trends in industrial production since 1985-86 also do not seem to support some of the recently propounded hypotheses. For instance, evidence does not suggest that growth during this period was concentrated overwhelmingly on chemical based industries. In fact contribution of this sector declined sharply after 1988-89 and that of metal based industries increased sharply. At the same time growth was not very much broad based and concentrated on industries that were characterised with high capital and import intensity. In 1990-91, however, this trend was reversed when many traditional industries including cotton textiles made major contribution to the growth in industrial production whereas import intensive industries like chemicals and electric machinery showed decline in growth rates.

(vii) Notwithstanding the arguments to the contrary, there have indeed been adverse trends in the import intensity of domestic production and exports. This phenomenon in the industrial structure had its impact on net value added and net export earnings. The close relation between imports and industrial production or exports is also highlighted in sharp decline in industrial production and exports consequent upon the import squeeze imposed on account of BOP crisis.

(viii) Finally, in the international context, it is worth noting that the improvement in performance of the industrial sector during the second half of the eighties was experienced not only by India but also by most Asian countries. Yet, India's performance was among the most dismal. Several countries which had realised high growth rates in early eighties, for instance mainland China, Indonesia, Korean Republic and Philippines to do so in the late eighties. Others like Singapore (despite severe recession in 1985-86, free trade but very interventionist state policy) and Thailand (with little state intervention) which had realised similar rates of manufacturing growth during early eighties, accelerated at a much faster pace.

The available evidence does not, therefore, lead to any unambiguous conclusion that the first major attempt at industrial policy reforms was successful either in terms of higher productivity or higher level of investment. There is also no evidence to suggest that any major self-sustaining structural changes occurred in the rate and pattern or growth of the industrial sector.

Recent Policy Reforms and Impact on the Industrial Sector

Several attempts have been made in the past to explain a rather depressing record of growth of the industrial sector. It is not the intention in this note to go into the details of these explanations. Nevertheless, in the context of a desirable follow-up to the recent policy reforms, it is essential to draw attention to three basic factors which continued to affect the viability of the industrial system. These are :

(a) continued restrictions on access to foreign investment and technology;
(b) absence of a viable exit policy; and
(c) inefficiency in decision-making mainly due to the persistence of a web of controls leading to procedural delays.

Since issues relating to industrial controls are too well-known, it may suffice to touch upon the first two issues mentioned above before attempting an analysis of the recent policy reforms.

It appears that one basic reason for differences in the growth rates was the usage and availability of foreign direct investment. Some of these countries like Singapore, Taiwan and Malaysia had very high rates of savings at 38-40 per cent and Thailand at 23 per cent but still attracted accelerating amount of foreign private investment. According to a recent study carried out under the auspices of OECD, between 1980-87, Japanese direct foreign investment increased fivefold in Thailand, four times in Singapore and sixfold in Taiwan. Singapore alone had by 1988 accumulated foreign investment of over 3.5 billion US dollars. It is interesting to note that reluctance of foreign investors towards India was most likely not on economic considerations but due to the perception of it being a 'hostile' country. Data cited in the same study indicate that in 1986, barring Singapore, India gave the highest rate to return on US foreign investment (of 21.1 per cent, against 21.8 per cent in

Singapore, 16.6 per cent in Hongkong, and between 12-14 per cent for the remaining Asian countries). The difference essentially was in treatment of foreign direct investment. In a country like Singapore, for instance, foreign investment did not attract restrictions, all industries were open for foreign investment, there were no limitations on remittances, same legal system applied to all investment, no conditions were imposed on local equity participation and all foreign firms were eligible for incentives on equal footing with local firms. No wonder, when compared with India, Singapore and in fact most east Asian and ASEAN countries appeared haven for foreign investment.

Another major reason for the poor viability of the Indian industrial system has been the growing sickness in both private as well as the public sector. For instance, as on December 31, 1991 there were as many as 1,117 companies registered with BIFR as 'sick' with estimated accumulated losses at around Rs. 4,850 crores. In the public sector, in March 1990, there were 102 loss making units with accumulated losses at over Rs. 10,000 crores. During April-September, 1991 alone, 98 loss making PSUs incurred losses of over Rs. 2,000 crores. Considering that another 85 profit making PSUs made total profits of around Rs. 2,460 crores, the net profit of PSUs during the first six months of 1991-92 came to only Rs. 356 crores implying a very poor rate of return. It is equally important to note that deterioration in the commercial viability of these enterprises has occurred in some major sectors like coal and lignite, petroleum, financial services, heavy, medium and light engineering, consumer goods and textiles. Despite this magnitude of the problem, there is hardly any operationally significant scheme to prevent industrial sickness.

The extent of and reasons behind industrial sickness vary from sector to sector. Instances of sickness are quite frequent in mill sector of the textiles industry, engineering industries, tyre, glass and aluminium industries. While there are reasons which are common to all the industries, like the lack of an exit policy, there are others which are specific to the particular industries. In the textiles sector, for instance, there are whole lots of constraints imposed by labour policies, trade policies, bureaucratic control on capacity, production and relocation and taxes on certain inputs. Severe sickness is often accompanied with state incentives for fresh investment depressing the profits in the sector. In the engineering sector, exit constraint made it impossible to inject fresh capital and technology. In the tyre industry, continued support to loss making units prevented technological innovations. The radial tyre technology introduced recently is 20 years behind the rest of the world. In aluminium sector, sickness has been hidden under the retention price scheme. In glass, protection of the existing firms prevented the introduction of float glass process which has decisive cost advantage over older technologies in vogue and which was introduced over 30 years back in the world.

Due to the apparently fast increasing sickness (at end 1990-91, over 2,350 units, excluding SSI units) and, therefore, deteriorating employment situation and increasing financial burden, it has been difficult for the government to come up with a clear exit policy. BIFR (through SICA 1986) as an instrument of exit policy for the non-SSI sector has not been effective as it does not capture incipient sickness. Moreover, as detailed in a recent review of BIFR, it does not have powers to tackle the problem. Also it cannot take a total view of the problem as it deals with only individual cases. To prevent industrial sickness and to facilitate an efficiency oriented exit policy required dealing with anachronistic hurdles like Urban Land Ceiling Act, Industrial Disputes Act, some anti-monopoly provisions concerning takeovers and mergers etc. Most important of all, it required severely narrowing down the objectives of IDRA.

To deal with the obstacles, some of which have been discussed above, the government issued on 24 July, 1991 a statement on industrial policy with a view to "...unshackle the Indian industrial economy from the cobwebs of unnecessary bureaucratic control." The major steps announced include :

Industrial Licensing Policy

(i) Except for a negative list containing 18 industries, licensing will be abolished;

(ii) Ares exclusive to the public sector will be restricted to eight sectors;

(iii) CG imports will be allowed automatic clearance where FE availability is ensured or where CG imports are less than 25 per cent of the value of plant and equipment and less than Rs. 2 crores.

(iv) Locational restrictions will be eased for industries of non-

polluting nature and it will be made more flexible for large cities requiring industrial regeneration.

(v) PMP will not be applicable to new cases. Scope of broad-banding will be widened and all expansion of capacity will be exempt from licensing. Also, mandatory conversion of loans from FIs in new projects will be abolished.

Foreign Investment

(i) Foreign direct investment will be allowed upto 51 per cent equity, with no bottlenecks. This would, however, be subject to the condition that foreign equity covers the foreign exchange requirements.

(ii) Payments of dividends would be monitored to ensure matching of FE outflows with export earnings.

(iii) Majority foreign equity holding upto 51 per cent will be allowed for companies engaged primarily in export activities.

(iv) A Special Empowered Board would be constituted with a view to attract large foreign firms to invest in India.

(v) Foreign technology agreements will be automatically allowed in high priority industries. No permission will be necessary for hiring foreign technicians.

Public Sector

(i) Area of exclusivity of the public sector will be limited to strategic, high tech and essential infrastructure industries.

(ii) BIFR will be amended to include Public Sector Undertakings (PSUs). A social security mechanism will be created to care for the affected workers.

(iii) A part of the government shareholding will be disinvested to raise resources.

(iv) Management of PSUs will be made more professional and autonomous.

MRTP ACT

(i) Threshold limit of assets in respect of assets in respect of MRTP companies and dominant undertakings will be removed.

(ii) MRTP Act will be amended to give more teeth to the MRTP Commission in matters concerning controlling

and regulating monopolistic, restrictive and unfair trade practices.

Along with these, several other changes were announced in trade policy, exchange rate policy, fiscal policy, and policy concerning financial sector. Some more policy changes are likely to be announced after the government decides on the comprehensive recommendations of Narasimhan Committee on the financial sector reforms and the Chelliah Committee on reforms in taxation. In addition, the government has to announce its approach and methods of implementation of an exit policy, primarily for the public sector. It may take two to three years to get a complete picture concerning the extent and impact of these reforms.

Apparently, the most important measures directly complementary to the industrial policy are those that affect trade. These essentially relate to :

(i) measures first announced in the Statement on Trade Policy on August 13, 1991 and concerning replacement of REP by EXIM Scrip; several export promotion measures and decanalisation of items;

(ii) announcements made in the Union Budget on 29 February, 1992 concerning replacement of EXIM Scrip with partial convertibility and a dual market for foreign exchange based on a liberalised exchange rate mechanism (LERM);

(iii) announcements made in the new Import-Export Policy on March 31, 1992 for 1992-97 concerning decontrol of the trade regime except for a small negative list of import and export, elimination of actual user condition, liberalisation of capital goods import and a scheme of export related import of capital goods, introduction of value based advance licenses and a more broad based policy concerning deemed exports; and

(iv) announcement made in the Union Budget for 1994-95 to reduce peak rate of tariff to 65 per cent and to make the rupee convertible on current account.

In addition fundamental changes in tariff structure recommended by the Chelliah Committee and accepted by the government will affect the industrial sector. These changes would include

(a) reduction of the general level of tariffs;

(*b*) reduction of the spread or dispersion of tariff rates;
(*c*) simplification of the tariff system;
(*d*) rationalisation of the tariff rates along with the abolition of numerous exemptions and concessions; and
(*e*) abolition of the practice of making changes in the effective rates through notifications.

It is difficult to make an accurate forecast about the intensity of these reforms and their likely impact on the economy in general and the industrial sector in particular. This is because these reforms work with a time lag extending to five years depending on the speed with which they are implemented. It must also be noted that the impact of the structural adjustment programme has been affected by the demand depressing stabilisation programme which was aimed at specific objective of dealing with the fiscal and payments deficits. Furthermore, the industrial scene, during the pendency of these programmes, is distorted by the escalation in cost-push inflation which occurs partly due to exchange rate alignments in the wake of convertibility and partly due to freeing of prices, spread of industrial sickness due to greater degree of import competition, growing pressures on infrastructure on account of cuts in resource allocation and adverse effect of import compression on industrial production and exports and so on.

Notwithstanding, following observations are still warranted on the present scenario :

(*i*) From no growth in 1991-92, the general index of industrial production accelerated to 2.3 per cent in 1992-93, 3.0 per cent in 1993-94 and over 7 per cent in first half of 1994-95. The most notable fact is that manufacturing sector which experienced an actual decline in production by 1.5 per cent in 1991-92 has recorded the strongest revival as the index for this sector has shown growth by over 8 per cent so far in 1994-95.

(*ii*) Going by the use based classification of the index of industrial production, the data reveals strong recovery in the capital goods sector which increased by 18.8 per cent during first four months of 1994-95 as compared with a decline of 9.2 per cent in the corresponding period of 1993-94. This is likely to have major impact on revival of the industrial sector.

(iii) Consequent on policy reforms and stabilisation measures, the decline in production in some industries since 1991-92 was broadly in line with a *priori* expectations on account of higher import dependence, demand recession and cuts in resource allocation. Manufacturing sectors which witnessed decline in production included textile products, wood and wood products, leather and fur products, rubber and plastic products, metal products, machinery and machine tools, electric machinery and appliances, transport equipment and other manufacturing items. Sustained increase in industrial production occurred only in food products; rubber, plastic, petroleum and coal products; and basic metals and alloys. However, barring few sectors like textile products and electrical machinery and appliances, the other sectors have witnessed strong revival in 1994-95. Of these, notable ones are cotton textiles, paper products, leather goods, chemicals and machinery and machine tools.

(iv) There has been a sharp increase in inflow of foreign capital since the new policy was announced in July 1991. The total net capital inflow in 1993-94 amounted to $9 billion as compared with $3 billion in 1992-93. Of these, the inflow of foreign investment amounted to $4.11 billion in 1993-94 as against $433 million in 1992-93.

(v) The revival in the industrial sector had favourable impact on exports. Total exports increased by over 19 per cent in terms of dollars in 1993-94 and by another 13.6 per cent during April-October 1994. Export of manufactured goods increased by 19 per cent in 1993-94 and by around 16 per cent in the first half of 1994-95.

These trends clearly suggest that the reforms have had favourable impact on the industrial sector. With favourable trends in foreign investment and revival of domestic and external demand, the industrial sector is bound to come out of recession in 1995-96 with growth rate touching around 9 per cent. This level of growth rate is sustainable in the medium term even beyond the Eighth Plan period. It is, however, of crucial importance that the policy reforms be continued without let or hindrance. While some element of recession in domestic demand is very much a part of the stabilisation programmes, experience suggests that a more expansionary credit policy could minimise the adverse impact on the industrial sector.

III

CONCLUDING REMARKS : SOME SUGGESTIONS CONCERNING THE EMERGING INDUSTRIAL SCENE

This note began with the basic premise that there had emerged long before a consensus for relaxing the industrial controls, reforms in the public sector, increasing role of the private sector and increasing participation by foreign private investment at least in priority areas where the shape of capital and technological inputs had been going from bad to worse. The policy reforms in 1985 were in the right direction but the favourable impact was limited to few sectors.

Empirical evidence relating to the post-1985 period suggested conflicting trends in the performance of industries in terms of industrial production, installed capacity and capacity utilisation. This was because the measures were half-hearted and there did not exist a long-term plan for the industrial sector. Many dynamic sectors suffered from increasing import intensity, and there was widespread fear that net value added in these industries was much lower than the gross value added. In retrospect and considering the developments in the Asian region in the 1980s, it was more opportune time for comprehensive reforms particularly those concerning foreign private investment. A worthwhile exit policy could have made the situation radically different from what it exists today.

In the short-term, some uncertainty concerning the end results of the new industrial policy are quite natural. These in turn make it necessary to think of alternatives, strategies and sources of development to sustain growth on a long-term basis. Such innovations are required in five major areas, *viz.* domestic demand, exports, foreign investment, infrastructure and public sector reforms. While some effective steps have been already taken in some of these areas, it would be worthwhile to reiterate the approach in this regard. It is in this context that following observations and suggestions are warranted :

(i) *Recession*

This is the most important area where policy initiative is required on an urgent basis. In 1991-92, the needs to overcome the BOP crisis and the inflationary pressures were over-riding. There was, as a result, a credit squeeze and a foreign exchange squeeze which affected the demand for and supply from the industrial sector. In retrospect, the credit policy for slack season of 1991 could have been more expansionary to make industrial recovery possible. The credit policy for 1992-93 along with the removal of restriction on imports of industrial inputs has contributed to recovery with a time lag. While concern for inflation are legitimate, there is now a strong case for a more flexible interest rate policy.

(ii) *Export*

Increase in exports is necessary both from the point of view of BOP as well as to sustain a higher level of demand for the industrial sector. Any deceleration in exports has, therefore, to be taken as a serious setback. In view of the increasing competition among the trade rivals and tough international regulation resulting from the Uruguay Round negotiations steps would be required to increase competitivity of exports.

(iii) *Foreign Investment*

In the medium/long-term India's ability to attract foreign investment holds the key. A quantum jump is required in the quality of each phase of production and export activity. This is a stupendous task and would require increase in the rate of investment, particularly foreign investment. Considering the trends in the recent past, it is a difficult task and would require additional efforts than mere announcing the changes in policies. In this regard it is worth noting that even though global foreign investment increased sharply from $47 billion in 1985 to $132 billion in 1989, the share of developing countries declined from 24 per cent to 13 per cent during this period. A practical approach in this regard is to concentrate on efforts to attract Japanese investment.

Japan at present accounts for around half of the global foreign investment in Asia and the Pacific. The major beneficiaries in recent years have been China, Malaysia and Thailand. Others with smaller share include Indonesia, Korea and the Philippines. Even if some of the additional investment is diverted to India, it would make significant impact on industrial efforts.

iv) *Public Sector Investment/Infrastructure*

The role of the public sector has been redefined in the new industrial policy. The experience of some of the highly successful economies like Japan, Germany, Singapore and South Korea provide testimony to the fact that guidance and intervention by the state in industrial infrastructure is both necessary and desirable. In the transition, the role of public sector should assume greater significance in areas like energy, transport, communication and irrigation. This is because *(a)* during the last two years no significant new projects were undertaken in sectors like oil, coal, power, railways and irrigation, and *(b)* even after opening up of the power sector to the private sector, no major private sector initiative has been reported. However, special efforts would be required in the capital goods sector which has suffered the most due to the recession and stabilisation programme. While fresh investment will be limited due to the resource crunch, efforts towards improvement in the efficiency may require only marginal investment and, therefore, needs to be undertaken on a priority basis. In the power sector, there is still considerable scope for improvement in the plant load factor (PLF).

(v) *Public Sector Reforms*

The reforms in the public sector must clearly go beyond mere planned disinvestment of equity. The need for a viable exit policy, particularly for public sector needs to be reiterated. Under the prevailing conditions, implementation of some of the reforms, particularly those concerning the handing over to workers' co-operatives or closure of those sick public sector units which cannot be revived may pose difficulties. This is, however, necessary both for improvement in the productivity of the industrial system as well as for clearer signal to the foreign investor.

A part from these five major areas of policy initiatives, constant review needs to be undertaken of the reforms in procedures to minimise time delays in investment decisions. The secretariat of the Foreign Investment Promotion Board needs to track the progress in follow up action too, after the proposals have been cleared. Also, to sustain effective demand, acceleration in generation of employment opportunities will be essential. A recent review of employment situation carried out by the Planning Commission indicates that the growth rates of employment in the organised as well as unorganised manufacturing sectors has gone down sharply since the mid-seventies. In the organised sector, in fact, growth rate of employment during 1983-87 was only 0.06 per cent. It would, therefore, be necessary to raise the rates of saving/investment in the economy and restructure the industrial sector in favour of labour intensive industries. This type of strategy will also help in export efforts and in minimising the adverse impact of reforms on poorer sections.

To avoid phenomena like higher import or energy intensity, which take growth performance, improvement in productivity of the entire industrial system, would be necessary. To achieve this, incentives to the industrial units should be related to the realisation of favourable trends in these parameters. Finally, significant expansion in industrial production is possible through better utilisation of existing capacity. A concrete programme of action needs to be devised on the basis of a detailed review of each sector with a view to identify bottlenecks and requirements for balancing equipment or to take any other necessary action.

An important aspect of the developments in the industrial sector is the need to implement the reforms within a specific time-frame and implement these in a co-ordinated manner with an appropriate sequencing. This makes constant reviews of the industrial policy all the more important. The mechanism of periodical sectoral reviews should be strengthened and issues concerning various bottlenecks be considered more often at higher level.

10

Emergent Situations and Government Organisation

Adjusting to Changes or Preparing the Conditions for Change

One of the cardinal features of post-industrial society is the rapidity of the persistence of change. Government organisations must constantly adjust to change. It will readily be agreed this is one of the basic problems we face today. One of the principal elements tending to block change is the extremely stable and impervious nature inherent in government organisations. Bureaucracies, especially government bureaucracies are always rigid and slow moving. Nevertheless one has not grasped the complexity or even the real nature of the problem if one thinks only in such simplistic terms, *i.e.* the rigidity of bureaucracy versus the necessity of adjusting to change from without.

Passive adjustment to that which develops independently is undesirable and presents great risks. In order to adjust successfully one should himself be an innovator, that is, take an active role in the process of change. This is true of any type of organisation, but especially for government organisations given their present social and cultural context.

Why? Because the basic problem confronted by post-industrial society is change in the modes of social control. Today we cannot govern ourselves with the same methods employed only thirty years ago. We must develop new methods that are in step with our time. Moreover we must generate modes of social control that enable us to handle problems of extraordinary complexity. This is an irreversible process. On the one hand, it is the direct consequence of our economic and social development, and on the other, of the growing freedom of choice open to all members of society who have become full-fledged partners in the social game.

To answer this challenge the role of government organisations is fundamental. These organisations are the pivot for the functioning of crucial social mechanisms in need of change. To develop a more open, more flexible, more democratic and more efficient system out of our present morass, adjusting passively to evolutionary drift will simply not be enough. We ought to promote innovative changes in our government organisations and use them to encourage or, even better, to create those conditions required to sustain changes within society as a whole.

The Basic Problems of Social Control and Their Impact on Government Organisations

From a sociological viewpoint, government organisations deal basically with the management of the social fabric; they are a very important cog in the wheel of social control. What does this imply?

People co-operate, exchange and communicate with each other to the extent that they possess languages, codes, and habits, and are protected by norms. They learn to play social games and to observe their rules. Even if these rules and constraints are internalized by individuals during the process of socialization, this is not enough. Not only should contracts be honoured and rules obeyed but people's learning capacities should be developed. New rules and games are constantly elaborated to take into account the new techniques and options available. All these emerging games are systems of professional, social, and cultural exchanges, forming the social fabric without which we could not live.

Admittedly, a good part of the learning of languages, codes, habits, and games is acquired during socialization and enforced through the pressure of key social groups and public opinion. Another part, however, which is seizable and growing can be considered as a much more conscious social construct. The social fabric does not support itself. It needs to be sustained by institutions. Furthermore it does not develop without constant innovation.

Conscious management intervention becomes more prevalent because of the acceleration of change. The more changes and developments there are, the more likely complexity will arise. And the more complexity, the more dense the social fabric. Therefore, we must possess the capacity which enables us to manage difficult innovation.

This does not imply that the powers of the traditional state in great civilized countries should be extended and made even stronger. Decentralised institutions could take over a great deal of the burden. It is true that administrative and governmental organisations in the broad sense will not wither away, it is not true that the totalitarian state is inevitable. A complex and innovative system of local, national, and international public organisations however, should be built, as well as a network of private collective institutions to support them. For all these reasons public administrations have become one of the most important new frontiers of post-industrial society.

But let us return to the problems currently facing us : in all highly developed societies government organisations face a basic crisis. This is the direct result of the last three decades of economic growth which has brought about an exponential increase in the complexity of human relations and the decision-making systems that are required to deal with them. Meanwhile the traditional instruments of social control which make it possible to manage contradictions and conflicts have tended to disintegrate.

On the one hand, society tries almost naturally to fill this void and generates all sorts of interesting initatives. On the other, capacity to mange and govern complex social systems or decision-making sets such as ours has significantly diminished. One of the most important elements contributing to this situation is the increasing demand of the citizen to participate in decision-making. This is largely due to the greater freedom and expectation of the individual. New instruments of social control and new decision-making mechanisms must be sought to answer this legitimate demand which can be a great source of progress if it is properly handled, but can lead to disintegration if it is not.

Decision-Making Problems in an Open System

The processes through which decisions are made, implemented, and evaluated are complex and frequently opaque. This implies that in an open system the study of decision-making must be multilevel (individual, interpersonal, organisational and environmental) and encompass multiple variables within each level. Everywhere the number of participants, be they persons, groups, or institutions to be consulted and dealt with has increased tremendously. Indeed the whole decision-making process has been grinding to a halt. Undoubtedly productivity has increased, but we should keep in mind the number of steps required to maintain this productivity. Given the problems of overload, the whole process of decision-making has become virtually unmanageable.

The superiority of democracies has often been attributed to the fact that they are open systems. But open systems are richer and more capable of achieving better performance only if they are manageable. They are threatened by entropy if they cannot maintain the necessary rules and regulations. Western democracies have been open systems only in part. Their mode of social contract especially consisted of a subtle screening of participants and demands. And if we speak of overload, notwithstanding the progress made in handling complexity, it is because this traditional model of screening and government by distance has gradually broken down to the point that the indispensable regulations have all but disappeared.

There are a number of interrelated reasons for this situation. In the first place social and economic developments have made it possible for a great many more groups and interests to coalesce. Second, the information explosion has made it difficult if not impossible to maintain the traditional distance deemed necessary to govern. Third, the democratic ethos make it difficult to prevent access and to restrict information, while the persistence of the bureaucratic processes which had been associated with the traditional governing systems makes it impossible to handle them at a low enough level. Because of the instant information model and because of this lack of self-regulating subsystems, any minor conflict becomes a problem reaching the highest levels of government.

These convergences and contradictions have given rise to a growing paradox. While it has been traditionally believed that the power of the state depended on the number of decisions it could make, the more decisions the modern state is obliged to handle, the more helpless it becomes. If decisions bring power, they also bring vulnerability. The modern Western state's basic weakness is its liability to blackmailing tactics.

Overload is clogging all industrial or post-industrial social systems for another reason : the natural complexity which is the result of organisational growth, systematic interdependence, and the shrinking of the world is such that fewer and fewer consequences of any decision can be treated as acceptable externalities. In order to reverse the general trend in Western societies, governing capacities must be improved. It would seem that politicians and administrators have found it easier and more expedient to give into complexity. They tend to use it as a useful smoke screen and even profit from it. One can give access to more groups and more demands without having to say no, and one can maintain and expand one's own freedom of action or, in more unpleasant terms, one's own irresponsibility.

Beyond a limited degree, however, the outcomes of a system cannot be controlled, government credibility declines, decisions suddenly erupt, citizen alienation develops and irresponsible blackmail increases, thus feeding back into the circle. One might argue that the Lindblom model or partisan mutual adjustment would give a natural order to this chaotic bargaining, but this does not seem to be the case because the fields are both poorly structured and unregulated.

The problem is exacerbated in older societies whose traditions have prevented the construction of decision-making systems on more open premises. European countries, such as Britain and France, may pride themselves in possessing the best possible elite corps of professional decision-makers who in many ways are better trained or at least more carefully chosen than elsewhere. This does not seem to be particularly helpful. Indeed it may even prove to be counter-productive. The seeming paradox can be understood if one accepts the idea that decision-making is carried out not only by top civil servants and politicians but is the product of bureaucratic processes taking place in complex organisations and systems. If these processes are routine and cumbersome, and these organisations and systems overly rigid, communications will be difficult, regulation will be vulnerable to blackmail, and poor structure will increase the overload. Despite all their sophistication, modern decision-making techniques have not brought improvement because the problem is political or systematic and not technical.

I do not wish, however, to overemphasize the general drift toward irresponsibility and impotence in Western states. While problems are threatening, the capacity to handle them seems to have diminished. But there are still many areas where government performances are satisfactory compared with those of the past. Ours are still civilized societies whose citizens are well-protected and whose amenities and possibilities of enjoyment have not only been maintained but extended to a great many more people.

There are growing areas, nevertheless, where governments' capacity to act and to meet the challenge of citizens' demands has been drastically impaired. Almost everywhere secondary education and the universities are affected, frequently metropolitan government (in terms of land use) and urban renewal issues are also threatened. This impairment of capacities is also becoming prevalent in many countries in terms of collective bargaining, income redistribution, and the handling of inflation.

Why is it so difficult to pace these problems? Why is it so difficult to construct the indispensable new regulations?

The linkages between the individual and the system are complex. A basic contradiction exists between the necessity of social control and the increasing demands of the individual on the one hand and on the other a refusal to put up with the traditional disciplines associated with these social controls. Everywhere in the West there is a near collapse of the traditional authority ethos which was buttressing the social control process. This collapse is partly due to the disruptive effect of change, but may also be viewed as the logical outcome of a general evolution in the individual's relationship to society.

Everywhere the individual's freedom of choice has increased tremendously. With the decline of old values, choices and options also seems possible. Not only can people choose their jobs, their friends, and their mates without being constrained by earlier conventions, but they can easily terminate these relationships. People whose range of opportunities is greater and whose propensity to change is also greater can afford to be much more demanding while refusing to be bound by lifelong relationships. This is, of course, even more true of youth. The questioning of sexual freedom and the role of women in society poses many additional problems. In this context, traditional authority is questioned. Not only does it run counter to the tremendous new wave of individual assertion, but at the same time it is losing the capacity which it has maintained for far too long to control people who previously had no alternatives.

The late sixties was a major turning point. The amount of underlying change was dramatically revealed in the political turmoil of the period which forced a kind of moral showdown over a certain form of traditional authority. Its importance has been mistaken inasmuch as the revolt was understood to be aimed at political goals. What was at stake appears now to be moral much more than political authority—churches, schools, and cultural organisations more than political or even economic institutions, were the targets. Indeed one aspect of the change in values can be seen in the decline of legitimacy of hierarchical authority, patriotism, religion, and so on.

Such a disastrous drifting of Western states is not inevitable, it is not even likely. But the possibility must be taken seriously as a measure of present vulnerability. To prevent the undesirable, Western nations should try to go beyond their present dire constraints and face, at the same time, the challenges of the future.

They should especially try to accelerate the shift away from their old model of fragmentation, secrecy and distance which produced an acceptable balance between democratic processes, bureaucratic authority, and some aristocratic tradition, and experiment with more flexible models that could produce more social control with less coercive pressure. Such experimentation, which is bound to succeed in the long run, seems dangerous in our present vulnerable situation. For we naturally hesitate to jeopardize what remains of the old means of social control as long as one is not certain of the quality of the new means. Innovation, nevertheless, seems to be absolutely indispensable. It must be careful innovation, but it is the only possible answer to the dilemma of democracies.

To meet this challenge government organisations are central not only because they are our societies' basic instruments of action. But they are even more crucial because they are also the problem, the matter, and even the object of the action.

The Nature of the New Administrative Tasks

To understand how government organisations are to meet these concrete challenges it might be interesting to begin with some remarks about the nature of the tasks their members perform and about the change of equilibrium between these tasks.

The nature of many administrative tasks has changed a great deal. It has diversified and it seems it will diversify even more. Yet the tradition of personnel management of government organisations is a tradition of uniformity and impersonal handling. Only differentiation will make it possible to attain the degree of discretion required to do a good job. This in turn will bring government employees to feel there is real meaning in their task. If the task loses this significance, not only are citizens hostile and alienated, civil servants also lose their morale. Regulations cannot be efficient and humane without a deep understanding of the nature of the tasks to be accomplished.

In addition to routine clerical and administrative work, only two kinds of tasks were traditional in government organisations upto the twentieth century : political decision-making tasks and judicial tasks. The extraordinary rise of government organisations throughout the civilized world during the first half of the twentieth century has brought forth many new tasks whose nature is quite different : these are managerial tasks of expertise, or coaching tasks.

Judicial tasks may be receding, and true enough, in the narrow sense, tasks of this nature have not followed the spectacular inflation in the general public administration. Yet they remain much more fundamental than one may think because many non judicial jobs in the narrow sense carry a basic judicial orientation. Financial tasks are an example. It is not desirable that our tax inspector have an entrepreneurial spirit. What we prefer is a tax inspector who is above all fair, honest, and who should also be understanding and humane. A tax collector should not be paid on the importance of his returns. For our own sake he must be protected against undue political interference either national or local. His independence must be maintained as regards other citizens. We prefer access to be a bit difficult rather than to face favouritism, pressures, and blackmail. Just as Ceasar's wife, the tax collector should be above suspicion. All great administrative systems have found ways to give him, and us, this kind of protection. Bureaucratic procedure is usually the price to be paid. Certainly some other costs could be avoided but this worthwhile area is not central here.

What is central is the extension of this mode of personnel

management corresponding to the needs of such tasks to domains where it is clearly counter-productive. Undoubtedly there are quite a number of tasks of inspection and control pertaining to the implementation of labour legislation, health and environmental regulations for which some of this kind of protection is required. It would not be desirable, however, if the eminent position of the controller gives too much importance to the control of conformity at the expense of the actual objectives of the controlled activity : one should not go too far. If theoretical judicial constructions are put above practitioners' experience, citizens will have to slave under a bureaucratic state. This is where ombudsmen are required (the police is certainly one of those domains where this would be advisable).

But there are much clearer dichotomies between the traditional functions and the new and burgeoning kinds of tasks which increasingly represent the future of post-industrial society. First of all are managerial tasks. If a judicial task requires double protection, that of the responsible civil servant to be doubly protected both against this superiors and against the public, this kind of isolation is disastrous for managerial tasks. For these tasks, human relations should be as strong within the hierarchy as with the public. Measurement of performance should be the yardstick, not equality of treatment.

This is not a trivial matter. In all countries, government organisations must perform management tasks, and in many countries entrenched state monopolies, new state office ventures, and even nationalisations carry a tremendous weight within the public service and influence the entire economic activity. When these tasks are performed under the same general personnel management rules which were the rules initially developed for judicial protection, bureaucratic dysfunctions become more and more stifling. This is, to my knowledge, the most important factor contributing to bureaucratic inefficiency.

One could, of course, conclude that government organisations should never engage in managerial tasks. Undoubtedly, the telephone and the postal services could be run by private firms. However, one should not forget that it is extremely difficult to impose such a reversal when the activity concerned will, in any case, remain a *de facto* monopoly. Furthermore, management tasks will always remain within the basic public domain : roads and bridges, health services and education are only a few examples. All these tasks should evolve within a completely different organisational system. This implies a rethinking of bureaucratic traditions, rules and principles and the acceptance of personnel differentiation.

The development of managerial tasks, however, could be curtailed to some extent. This is not the case with tasks requiring expertise, the increase of which has already been spectacular. This increase will continue until such tasks become the dominant intellectual tasks within government organisations.[1] The modern state cannot help but intervene to an increasingly large extent, and this in turn cannot develop without public regulation. The modern state has a direct responsibility for the overall management of the economy in providing education, in maintaining employment, in developing exports. But it now has or will have as much responsibility in improving working conditions, in restructuring industrial branches, in keeping the environment clean, in improving the quality of life, in developing and maintaining complex communication systems, in stimulating research. For all these tasks, a grater number of experts are required whose relationship to the environment and to public service cannot be the same as existing judicial or managerial personnel. Spectacular failures have taken place in many countries merely because one could not call on the proper expert. Experts should not be hindered by bureaucratic rules. Nor should they have tenure. This would imply work by contracts. Thus they would enjoy considerable benefits and salaries to compensate for job insecurity. This does not mean, however, that they could not subsequently apply for tenured civil service jobs after some years of experience. Since their performance cannot be measured in a quantitative way such as those of managers, consultants should be dependent on another kind of sanction taking its point of departure from the scientific community. Therefore, public service should open up to the scientific community which is the only institution that can provide simultaneously the training, the norms, and standards, as well as alternative employment for the experts that the public service will increasingly require. Instead of isolating these potential human resources as todays' public service usually does, it should attempt to build open systems for handling problems of expertise.

All manner of diagnoses have been offered to explain the disappointing performance of administrations. Many no doubt will have to be seriously studied, but one especially emerges as a clear source of grief. In many countries, leaders of government organisations have not yet understood that their freedom of decision is deeply impaired because the in-house experts on whom they rely are dependent on them. The latter, in turn, enjoy a virtual monopoly on giving advice. It is for this reason that decision-makers are for all practical purposes dependent on them. Decisions could be made with greater freedom if leaders had easy access to a variety of experts whose standards of excellence have been proven in the outside community. Bureaucratic expertise is simply technocracy; not only a threat to the citizen, but a menace for the politician as well.

A plethora of new tasks has emerged which require fresh thinking : arbitration, especially in labour questions present difficulty and politico-administrative tasks that pose the problem of the specific organisation of each nation's political system are a few of many areas requiring immediate government attention.

I would also like to say a few words about the tasks that have arisen in all countries parallel to those requiring outside expertise. These would include the sponsoring and coaching of many creative activities calling for state intervention. New fields in culture, the environment, and quality of life, to name but a few, require the service of those with specific knowledge and skills. Here again, tenure positions should not be available. The difficulty in this area is that, unlike in the scientific community, support is difficult to obtain from the outside community.

It is clear that government administrations are not rational animals with central nervous systems pursuing a single set of objectives. Rather, efforts should be made to utilize the great variety of both public and private institutions which deal with these questions in order to develop both open and responsible employment markets.

From the preceding discussion, which is certainly much too sketchy, one may glean a better understanding of the problems of overall management and regulation of government organisations. The primary problem, at the risk of repeating myself, is to shift from one model of fragmentation stratification, secrecy, and distance which characterized the old bureaucratic state to a more social control with less coercive pressure.

But in order to achieve this indispensable goal, steps should be taken to change the structure of the problem to be dealt with. We certainly will not achieve more social control and less coercive pressure if we continue to believe in the same hierarchical model of management control. Changes for all practical purposes have already been made. Otherwise the whole system would have crumbled. The basic problem is in fact somewhat different. Many of our leading civil servants and statesmen in most countries still believe that what is crucial is to first make a good decision intellectually and subsequently use the bureaucratic machine to implement it in a hierarchical manner. They remain to be convinced that their task is not to impose an abstract good on resistant citizens. It is to understand the complex system on which they wish to act and to utilize its potential resources. In this way the system can evolve and enrich itself in a promising direction.

Administrative know-how should take only second place to a real understanding of the ways in which a society functions. This is why vital expertise must become more and more central to government organisations.

Past administrative tasks should not be forgotten in the process. The fact that tradition will no longer dominate should not be an impediment; on the contrary, it could and should facilitate new growth. The solution should not be replacing one kind of leadership with another, but accepting and even imposing differentiation as the basic principle of post-industrial government organisations.

This primacy of knowledge and differentiation will lead officials to methods other than managerial interference and universal rule. This would imply that significant political decision-making initially at the national level, but also at the regional and local level, will be gradually divorced from the operational level.

I will return to these two general proposals in my conclusion. But let me first attempt to tackle the problem in the few areas where the breakdown is such that it is urgent to intervene.

Some Basic Administrative Crises

The crisis of social control does not affect all parts of government organisations equally.

The courts may be strained and sluggish but normally function Fiscal systems (despite great criticism) perform amazingly well.

Older divisions of the administrative system often operate in a more satisfactory manner. In a sense, aloofness from the public is maintained because of the judicial aspects of the tasks at hand. Here too, adjustment, although slow, is not unhealthy.

In most countries there are domains which are weaker, and therefore, breakdown is more likely to occur. These are the areas in society where changes have been so fundamental that the systemic context in which government organisations operates can no longer exist.

In this respect spheres of particular vulnerability are : urbanization, city and regional government, industrial relocation, and industrial choices, health and welfare, education and culture, environment. In all these areas the breakdown has occurred because demand has increased. Operating conditions have changed to such an extent and have become as complex that they are no longer manageable with conventional bureaucratic tools. To further the dilemmas, freedom of choice of the partners prevents any authoritarian or even natural automatic regulation.

To illustrate the above one has only to look at the problems raised by the consequences of urbanization. Our administrative system has been developed for societies in which half the population was still rural. When big cities and suburban sprawl predominate and rural life becomes marginal, a breakdown is likely to occur. In a careful analysis of the French territorial administration we have been able to demonstrate the striking dichotomy between the feelings of the rural minority and those of the urban majority on the subject of public administration. Those living in rural areas, although critical, were reasonably content; more significantly, they were realistic and understanding. By contrast, city, especially suburban citizens, were not only hostile, but disgruntled to the point of alienation, and completely unrealistic. Hope had been lost largely due to the poor relationship between the city inhabitant and the administration. Access (we had resounding proof) was considerably easier for rural citizens than city inhabitants. Information was more readily available to the former than the latter. Conversely civil servants were much more knowledgeable, understanding, and tolerant in the rural areas with which they were more familiar, whereas in the cities they found themselves in what they considered to be alien territory. (It maybe that France presents a special case inasmuch as it was hit harder and later by the last wave of urbanization). In one way or another, in all countries, federal and local government and the relationship between the two pose serious problems.

Progress will not be made as long as new forms of active decentralization do not develop. Strong self-government closer to the people is required. Today big city government is far too distant and bureaucratic. At the higher level, strong regulative agencies are needed in order to allow resource allocation markets to function. Citizens' grievance committees facilitating access and redress should be encouraged. Each society, however, must develop its own solution. There cannot be any overall formula since models of decision-making and access have historical roots. They differ profoundly from nation to nation.

Environmental problems will accelerate the crisis. Due to the absence of strong regulatory bodies, citizens groups become more prominent. The intervention of new multiple 'people's interests' to block any move allegedly detrimental to the environment will make any decision impossible. At the same time pressure to act in order to alleviate the problems of employment, industrial relocation, as well as solving the energy crisis make it equally impossible not to act.

There is another universal blight to which many countries have succumbed in a variety of ways. This is, on the one hand, a longing for a strong, rational industrial policy, and, on the other, the impossibility of achieving this goal. The urban breakdown may be ascribed to the acceleration of the move from the country to the city; the environmental crisis due to the physical consequences of accumulated industrial growth. Industrial policy problems emerge from the growing world-wide nature of most economic markets. State intervention in the economy has frequently developed in two quite unrelated directions : first macro-economic management that functions primarily through financial regulations and second protective subsidies which help diminish, if not prevent, risk of foreign competition. The very large scale of world industrial relocation has made the latter, slow-moving and bureaucratic style of management more and more crucial for the success of the former as well as for maintaining social peace. But in most countries the tools required to improve the situation have not been discovered. What is particularly dismaying is the lack of concrete knowledge of reality and faulty reasoning. The question of markets is indeed an area where expertise is lacking. But to elicit expertise one should depart from the traditional opposition between market liberalism and 'dirigisme' planning. Markets are indispensable. Intervention that prevents the working of markets inevitably leads to absurdities and is doomed to failure. But markets are not the natural outgrowth of liberal principles. Thus intervention is necessary, even strong intervention in order to build more sophisticated and more adequate markets. But for this worthy goal both fresh views and innovative government agencies are called for. Indeed what we must try to do is to anticipate the problems and see to it that the necessary steps are taken before it is too late. This is certainly one of the basic challenges of the immediate future.

Another stumbling block of a completely different nature is health and welfare. Public financial agencies the world over are sorely challenged when confronted with the economic forecasts in this domain. Paradoxically the breakdown of health services may be attributed to the very success of medical technology. Providing equal access for all citizens to the newest medical techniques becomes increasingly difficult because of precipitously rising costs. Nowhere have there been discovered regulatory mechanisms which ensure equality of treatment, efficient service and financial accountability. There seems to be no way out of the vicious circle : the more demands satisfied, the more new demands raised, the more money spent, the more money to be spent. Neither the medical community nor public administration has been capable of finding solutions. Fresh points of view as well as large scale experiments to explain new alternatives must be encouraged.

Furthermore a tremendous effort in research and training is required to change the proclivities of the medical profession so that it will accept a new and open relationship with its environment. Physicians will price themselves out of our reach if citizens are not trained to take on part of the burden. Of course, the state is not compelled to take on this task. Yet if it supports the medical profession as it currently functions, change cannot be contemplated. Government organisations, as a duty to public service, must encourage research and experimentation in order to develop new regulatory practices.

The same holds true for welfare where vicious circles develop around the complexities of administrative handling of multiple assistance by a huge and inefficient petty bureaucracy. We must shift from a judicial resource allocation process to an innovation kind of systems management which could prove in the long run not only more efficient but less costly. This would be, however, in contradiction to the prevailing civil service ethos which would do well to be in tune with the new mood of the citizenry.

Last but not least, education and culture is another domain where breakdown is imminent. The situation, however, widely varies gives the degree of decentralization achieved by each country. In some, education falls under the jurisdiction of provincial, or local government. Even though decentralized systems adjust more efficiently and have proven more capable of sustained innovation, all educational systems are presently threatened. Here again, new expertise, and new revolutionary thinking should be forthcoming. Society can no longer afford estrangement from its youth. The gap between educational training and employment expectations offers a striking illustration of this problem. New relationships—systemic regulations between school and the outside world, youth and adults, teachers and the scientific community–should flourish. Administrators can no longer count on outdated bureaucratic tools, but thus far have found nothing to replace them. The present system and the legitimate fears of the bureaucracy are serious impediments to change. Innovative experiments in this area would seem possible. Although to my knowledge, at this date, only a few have been attempted.

One would like to shield culture from the bureaucratic harness. Shouldn't there be advance preparation in order to avoid the collapse of all art and cultural markets which will certainly force public authorities to intervene?

Without public regulation the build up of the complex communications systems of the future will be impossible. The cultural implications abound throughout. In order to avoid tragic errors, a tremendous effort in research is indispensable.

The scientific communities themselves are not immune to bureaucratic evils. The management of science by government organisations is another acute problem calling for immediate intervention. In many countries, scientific creativity is being stifled by the bureaucratic spirit.

How to Make Government Organisations Active in the Process of Change

In a very important sense, government organisations are laboriously slow to change. At best they merely keep up in these times of rapid change. Thus, may we not be asking too much when we pose the question of ways in which government organisations could take an active role in the process of change?

We must bear in mind that piecemeal adjustment is ineffective; it runs against the systematic regulations of the traditional bureaucratic system. Only severe restructuring will bring about progress. Until the present, this solution has been carried out in such a way as to prove even worse than stagnation. Without a deep understanding of the human psychology, all efforts at systematic restructuring are bound to fail. The only insurance against failure is experimentation and innovation. Administrative leaders must once and for all depart from brilliant and idle talk on principles and come to terms with reality. For only in this way will it be discovered how things really work. Bureaucratic irresponsibility is the curse of modern government organisations. An active policy in the change process is the only way to bring realism back into public management.

Four kinds of general orientations seem to me basic for such a purpose :

1. Knowledge, especially new knowledge about systemic regulations of the social fabric.
2. A new mode of reasoning for state and public intervention.
3. Reviewing organisational controls and personnel management.
4. A new relationship between government organisation and politics.

We will try to develop these four points very briefly.

The first may already be obvious from what we have said. Knowledge is indispensable in all the domains where systemic breakdowns prevent government agencies from answering demand. Let me add a few words about the kind of knowledge that is needed and the way to acquire it. We have a great deal of technical knowledge pertaining to a number of subjects. We assume that our administrative know-how acquired from the past will be able to apply this knowledge in a productive manner. But the technical knowledge is, at best, irrelevant, and at worst it prevents understanding reality. What we need is fresh knowledge about the way the relevant human, economic, and technical systems work. We also need to know more about how to guide and influence systems, that is systems as a whole, in order to learn about new relationships, new games, and new regulations. This can be achieved only through the introduction of a great many more experts with the development of an appropriate institutional and scientific backing. This is, for me, the most important investment any government should make in public administration. For an active role, present expertise is insufficient most of the time.

But new expertise will not be accepted without a change in the mode of reasoning. This brings me to my second point. The only way to change the mode of reasoning is to first bring in new expertise and then to prove its value. For this, one should invest as early as possible in new training so that senior government officials abandon their faith in government by passive decision-making, neutrality and relentless control. They must begin to trust their own capacity to manage complex systems by intervening only at key points. They should also be trained to apply differentiation which considerably strengthens the capacity to manage large scale organisations.

References

1. Daniel Bell foresees the "post industrial society" as one in which the creation and utilization of knowledge provides the basis for a new system to emerge.

11

Perspectives and Retrospectives

At the end of an introductory treatment of bureaucracy as condensed as this, it would hardly make sense to attempt a listing of conclusions. For the most part, the conclusions are woven into the discussion and have been presented in its course. Too much of the discussion would have to be repeated for a meaningful restatement of the conclusions. But we should perhaps not miss the occasion for taking another look at the subject from a distance, for asking some larger questions about it, and for venturing at least tentative answers.

First we may ask whether technological developments will significantly modify in the predictable future the structure and working of the administrative system of modern government. Will the advent of machines with "brains" reduce manpower to the pulling of switches and thus usher in the demise of large-scale organisation as we know it? Will a machine-controlled rationality, operating without constant direction, supersede day-by-day supervisory authority? Next we need to consider what is the relative success of the merit bureaucracy as a means of accomplishing sound choices in the conduct of public affairs. Is the citizen being choked by merciless "processes"? Are decisions truly made, or do they mostly "happen"? And, finally, we should give some thought to the possibility of coming to a more satisfactory interlocking of political responsibility and administrative responsibility, to a better definition of the proper role of each, and to a clearer understanding on the political level of what use to make and not to make of the administrative machinery.

Effects of Technological Evolution

Progress of Automation

Continuing advances in applied research, especially the recent development of electronics, have stimulated popular speculation about a push-button world. In that world, it is assumed, much of the mental as well as nearly all of the physical labour could be left to obedient robots. This is the vision conveyed in Orozco's painting in the library of Dartmouth College, which shows a hulking worker reading a book, perhaps Shakespeare or even T.S. Eliot, while the gleaming control room is filled with the hum of gigantic engines that need only occasional attention.

Utopia, however, is not likely to come upon us like lightning. As a matter of fact, the progress of automation has been quite gradual and relatively inconspicuous. It can be traced far into the past and offers little promise of changing Western man's environment abruptly. The abacus, for example, has been in use for a long time, and, although representing an innovation no less startling than today's computing monsters, it has not wrought telling social change. Similarly, one finds no evidence of revolutionary transformations where automation in its modern characteristics has been introduced into office work, as in the insurance business. Displacement of labour has not been dramatic. The structure and the basic operating processes of the enterprise have barely changed. The biggest gain has been in speed and accuracy of performance.

In appraising the foreseeable impact of automation in our time, it is probably more important that large-scale organisation has been built up to its contemporary order of magnitude without basic change in administrative technology. While the past half-century witnessed a striking growth in the size of organisations both public and private, the administrative devices relied upon for direction, co-ordination, and control have hardly changed at all. Except for modern frills, they would look like old stuff to a Roman governor. Thus the dimensions of large-scale organisation have been permitted to outrun the optimum of efficiency that these traditional devices can be expected to contribute. One of the most important effects of automation may be to redress the balance, to give large-scale organisation an operating technology that would enable it to function with greater ease and versatility.

For one thing, automation is likely to furnish a strong incentive to cut down the welter of routine controls. The scientific principle embodied in machine operations, the impersonal objectivity of a technical process that neither gets rattled nor falls asleep, the predictability with which it grinds out predetermined results at a clip—these factors have little reason for watching every turn of the wheels. Few things would do so much to diminish the bureaucratic cumbersomeness of large-scale organisation as reduction of internal controls to a limited number of key points. The proliferation of internal controls has flourished in public administration. It is particularly marked in administrative systems that have suffered from an excess of legislative superintendence and from a deficiency of professional spirit. In such systems automation may prove itself a liberating force by leading to a disposal of many of the reviews piled upon reviews.

But automation will also give impetus to fresh ideas about the engineering aspects of administering governmental functions. For example, it is no doubt only a matter of time before customer contacts between the government and the public will be confined to "application houses." All requests from individual citizens, to be made on standard cards ready for punching, will go to the nearest "application house," which will serve as the joint receiving point for all governmental agencies. Action upon such requests will be noted in the form of a small metal disk containing everything that needs to be said in a single line of jumbled code letters and figures, together with the serial number of the applicant. Personal appearances at the "application house" will be discouraged in the name of economy and efficiency; but there will be psychologists on duty at all times. "Processing" of each request in the agency having jurisdiction will be greatly accelerated by the absence of agitated or confused applicants wandering about the halls, and the textbooks on public administration will deal with "public relations" simply by running an index entry, "see Application house."

"Operation Scatterbrains"

New approaches to administrative technology are also bound

to come to the fore as nations persist in preparing themselves for the disaster of a thermonuclear or similarly devastating attack. Here we must start with the premise that the concept of the capital city was totally obsolete even before the end of Second World War. To be sure, halfway measures will have some appeal while public opinion gropes for a comprehension of the peril. Short of ignoring the threat as beyond effective defense, however, desperately little choice remains. It is reasonable to suppose that eventually only one formula will prove practicable—complete dispersal of government as a normal, peace time method of operation. This would mean not only that the directing and planning elements of the executive branch would be scattered throughout the country (hence "Operation Scatterbrains") but also that the regional and local centres of field administration would be disbanded. Way off the highway, for instance, a hiker emerging from the forest will come upon a fence with the sign. "Visa Division, Department of State."

Under such circumstances many adjustments will be necessary in the familiar forms of carrying on administrative work. Ordinarily, it will no longer be possible to use the lunch period for a relaxed discussion of current business with one's opposite in another agency or even in another division of one's own department, for their locations may be a thousand miles away. A conference that actually brings the participants together in one room will be an unusual occurrence except for those stationed at the same location. With division chiefs at many different places, there will be no chance for them to drop in on the department head for a few minutes to set him right on this or that or to get his "line" on something for which guidance is needed in a hurry. But refinements in communications will compensate for much of the loss of physical proximity. Group discussions, for instance, will be carried on over vast distances by means of desk sets that not only will carry the voice but also will show the face of each speaker. One of the pleasant things about this type of conference will be the participants' chance to yawn freely out of range of the screen.

But even "Operation Scatterbrains" will leave intact the basic elements of administrative organisation and procedure as these are known at present. The level-by-level structure of authority will remain, although many intermediate controls may have been cleared away as unproductive and burdensome. The number of needed specialisations will be substantially larger, and each will be narrower and thus more self-contained than today. Lining up these specializations in the accomplishment of broader purposes will require, on a scale even larger than the present scale, a trained capacity for planning, direction, and co-ordination. That entails seeing the parts in relation to the whole, achieving the necessary degree of unity of operations, and sustaining an alert sense of responsibility. These essential qualities will continue to be in great demand in the administrative system. So will the kind of mind that not only can comprehend the working rhythm of vast and intricate machinery but also can recognize the axiomatic subservience of its output to the public interest.

On balance, then, we may expect an uninterrupted and widespread influence of technological developments upon public administration. The effects are bound to result in numerous changes over the entire range of operating processes. Thus they will modify in many particulars the institutional environment. But it appears unlikely that the outcome will be a new administrative world that would baffle the practitioner of our day. He may take delight at the wealth of novel gadgets and the surprising ways of doing the same old things. But, as he looks about and sniffs the air, he will happily conclude that bureaucrats are still bureaucrats.

Problems of Decision-Making

Functionary or Common Man?

To an important extent administration attains its ends by the making of decisions. As spheres of decision-making, administrative systems operate differently depending on various controlling factors. We come to grips with these factors when we ask : What images prevail within the individual administrative system about its own role? What working doctrine governs its actions? What kinds of men tend to emerge in its top cadre? In a certain way each of these factors may be seen as a consequence of the others. In some respects, however, each factor has an independent impact. Fundamentally, the combination of factors can be reduced to two alternatives that manifest themselves in the predominant characteristics of the particular administrative system. On the one hand, the administrative system may serve as a self-reliant source of technical competence. On the other hand, it may function as a response to impulses that play upon it from the outside.

Viewed from a different angle, in the first instance the bureaucracy regards itself as a separate body. It derives its identity from being unified for the performance of functions that are peculiarly in its charge. This gives the civil servant the distinctive marking of the functionary. In the second instance the bureaucracy looks upon itself as identified with the people. It expects its cue from the people or from those acting on its behalf, content to be a transformer of popular drives into governmental operations. This casts the civil servant as the common man's brother and thus as the common man himself.

As functionary the civil servant has come to life in the prototype of the guardian bureaucracy—dutiful, dedicated, and deferential to authority but also acting like the common man's self-assured mentor mounted on a pedestal above him. In the prototype of the caste bureaucracy the functionary consciously isolated himself from the people, allying his own interests with the interests of the few and placing both above the interest of the many. At the same time a narrow-minded authoritarianism sapped the spirit of service and filled the void with a ritualistic devotion to set ways and empty formalities. At the opposite pole the common man's version of civil service came to flower in the patronage bureaucracy of the spoils system. By throwing out the functionary altogether, this prototype promised to make public administration the domain of the ordinary citizen and thus the people's agency. In actual fact, however, the citizen first had to qualify as a partisan; and he was bound to lose out in competition with those who made their living as partisans. As a result, the patronage bureaucracy as an institution of popular rule had all the ills and little of the dignity of administration by amateurs. Indeed, office-holding appealed to the office-holder mainly for what he could get out of it for himself, for his political friends, or for those who were willing to show their appreciation of favours received.

None of these three prototypes as such commends itself for public administration in our day, in a setting dominated by democratic choices, middle-class values, and technical competence. Having rejected these prototypes, however, we are still raced with the necessity of a basic choice. The choice is between the civil servant as fuctionary and the civil servant as common man. Is he to withdraw into a fraternal order with its own point of view, standing apart from the general public to that extent but developing from his sense of mission the stamina of fearless advice coupled with the self-discipline of faithful service to each lawful government in power? Or is he to think and act like everybody else, being part of the multitude, offering his counsel when there is an opportunity for doing so, but not letting his better insight get in the way of what is asked of him? Even when the choice is not presented quite in these terms, it nevertheless raises a real issue. Do we want a bureaucracy that has the courage of its integrity, capable of displaying administrative statesmanship but likely to talk back to us on occasion? Or do we want a bureaucracy with its "ear to the ground," rarely making much of a fuss over anything but so relaxed in its professional attitudes that we can walk straight through it?

The Purpose of Democratic Administration

It has become popular to talk about "democratic administration" without always making clear exactly the intended meaning of the phrase. Obviously, under auspices of democratic government the administrative system must simultaneously reflect a consistent democratic orientation and answer to those exercising political control. Moreover, if only for reasons of good management, each public employee should have assurance of fair treatment and proper recognition of his rights. It is no less important that the individual participant's contribution to the group process of administration be made the object of frequent acknowledgment and thus be removed from the cold shadow of hierarchy. But democratic administration, above all, is to be a source of strength for democracy. To give strength, it must have strength to give. It does not give strength if its voice is that of the echo, if its attitude is that of an errand boy who mistakes public whims for manifestations of the general interest.

This does not mean that a politically unmanageable bureaucracy is preferable to one too limp to manage itself. They are equally undesirable. But a civil service is not likely to develop its full potentialities in public spirit and technical competence unless the facts of its existence allow it to think of itself as the colour guard of the common good. To this end it must have an identity of its own, built upon the consciousness of its public function, a function worth performing in exact proportion to the benefits accruing ultimately to the people. Expressed differently, the civil servant should be a functionary first; he is not free to emulate the common man when that impairs his role as functionary.

The Administrative End Product

But ideal and travesty live close together. When stressing the link between the civil servant and his public function, when speaking of him as a functionary in this sense, we would not like him to turn into a stuffed shirt, a haughty formalist, or a petty tyrant. On the contrary, we want him to be profoundly concerned with what the common man thinks as well as with what the common man needs. Function provides great temptations to become self-contained, to retire into an ivory tower, and to resent intrusions from the outside. In meeting these temptations, nothing is more helpful to the functionary than to see himself through the eyes of the common man. In this respect it makes quite a difference whether or not the top cadre in the administrative system, by the nature of its composition, finds it difficult to use the eyes of the common man. There should never be a shortage of higher civil servants whose own social background connects them with the outlook and the worries of the common man.

Ironically, where the civil servant shuns the insignia of the functionary, where he self-consciously plays the part of the common man, public administration is far from breathing a distinctive popular vitality. On the contrary, a civil service consciously accepting the primacy of public opinion is prone to attach correspondingly greater value to precedent and procedure as anchors in the winds of pressure. The written rule becomes more important as a railing to which to hold when the waves of public sentiment sweep freely across the deck. To put it differently, when the civil servant can trust his resources in knowledge and experience to give him something to stand upon as particular administrative issues arise, when his counsel carries weight with his political superiors, when he will not be accustomed to a reversal of his department's position as soon as a storm is building up—in these circumstances he will have a freer attitude toward prescriptions embedded in fixed routines. Then he will more often act on the "rule of reason," assuming personal responsibility for his action. Lacking such assurance, he will hold on to the letter of the manual for dear life. As a result, an administrative system dominated by the idea that it should live close to the people may provide a particularly hospitable climate for the flowering of "bureaucracy."

But, even when there are no special incentives in this direction, large-scale organisation and "red tape" are intimately connected. It would be difficult in a large-scale organisation to point to a single decision of some consequence that is reached without being part of a specified operating method, pinned down by checks and balances, reviews and concurrences, supporting files and staff papers. Indeed, it might not be too much of an exaggeration to sum up the progress of modern management, and especially of public administration, as an elaboration of the methodology of decision-making. Time was when the making of decisions was the lonely task of the man in authority. Today's decision-making is a group process, enveloped in procedure and yet frequently eluding responsibility. Authority can be outflanked by personal or group influence, internal as well as external, despite the fact that such influence may simply be the product of sundry interests that happen to converge at one point. Much of what has been written in recent years about the "executive function" in the context of the large-scale organisation centres upon the need for coming to decisions safely. Much of the institutional development has been along the same path, ranging from the creation of special management staffs to the establishment of committee machinery. But the plural character of group action has retained a good deal of its irrationalities.

In the operating experience of the administrative system these irrationalities burst forth at various points—in the struggles over jurisdiction, in the intransigence of specialization, in the contest for position. They flare up also in the relationship between the career man and his political superiors. They come alive further in the relations between the department and the larger world surrounding it—the legislature, the political parties, the interest groups, and the general public (which acts mostly in the form of special publics). In each general area the frequency and the intensity of unproductive clashes are minimized when conflicting positions can be adjudged by reference to a commonly accepted standard. In the clash of division heads, for instance, that standard may be established departmental policy. In the argument between the career man and his political chief, the standard may be found in governmental practice of long standing. In the collision of the department with the outside world, the most important standard would be the government's programme; and, if that programme has its foundation in the platform on which the governing party or parties triumphed at the polls, the programme is likely to be respected as a valid standard by the parties, the interest groups, and the citizenry alike. To the same extent that such a broader coherence is superimposed upon the group process, the shredding effect of self-centred motivations will be kept in bounds. When this broader coherence is feeble, the productivity of the group process as a source of decisions is likely to be low.

The Problem of the Right Decision

No doubt the modern bureaucracy, in the organisation of its technical competence, possesses a tested methodology of decision-making. In addition, this methodology is rather well adapted to the making of decisions of the political level of action, provided sufficient strength and unity exist on that level to permit a satisfactory linking of administrative responsibility and political responsibility. But the emphasis placed on the manner of reaching decisions—above all, on the procedural approach—has its obvious limitations. To be sure, to rely on a soundly conceived and well-understood way of coming to decisions in itself contributes to the likelihood of reasonable results. But the procedural safeguards are too easily and too often converted into criteria for the evaluation of the decision reached. It is one thing to say that the decision was made in meticulous conformance with applicable procedure. It is quite another thing to say that it was the right decision.

Who could say that it was or was not? Who could claim to be the authentic source for such an answer? In an age preoccupied with relativity, it is hardly surprising that nobody seems eager to press this claim. It is least surprising that the career man eschews an answer. He may venture to express the judgment of the "expert," with due caution, but he would decline to enter the realm of "political judgment."

At first glance this may appear to settle the matter. Yet the conclusion does not satisfy. For it is clear that it inflicts defeat upon the rationality of public administration itself. That rationality requires a deep concern with whether decisions are right or wrong-before they are released upon the public. In this screening operation the career man's appraisal is a critically important factor. His is the analytical responsibility in any event. How can a proposed decision get by unless, on the judgment of those having technical competence, it is a suitable response to an understood need? For that matter, the response should be the best response conceivable, in terms of both what the law authorizes and what the need calls for. This entails also an evaluation of alternatives. Obviously, there can be no assurance about what would be the best response if no informed and imaginative search is undertaken to measure out the range of feasible choices. Nor must we overlook the point that in marshalling the sharp force of authority it is a rule of reason, if it were not a rule of law, to select the mildest means that meets the purpose.

In all these matters the initial responsibility for judgment lies with the civil servant, as one well equipped to judge; and in the absence of an overruling political judgment his judgment is final in fact. He cannot be expected to do this sifting of considerations if he is meant to go by rote, especially if his political superiors insist that he simply carry out their orders precisely as they are given. But the situation is different when the sifting hand of the career man is welcomed, when the public has reasonable confidence in his judgment, and when it is widely recognized that for good performance the engines of administration must be lubricated with the oil of discretion. Under such circumstances it would be preposterous if the civil servant confined himself to periodically checking the links in the chain of decision-making. Beyond such concern with procedure, he should exert himself to make sure that each proposed decision is the right decision. Nor should he stop when he comes to the boundaries drawn around the rationality of day-by-day utilitarian choices—when he has assured himself of the means-and-ends relationships of administrative purposes, the attainment of economy and efficiency, the calculus of benefits. The right decision must meet a higher test. It must accord with the general interest, the constitutional spirit, and the moral principle. Nothing short of this will do.

But does not such a view of the career man's responsibility collide with his functional role as an agent of those exercising political control? Indeed, is there anyone entitled to speak with final authority on the general interest, the constitutional spirit, and the moral principle? These questions must be answered. Let us admit that there are many critically important matters on which nobody is entitled to speak with final authority. Can they, therefore, be ignored? They must be coped with, and every honest attempt in this direction adds to dealing with them as adequately as their nature permits. To be sure, as this contest for better solutions goes on in the conduct of governmental functions, the administrative judgment is obliged to yield ultimately to the political judgment when there is a difference between the two. Moreover, the political judgment must furnish policy guidance for the operation of the administrative judgment, to insure the primacy of political responsibility. Again, however, the alternatives are clear. It is one thing for the career man to fall on his face whenever his advice is received coldly by his political superiors. It is quite another thing when he is meant to play his part in a virile contest for a decision that draws strength from being supported by the administrative judgment as well as by the political judgment.

Decision-making in the administrative system is most likely to turn out an acceptable end product when the bureaucracy is a responsible partner of the political leadership. This provides at the same time the most satisfactory setting for the career man to function as the monitor of good administration. Perhaps the greatest contribution that can be made by the higher civil service is to keep its eyes on the things that roll off the administrative assembly line. How well do the "finished goods" serve the needs of the general public? How closely do they fit the legitimate interest of the individual citizen as applicant? No more effective antidote to "bureaucracy" can be hoped for than that which the critical mind of the career man itself is able to supply. But his mind needs to be alerted to the urgency of this task. His thinking needs to be lifted above the daily drag. And his loyalty needs to be focused upon the record of the political system rather than the record of his department.

How to Use the Bureaucracy

The Political Aspect

To speak of decision-making in the administrative system as

a partnership of the bureaucracy and the political leadership makes sense only on the assumption that each sees the other in these terms and acts accordingly. As a practical matter, however, the assumption is a considerable distance away from the facts, more so in some countries than in others. One way of making the distance conspicuous is to compare the mass of formally adopted working rules that govern legislative action and administrative action, respectively, with the paucity of equally specific rules that centre upon the operating relationships between both elements. This is not to say that there ought to be more rules on the subject. Rather, there ought to be a fuller understanding, on both the political level and the administrative level, about how to get the largest returns from the desirable interlocking of responsible direction and responsive operation.

Those in political control should recognize that they are depriving themselves of the advantages of effective machinery for giving application to their policies when they fail to create the conditions for resourceful public administration. As a minimum, this would entail a measure of self-restraint by the political leadership in the manner in which it pursues its aims, especially in the use it makes of the administrative system. Moreover, it is distinctly a responsibility of those in political control to take the initiative in defining, in sufficiently precise terms, the working relationships between the political level and the administrative level.

The Administrative Aspect

But it is clear that significant advances in the functional efficiency of the "administrative state" cannot be expected without corresponding changes in the working style of the administrative system. In this respect perhaps the most important thing is the acceptance within the higher civil service of a reorientation toward its role. The men of the top cadre must shift their attention from watching "processes" to measuring their impact, from "getting things done" to giving each citizen his due, from the technology of administration to its effect upon the general public, from utility to ethics. Not what is being said but what is being done will decide whether the "administrative state" will stand out eventually as a benefactor or as a destroyer. It is for the civil servant to realize that much of what can be done must be his doing.

Responsible administration cannot unfold its full strength except within a governmental structure that subordinates technical competence to political control. But this relationship is not likely to have as much substance as it needs to have if its elaboration is left to a few basic principles. In the overdue elaboration of the relationship between technical competence and political control, a large share falls to the bureaucracy, to its working doctrine, to the ideology of service that it may infuse into the administrative system.

Appendix

A Comment on Scientific Establishment and Decision-Making

Comment by Sir C.P. Snow

I am going to begin quite a long way back. How are decisions made? This may sound like a trivial question, but it is the kind of question which society has never seriously examined. The concepts which people have of how decisions are made in our kind of society bear surprisingly little reference to the truth. You are the most legalistic people on earth by miles, and so you are always inventing legalistic diagrams of responsibility and are frightfully upset if they do not seem to correspond to reality. But usually they do not. We all know that even in non-secret decisions there is a great deal of intimate closed politics, a subject to which I have given probably too much of my literary life. In your country, you elect a President; he initiates legislation (that is, he takes a decision as to which legislation to produce), and then the Congress takes the decision as to whether this legislation is to go into action.

In my country the procedure is more vague, but very similar : the country elects a government and that government collectively lays its decisions or its suggested decisions before the House of Commons. Those are the legalistic diagrams; and yet, in depth, I suspect that many of the most important decisions, although they may finish up with this format as a kind of rationalization after the event, do not take place in this way at all.

I believe that the healthiest decisions of society occur by something much more like a Brownian movement. All kinds of people all over the place suddenly get smitten with the same sort of desire, with the same sort of interest, at the same time. This forms concentrations of pressure and of direction. These concentrations of pressure gradually filter their way through to the people whose nominal responsibility it is to put the legislation into a written form. I am pretty sure that this Brownian movement is probably the most important way in which the ordinary social imperatives of society get initiated.

Let me take two examples, one from my country, which has happened, and one from yours, which I think will happen. The one from my country which happened was the introduction of a National Health Service. All over England there had been people thinking, unconstrained by their party politics, that this was the kind of thing which our society must really set about, that health was too important a matter to be left entirely to the kind of money which you could reach for. This thinking was surprisingly general. One heard it on all hands. It was not a Labour matter, it was not a Conservative matter. It was weighted more on the Left than on the Right, but not very much more. Any government both could and would have had to find expression for this concentration of pressure. It was a perfect example, I think, of the way in which this anonymous Brownian movement finally found its way through into the written legalistic act.

As I go about the United States, I believe that a similar process is taking place here and now. I believe that all over this country there are people saying that although your college education is wonderful and can do everything which you ask it to do, your elementary and high-school education in certain respects leaves a great deal to be desired. I think that one feels and hears this kind of dissatisfaction everywhere one goes. I, myself, believe that the broad social generosity of your educational programme is a fine thing. I believe that in strategy, in intention, your education is incomparably better than ours, but I have been in high schools where I felt it would be a good idea if the children sometimes were taught something. I am just saying that as a friendly outsider who knows you pretty well, but I have heard it in much more virulent form from my American friends. Although the ramifications and the interconnections of the federal system are the devil's own business to cut through, I am quite sure that within the not very distant future we shall see the widespread demand for a revised elementary and high-school curriculum enforced upon the people who in theory make the decisions.

Decisions in Secret by the Few

This Brownian movement is one of the ways in which any type of healthy society, not only a parliamentary democracy, makes some of its decisions. But the particular social situation in which we now find ourselves drives us into a very different kind of decision. We happen to be living at the time of a major scientific revolution, probably more important in its consequences than the first Industrial Revolution, a revolution which we shall see in full force in the very near future. We also have seen the two biggest political revolutions of all time and the two biggest wars of all time, and all this has happened within approximately forty years. This has meant a tempest of history which is not yet over and a rate of change which is going to accelerate more and more. We are not going to have a stable intellectual or social world within our lifetimes. That is the situation. As a result, many of the cardinal decisions of society are being taken in a way of which we are all aware, but which none of us like, a way which alters the entire structure of democracy and brings with it numerous consequences. This is what I was trying to say in the Godkin lectures in a neighbouring institution.[1]

Unfortunately, partly through my own fault, the message that I was trying to convey got somewhat overshadowed by a personal anecdote.* I had to tell a personal anecdote because it demonstrated one of the essential features of this new type of secret decision which is taken by very few people—that personalities matter very much more than they do in open, nonsecret politics. It is a curious irony, but I think there is no doubt of the fact. However, I showed poor literary tact in letting the personal story from which I was drawing examples obscure what I was trying to say. Now I can try to extract slightly more sharply the lesson I was wanting to be drawn. And this is that decisions which are going to affect a great deal of our lives, indeed whether we live at all, will have to be taken or actually are being taken by extremely small numbers of people, who are normally scientists. The execution of these decisions has to be entrusted to people who do not quite understand what the depth of the argument is. That is one of the consequences of the lapse or gulf in communication between scientists and nonscientists.

---

* The anecdote is the Tizard-Lindemann story recounted in Reference 1.

There it is. A handful of people, having no relation to the will of society, having no communication with the rest of society, will be taking decisions in secret which are going to affect our lives in the deepest sense.

I chose simply for convenience, because its was far enough in the past, two particular decisions in my own country. One was the matter of how we should defend overselves before the Hitler War. The decision was taken to give highest priority to the radar chain. No more than fifty people, and at the point of action no more than five or six, were involved in that decision. My second example was the decision in 1942 to make strategic bombing, the bombing of the civilian population, a major part of the British war effort.

The second is a slightly different example from the first, because to some extent the decision to make bombing a major activity had some of the features of the Brownian movement which I described. That is, before the war and during its earliest years, a lot of English people felt with remarkable lack of strategic judgment that this was the one thing which we could do and ought to do. It was a great mistake, and it probably affected the judgment of those who finally had to take the decision. The final decision, of course, was taken again by very small numbers of persons, and you know the consequences. We certainly disturbed the process of the war, and in my view, we certainly lengthened it.

These are characteristic decisions which in society now are being taken in secret by scientific persons and scientifically minded persons. As I look at it, it seems to me that there is very little to recommend this method. It may be partly inevitable, but some of it is not at all inevitable. The procedure would have nothing to recommend it were we not in the state of exaggerated world tension that we actually are. It has nothing to recommend it but speed.

As a general rule, very small groups of people are less wise than larger groups of people. Very occasionally, small groups can produce pieces of imagination and initiative which large ones would not. But, by and large, that is not true; by and large, maximum errors of judgement occur when concentrations of power result in decisions being taken by the smallest possible number of people. In fact, when I reflect on my experience as an observer of these things, the criticism I feel inclined to accept of my own attitude is that on the whole I accept closed and secret decisions too easily; that I have got used to them; that I know the way they work and in some ways find them even cozy; that I like them too much and do not realize how inhuman and contemptuous they tend to make the decision makers. I believe that is a criticism which I ought to take to heart.

A New Elite

Let us take this as the existing state of our world. And now, the computer comes on the scene. Previously, it seems to me, we have had two groups of persons in secret government : the circle of scientists who are knowledgeable about what is happening and which decisions must be made, and the larger circle of administrators and politicians to whom the scientists' findings have to be translated. My worry is that the introduction of the computer is going to lead to a smaller circle still. I am asking a question; I am not making a definite prediction. Instead of having the small group of scientists, knowledgeable enough to have something to add to the decisions, I am asking whether we are now running into a position where only those who are concerned with the computer, who are formulating its decision rules, are going to be knowledgeable about the decision. If so, instead of having a small circle of scientists and a large circle of administrators, we shall have a tiny circle of computer boys, a larger circle of scientists who are not familiar with the decision rules and are not versed in the new computer art, and then, again, the large circle of politicians and administrators.

It seems to me that it is going to require a tremendous effort to try to make all scientists in government literate in computers, and it is going to be quite impossible to make anyone else in government literate about computers at all. I know that you can do all kinds of things with these beasts. You can build in rules so that they defer to human judgement. Nevertheless, I suspect that the chap standing next to the machine, who really knows how it makes decisions, and who has the machine under his command, is going to be in an excessively influential position. If there is anything in this, we are running into an added danger.

What I would like to suggest is a piece of pure experimentation. The facts about the strategic-bombing controversies of 1942 happen to be exceptionally well documented. All the figures available in 1942 are there on the table. I should like to see two teams, one *pro* strategic bombing by inclination and one *anti* strategic bombing, both armed with their computer programme or programmes. It would be interesting then to see how the argument would have proceeded. Is this not a case where, with a little imagination, we could learn something from history?

Most decision-making, of course, consists of finding arguments to justify what you know you are already going to do. I would guess that in these circumstances probably the *pro* strategic bombing characters would have come out with approximately the same answer that they did in 1942, and the *anti* strategic bombing experts would have come out with exactly the same answer as they did in 1942. But I believe it would be a valuable piece of research to try to see what difference, in reasonably accessible historical situations, the introduction of the computer really would make. It may make much more difference than I think.

The Gadget Charm

My second apprehensive question concerns an intellectual danger with great practical consequences. Cybernetics, as named by its founders, is a beautiful subject with great intellectual variety, depth, and complexity. I suspect, however, that the computer in certain hands could easily become a gadget. Gadgets are the greatest single source of misjudgment that I have ever seen, or that anyone has ever seen in scientific decisions in our time. People get fascinated by gadgets. They love them. They want everything to be explained in terms of their gadget. They think it is the answer to everything on heaven and earth. All the bad decisions I have seen have some element of gadgetry in them. And I suspect that computers in government are going to get into the hands of persons with mildly defective or canalized judgment and become gadgets. It will be astonishing if that does not happen.

Society Left Outside

Clearly we have not yet reached the stage of real danger. But dangers are usually much better met if you have anticipated them. Most things can be coped with if you recognize them in time. I think that with a certain amount of administrative and experimental skill we can reconstruct certain historical situations with the aid of a computer and see how the answers turn out. It will need some historical imagination, some scientific imagination, and especially some psychological imagination, but I am sure it is worth doing. Otherwise, the obvious and glaring danger is that the individual human judgement is going to take a part which will get smaller and smaller as the years go by. I am inclined to think that for a society which is really viable, and certainly for one which feels itself to be morally viable, there is no substitute for individual human judgment; and the wider it is spread, the healthier and more viable this society is likely to be.

It is not only that I am afraid of misjudgments by persons armed with computing instruments; it is also that I am afraid of the rest of society's contracting out, feeling that they have no part in what is of vital concern to them because it is happening altogether incomprehensibly and over their heads. I suspect that the feeling of being left out, being outside the decision-making party, as it were, is one of the causes of the malaise of our society. We must not let it go too far. I am not in the least pessimistic about our finding our way through these difficulties and dangers. I believe that the computer is a wonderful subject and a tool from which we can get great service. But if we let the individual human judgment go by default, if we give all the power of decision to more and more esoteric groups, then both the moral and intellectual life will wither and die.

Panel Discussion

MORISON. I shall make clear at the beginning two things that would, in any case, become obvious as I go along. First, I do not know very much about the subject of these talks, the computer. And second, I have spent my life in that culture which, as Sir Charles suggests, tends to produce nervous apprehension and depression of the spirit.

I do know that the computer in its present form is a relatively new machine; so I thought I might say a word or two as a historian on the way new machines and men have got on together in the past. I also know that the computer is a machine that will give answers to certain kinds of questions and supply solutions to certain kinds of problems. So I thought I might suggest what some men in my culture think they have found out about the perplexing dialogue between question and answer, problem and solution.

As for the first topic, no more than Sir Charles am I a Luddite. One of the things you can learn from history is that men have lived with machinery at least as well as, and probably a good deal better than, they have yet learned to live with one another. Whenever a new device has been put into society—the loom, the internal-combustion engine, the electric generator—there have been temporary dislocations, confusions, and injustices. But over time men have learned to create new arrangements to fit the new conditions. Anything that has the power to build also has, of course, the power to destroy, and this applies to machines in the hands of men. But, on the whole, and more often than not, men have always succeeded in organizing mechanical systems for constructive purposes and for the enlargement of human competence and opportunity. No one, I think, who compares the condition of life for the average person in the seventeenth century with the average condition of life today in our society can fail to reach this conclusion.

Partly for this reason, I am not as much of a Luddite as Sir Charles may be. Take his first apprehension—that the computer may measurably increase the tendency toward closed decisions in our society. Obviously, we shall have to think about this. Machines can, beyond doubt, alter some of our views of things—the multiengine plane, for instance, has changed somewhat our sense of time and space. But there is, as I understand it, noting in the nature of the computer that will necessarily take us nearer to closed decisions—closed decisions such as those taken in the days of Wolsey or Richelieu or Caesar long before there were radar sets or computers. Both the machine and its progammers will have to work within a general scheme, a field of general decisions and determinations that can still, as Sir Charles says, be gathered out of the air if that is the way we want to do it. In determining the kind of life you want to have, the instrumentation is less influential than the nature of the culture you create to control what you want to use the instruments for.

For example, I do not believe that the rumble seat of automobiles increased the incidence, it merely changed the locus, of experiment in physical relations between boys and girls in the age of F. Scott Fitzgerald.

Then there is the apprehension about the computer as a fascinating gadget. It is obvious that there is always danger from the gadget-happy—whether the gadget is a machine, an idea, or a procedure. Amasa Stone, a very able man, killed a trainload of people because, against advice, he built a bridge at Ashtabula from a truss design for which he had an ancient attachment. I have no tonsils, nor have my brothers, nor have most of my generation, because an accomplished ear, eye, nose and throat man and his colleagues were all obsessed with the thought that the way to make a boy grow was to take out his tonsils.

In an age of new departures we have to live with all this, I suppose, but history suggests only for a limited period in each case. Over time the potentials of a new gadget are explored by trial and error until the real capacities are discovered and understood. Then, whatever it may be—Manichaean heresy, steam turbine, penicillin—it is fitted into a reasonable context.

I do not want to appear like a wise old head, made sager by my study of history than those like Sir Charles who have actually been there. Of course what he has said should cause any sensible man to think, and what I have said does not, I know, fully dispose of the complex problems he raises. Perhaps we can all talk about these things together afterwards. But now, I do not have much time, and I want to get on to a nervous apprehension of my own.

I think we may have more difficulty in exploring the full limits of the computer than we have had with earlier gadgets. I think there may be more danger in the period of trial and error than there has been with earlier devices. These earlier devices—looms, engines, generators—resisted at critical points human ignorance and stupidity. Overloaded, abused, they stopped work, stalled, broke down, blew up; and there was the end of it. Thus they set clear limits to man's ineptitudes. For the computer, I believe, the limits are not so obvious. Used in ignorance or stupidity, asked a foolish question, it does not collapse, it goes on to answer a fool according to his folly. And the questioner, being a fool, will go on to act on the reply.

This at least is what my culture tells me often happens. Let me give you an example. In the play with which you are all familiar, Hamlet had a problem which he defined for himself as follows : what had happened to the late King of Denmark and what should he, Hamlet, do about it? Framing the question accurately—a good programme—he took it to a ghost—the most sophisticated mechanism in the late sixteenth century for giving answers to hard questions. From the ghost he got back a very detailed reply, which included a recommendation for a specific course of action.

Responding to these advices, Hamlet created a political, social, moral, and administrative mess that was simply hair-raising.

The trouble was that he had got the right answer—the answer he deserved—to a question that was totally wrong. He had asked about his father when he should have asked, as any psychologist will tell you, about himself and his relations with his mother.

My culture says, in other words, that it is much harder to ask the right question than it is to find the right answer to the wrong question.

Some of you, like some of my students, may say that Hamlet is only a play, so what does it prove? I, therefore, shall give you some further evidence about questions and answers taken from real history. We asked ourselves once, in the first days of the Republic, what a negro was really worth and came up in the Constitution with the answer that he was worth three-fifths of a white man. Somewhat later we asked ourselves how to increase the income of the average citizen and decided the answer was to coin silver at a rate of 16 to 1. And still later we asked how we could limit the arms race between Britain and US, and worked out the answer that for every British light cruiser we could have 1.4 American heavy cruisers. About the same time we asked ourselves how to make the nation "self-substaining," and arrived at the answer of the Smoot-Hawley tariff which set an average ad valorem rate of 40.1 per cent for all schedules.

You will know, I am sure, that all of these answers caused us very real trouble of one kind or another. They did so because the questions they were designed to answer were framed in a wrong interpretation of events, a false conception of the actual problem. The answers supplied, therefore, gave the wrong solutions. They represented collectively what Ramsay MacDonald said of one of them : "an attempt to clothe unreality in the garb of mathematical reality."

The quotation from the Prime Minister suggests a further source of nervous apprehension—the tendency to simplify human situations and to do so, often enough, by reducing them to quantifiable elements. I have spoken of Hamlet so, by way of illustration, I will speak of him again, I remember two things my engineer-type students have said in explanation of his behavior. First, he had too much feedback in his circuits, and second, he was 16 $\frac{2}{3}$ per cent efficient, because he had one person to kill and he killed six. This, purely incidentally, is about the thermal efficiency of the average internal-combustion engine.

What I want to suggest here is the persistent human temptation to make life more explicable by making it more calculabe; to put experience into some logical scheme that, by its order and niceness, will make what happens seem more understandable, analysis more bearable, decision simpler. When you talk of 140 per cent of a cruiser, you can hope you have solved the underlying diplomatic issue you haven't dared to raise; when you pass a tariff with average rates of 40.1 per cent ad valorem to make a nation self-sustaining, you can assume that you do not have to look further for the causes of the worst depression in the nations' history—to which, incidentally, you have just contributed by passing the tariff. This is, I suppose, the way it does figure; and this seems to have been the human tendency from the time of Plato's quantification of the Guardian's role right on down.

I am not trying to suggest that the computer will soon bring us all under the cloak of the mathematical reality of its programmes. But today the tendency to work with quantifiable elements and logical systems seems to me accelerating. There are more tests and measurements (the brain of a candidate for college works within a precisely graded scale from, presumably, 1 to 800), more rational systems like those of Keynes and Freud to assist us in ordering the economy and the personality, more mathematical models, and more efforts, as in this School of Industrial Management, to reduce administrative sexperience to quantifiable elements. This, in the name of clarification and the advancement of general understanding, is quite obviously all to the good. The aim of pure reason, which proceeds upon measurable quantities, is, presumably, to introduce increasing order and system into the randomness of life. But I have here the apprehension that as time goes by we may begin to lose somewhat our sense of the significance of the qualitative elements in a situation—such things as the loyalties, memories, affections, and feelings men bring to any situation, things which make situations more messy but, for men, more real. My apprehension is that the computer, which feeds on quantifiable data, may give too much aid and comfort to those who think you can learn all the important things in life by breaking experience down into its measurable parts.

I hope it is evident that I am for order and logic. But I do hope also that it remains clear that in all the really interesting questions and problems of life the measurable and the immeasurable are all mixed up. I think from time to time of the Pythagoreans, those men who came to believe that "all things are numbers" and who were supposed to have put to death a man who suggested the idea of the incommensurable. Even in an inventory programme the risk one is willing to bear if he runs out of stock must be considered—and this risk is in part determined by the unknown size of the irritation of frustrated customers. Even in the strategic-bombing exercise suggested by Sir Charles, there is what might be called the Coventry factor to put in the programme—the unrequited feelings of men and women who had been bombed with no redress.

Still, I am no Luddite. What I want to do, first, is to find out all there is to find out about the computer. And I must say this is hard enough. In my cursory researches I have been told a great many different things by people who have at least thought more about it than I : that it is and always will be simply an idiot doing what it is told to do; that it can now design fractional horsepower motors and electrical circuits; that it can already throw old data into new combinations—introduce intellectual surprise; that it may some day write a sonata; and that, if we can get enough vacuum tubes hooked up right (10^{10} is the figure), we cannot exclude the possibility that it may feel its own emotion and have a will of its own. The spread between assumed present capacity and the foreboded potential is, in other words, considerable.

In any case the computer is here, and no doubt it is going to develop. Everybody, or almost everybody, seems a little uneasy about this, and why not? This is man's first encounter outside himself with something that is exactly like some inside part of himself. It is not, as many other machines have been, like his arms or hands or legs in the work it does, it is like him. How much like him we do not yet know. But regardless of what happens in the future, we have already made a machine that simulates some part, a small part, of what we alone have been able to do in the past by thinking. Even this small advance begins to raise the large question we have succeeded so often in avoiding—as Hamlet did for instance. What is in fact our true image, what is our real likeness?

To assist us in examining this question, I propose, not that we bust up the machine, but rather that we explore it in a series of experiments suggested to me by Sir Charles's idea of replaying the bombing problem. I suggest a continuing experiment in which the machine would be asked to reconstrue a series of situations out of the past—situations taken from my own culture—in which men have acted most successfully on their own. One could begin with simple things—a successful plant relocation—and work up through, let us say, the Army and Navy decision on how to use the plane against the submarine, and then on to the most interesting situations—our method of limiting trusts and cartels as revealed in the Sherman Act and its subsequent modifying judicial interpretations, or the miracle of Queen Elizabeth I's foreign policy. I suggest for each situation a series of experimental programmes—leaving some things out, adding some things, practicing ways to code things that seem uncodable, and so forth—to test various hypotheses and understandings by repeated trials against what may be called the real situation.

Some of the problems may be, at the moment, a bit far out, given the present state of the art. Also it is probable that the study of a particular past and nonrecurring situation would not produce the most desirable results. For instance, it has been suggested that a programme designed from evidence taken from the record of six or eight different revolutions might well be useful in the attempt to discover how to control common elements—both the stabilizing and the disrupting—that operate in all revolutions, including the one we are in today. Or a programme put to a computer on the problems of underdeveloped regions that are now developing under the energy of technology might well include data collected from the history of other regions that have passed through this stage of experience.

Whatever difficulties or defects there may be in these particular proposals, I am told a beginning of some sort could be made in the direction I suggest, and I hope it will be, for several reasons.

First, a good many people would have to learn some history—which is a good thing.

Second, it would be a way to capitalize on the ancient truth that fools persisting in their folly learn wisdom. We could acquire understanding of the uses of the machine without danger in a time of controlled trial and error.

Third, the machine would, therefore, become not so much a

problem solver as a learning machine, which is today in fashion. Used as suggested, it would force us, again without danger, out from behind the silly or distracting questions we like to ask to the real questions we have to ask—and teach us to ask them more correctly. It would thus help us to sort out the things that can be thought from the things that can only be felt, and advance a little of our understanding of how much feeling goes into what we call thinking. Perhaps some of the things we now classify as feeling may turn out to be more identifiable and explicitly definable, as the work of Freud indeed suggests, than we think. But if not, if they cannot be programmed as they say, at least by this exercise we may well find out more about their meaning and influence. What I am suggesting here is, I trust, obvious; that we use the machine which simulates to explore fully what it is simulating—what image, what likeness.

For some, this assault by mechanism upon what e.e. cummings calls the single secret that is still man will be distasteful and to some appalling. It is not—at least not to me. Over on the other side good friends of mine are using accelerators to find out the secrets of other marvellous structures. The more they find, the more they seem to stand with respect, indeed with wonder, before their findings. If man working experimentally can learn more about himself from something he invented, can learn who he is, and who he is not, then he will have learned enough, I should think, to use himself as well as the machine that simulates more wisely and constructively.

And if in this process he finds, at length, the full answer to the single secret—well, that is what my crowd has been trying to do for twenty-five hundred years.

WIENER. I think we have been talking a good deal about computing machines on the basis of rather a shady account of what these machines are, and an even shadier account of what these machine are going to be.

I shall not confine my remarks to computing machines; I am going to talk about control apparatus in general. The difference between the two from our point of view is not very great. The computing machine is a general-purpose device that can be programmed to do very specific jobs, and it may be at the heart of the control apparatus for certain applications. But let us talk in general about control and communication machines, rather than specifically about computing machines.

As has been intimated by Professor Morison, we are starting to hear about a class of machines just coming into being—the learning machine. I want to say something more about the learning machine, because I think that both the greatest part of the difficulties which we have been discussing and the greatest part of the possibilities for relieving these difficulties lie in this machine.

Take the learning machine as it now exists. One form of it is a machine for playing checkers. Now, it is possible to play checkers with machines that are not learning machines. It is possible to write down at any stage of a game all the successive moves that are legally possible for the next stage; to rank them on a scale of values involving loss of pieces, mobility, control, and many other factors (I believe about fifteen factors have been considered in one game); and then to give these factors certain weightings, established at the beginning. This procedure leads to a machine that is a checker-playing machine to a limited extent, but not a learning machine. If you were to play against this machine, it would feel like a rigid personality. (By the way, if you play correspondence checkers or chess, whether with a machine or a person, you do acquire a feeling for the personality opposed to you.) When a rigid personality makes a blunder, it always repeats the same blunder in the same situation.

A machine with a less rigid personality can be achieved as follows. The machine plays as before, but now keeps a record of all plays made and all games played. At intervals it is run in a different way. Instead of evaluating moves in terms of a fixed scale of evaluation, it evaluates the scale of evaluation in terms of the games played. It determines which scale of evaluation would have led to wins more assuredly than any other. There are various tricks of accomplishing this which I need not describe here; they are not perfect, but they are valid. The machine, having determined which scale of evaluation would have been most conducive to winning, adopts it for further play. That is learning.

Such a machine, if you use it for playing checkers, as it has been used, would have a more flexible personality. The tricks that once worked against it might fail with its increasing experience and its re-evaluation of various considerations. Such a machine has been developed by Samuel of IBM.[2] At first the machine was able to defeat Samuel fairly consistently. Later on he learned a little more checkers and was able to defeat the machine more often.

Nevertheless, the fact is that the machine can go beyond the person who programmed it. Even though Samuel caught up, there is always the possibility that the machine may catch up again later with more sophisticated programming.

The fact that a machine can defeat the man who programmed it means that having made such a machine does not give him completely effective control over it. If he had that, he would not let it beat him. Now, this is very important. Such a machine could be very useful in certain decision situations. It could be used to play games other than checkers : the business game, the war game, and the game of determining when to press the button for Armageddon—for the thermonuclear war.

How are you going to programme such a machine? Well, you cannot programme it based on prior thermonuclear wars. You would have to play the game according to a set of postulates which you constructed. You could make the machine learn to be more successful within the framework of these postulates. However, you receive no indication from this whether your postulates have the right values. Such a machine, in other words, can beg the question very badly and can be very dangerous.

What you have here is a situation not unlike that found in the folk tale, "The Monkey's Paw.' "The Monkey's Paw" is a story told by W.W. Jacobs of England at the beginning of the century.[3] An old soldier returns from India to visit a friend. He has with him a talisman that he says has the ability to grant three wishes to each of three people. The first owner of the talisman had taken the first set of three wishes, two unknown to the soldier, but the third one for death. That is how the soldier became owner. The soldier took the second set of wishes for himself, but declines to talk about them. His experiences were too terrible. One set of wishes remains. With considerable reluctance the soldier yields to his friend's request for the talisman. The friend's first with is for £ 200, and an official of the company where his son is employed comes in to tell him that his son has been crushed in the machinery. As a solatium, but without any admission of responsibility, the company has granted the father £ 200. The next wish is that the boy be back, and his mutilated ghost appears knocking at the door; the third wish is that the ghost go away.

The point is that magic is terribly literal-minded. It will give you what you ask for, not what you should have asked for, nor necessarily what you want. This will most certainly be true about learning machines. If you do not put into the programming the important restriction that you do not want £200 at the cost of having your son ground up in the machinery, you cannot expect the machine itself to think of this restriction.

"The Monkey's Paw" suggests a very real danger of the learning machine. The danger of these machines is greater than that of the simple computing machine, because you do not set down for it the tactics of the policy but only the strategy. You let the tactics work themselves out from the experience of the machine. The machine acquires a nature based on its experience.

So there are real dangers here. Is there any way of partially overcoming these dangers? The importance of learning machines is not how they act as pure machines, but how they interact with society. We thus are led to the concept of a system involving both human actions and machines. Is there any way in such a system to transfer values from the human being to the machine?

In a general, imperfect sense there is. Suppose you build a machine to translate a language. The value of the translation is a human value. The value depends upon whether people reading the translation will interpret it with the same meaning as the original. It is conceivable that you might attain a value system by having a complete logical code of translations, superperfect grammar; but this would not be a really profitable way to proceed. Instead, you would have the machine do exercises, just as a human pupil does exercises. These exercises would be marked by a teacher who possesses human values. The machine would modify itself based on these marks, just as the checker-playing machine modifies itself based on its prior wins. It is at least theoretically possible to transfer values from the human being to the machine in such man-machine organisations. I think that the possibility of reproducing human values is of great importance, but in itself has dangers too.

The last thing I want to discuss is the temptation of gadgets. What are the tempting things about gadgets? What are the tempting things about machines? What are the tempting things about an organisation with great compartmentation and high secrecy? These are the human questions that arise.

I am reminded here of the game of Russian roulette. At various times, in remote barracks and posts, officers have played this game of putting one bullet into their revolvers, spinning the chamber, and pulling the trigger, either at themselves or somebody else. This is obviously a means of expressing aggressive impulses either against oneself or against one's opponent. It is obviously a form of masochism or sadism. It is permissible, however, because one man has removed final responsibility for the act from himself, put it in the machine, and left it to chance. If he kills the other man, he has provided himself with a way (in his mind) of reducing his responsibility from what we ordinarily associate with murder to what we associate with manslaughter. He can blame chance.

This is very much like the game that is often played when a prisoner is taken before a firing squad. Each man in the firing squad has his rifle loaded with several blank cartridges and a single bullet. The result is that the men are more willing to fire because of the overwhelming likelihood that they will not kill the prisoner. This is a way of avoiding responsibility.

I am certain that a great deal of the use of gadgets for decisions, as it exists now and as it may exist even more in the future, is motivated by this desire to avoid direct responsibility. I am sure that a lot of the subdivision of effort in secret projects and highly compartmented projects has the same motive. The subordinate does not know enough about the project to feel responsibility, and the man in-charge can place responsibility with the system. I believe that one of the greatest dangers at the present time has to do with the attempt to avoid responsibility in order to avoid the feeling of guilt.

SNOW. I find myself in very close sympathy with both discussants, which is a rather tedious position to be in. I share Professor Morison's passion for history in a very amateur sense, but in my view he, like all historians, slightly underestimates those few occasions in human affairs where there is a genuine discontinuity. I believe that the amount of energy we can now trigger is so grossly different from the amount of energy we could trigger in the very recent past, that a great many decisions take on a quite disproportionate significance. It is a significance which is unique in history. This discontinuity makes some of the language and attitudes of history, not exactly inappropriate, but often not entirely adequate.

I found Professor Wiener's remarks fascinating, but he provided more dangers than I ever could have imagined. Though intellectually stimulated, I do not feel really encouraged. My state of mild apprehension has not been dispelled.

MORISON. I do not in any way discount or deny that there is really an absolute change today to which certain of the precedents of the past do not apply. This is one of the things that worries me as much as anything we have discussed. There are many precedents which suggest that we can learn from our small-size errors, and historians tend to rely on these. It is the really large error that we do not know how to deal with very effectively, and I share Sir Charles's concern.

WIENER. There is a real possibility that changes in our environment have exceeded our capacity to adapt. The real dangers at the present time—the danger of thermonuclear war, the computing-machine sort of danger, the population-explosion danger, the danger of the improvement of medicine (to the extent that we shall very soon have to face not letting people live as part of the policy of letting them live)—all of these dangers make one wonder whether we have not changed the environment beyond our capacity to adjust to it, and whether we may not be biologically on the way out. We may not be, but this is not at all clear.

SNOW. What Professor Wiener has said is very real. Our tendency is to laugh it off, but it is not something that I would laugh off too easily.

WIENER. I think that the over-all danger from the total situation is much greater than the danger from any of its particular manifestations, such as the atomic bomb or the learning machine.

SNOW. I agree.

General Discussion

MINSKY. I should like to address a remark to Professor Morison, and I shall try to speak as an antihistorian. The experiment that you propose reminds me of the experiment that I feel historians have been avoiding very skillfully for many years; namely, to take a precise area of history about which not everything is generally known, but many facts can be found, and then have a group of professional historians study the facts and predict the outcome. It seems to me that members of your profession, and social "scientists" in general, have meticulously avoided any such experiments.

What brings this to mind is your sanguine attitude about the way mankind will adjust to the computer—to this minor innovation or gadget. Your look back at history as a professional historian and see a continual sequence of successful adjustments to dreadful or complicated gadgets. I, as an antihistorian, look back at history and see the most horrible sequence of disasters, with billions of people (or at least millions, before the population reached the precarious state at which it could be billions) being wiped out every few hundred years in virtually every culture. I do not get the impression of mankind's being capable of surviving even minor dislocations. It happens that a number of people seem to survive these disasters and start over, but I cannot see the flow of history as a neat adaptation to innovations.

MORISON. I hope it was clear that in making my suggestion I was not above using the machine to improve the profession. I should agree with you that one of the things we as a profession have too much difficulty with is using the data in what you people would call a useful way, that is, to make generalizations and predictions. I think we have been timid in this respect. In fact, one of the reasons why I made the suggestion I did was to see what my historian friends would say. I thought it might force us all to think in new and different terms.

As for your second comment, I hope that I said (and I think I did) that we find it easier to live with machines than with each other. I think this is true. I think the disasters which you refer to were frequently not caused so much by machines directly as by our failure to accommodate to our fellow man.

WIENER. There is one thing about the machine; the machine habit is like the liquor habit. If we drink enough of it, and we already have, it is an awfully hard thing to stop. We have made ourselves dependent upon the machine, on the car, for instance. We are suffering from the way the train is breaking down, and we cannot give up the airplane. We have made ourselves more vulnerable to machine failure than ever before. We cannot go back to the old agrarian civilization. The soil is not there. The habit of raising crops, the habit of living off your own patch of potatoes, are just not there anymore. In an emergency we should have a terrible time adjusting ourselves, if we ever could, to the way not only that our great-great-great-grandfathers lived, but even to the way that our grandfathers lived.

HNILICKA. One of the basic problems of history and of mankind is that all our thinking and philosophy are based on a static situation. We always assume that the way things are now in their static form is actually the right representation. Would the panel be so kind as to comment on whether the machine might help us interpret future stability, not from the static point of view, but from the dynamic point of view, so that we cannot just catch up but actually predict what is going to happen?

SNOW. This is an extremely interesting point. It is clearly true that societies like ours find it extraordinarily hard to understand change. The problem is very large, and I think that the machine might help us here.

WIENER. I should agree that the machine might help. It is true not only that the equilibrium of society must be dynamic, but that its possible breakdown must be dynamic, too. If we have a catastrophe, the final catastrophe, it probably will not be because our world has broken down statically, but because, as the engineers would put it, the transients have reached the explosive point. The idea of a dynamic equilibrium must be supplemented by the idea of a dynamic disequilibrium and a dynamic collapse. These also can be studied to some extent on the machine.

HERZOG. I am a little curious why Sir Charles is so worried about scientists becoming an in-group in government. Certainly the militarists and the economists have been in-groups in government whom most of us could not understand. Does Sir Charles really think that scientists will do worse than politicians have done?

SNOW. I have been accused of some awful things in my time, but why in God's name do I get accused of this? Now, I have said very clearly that I should like to see many more scientists with direct responsibility in the affairs of government. There are two things that frighten me : first, the assumption of power by very few people of any kind (scientists happen to be an exceptionally important group with extreme powers, and I would hate to see a solitary scientific overlord in any country); and second, the danger of even a relatively large group of scientists, with the actual legal decision-making power, communicating across a void. Both of these things I have said. But I have never said that I am especially frightened of scientists; this would be an absurd statement for me to make.

BEECHER. The training of a person in values takes anywhere from twenty-one to fifty years, depending on where the person is reared, before he is judged worthy to make a decion. Is there any reason to suppose that we could reduce the time with a learning machine? Also, how are we going to get the input? Are we going to send the learning machine to Sunday school, and then during the week teach it not to take what it learned too seriously, as we do with our children?

WIENER. With respect to breadth and depth of learning, man will be far superior to any machine that we are likely to see for a long, long time; very likely for all time. One of the advantages of the machine, however, is its ability to work faster and do many things in the same time that a man does relatively few. It is conceivable that over a limited scope the learning of the machine can proceed more rapidly than the learning of man. This will not be done without effort, but it is at least possible.

MORISON. I should like to ask Professor Wiener to go a little further and talk technically about how value can be programmed. How far have we gone on this?

WIENER. We have gone only a small distance, but the possibility is very clear. Consider a translating machine. You grade it on its translation and use this grade to modify the translating programme, just as you use the past performance of a checker-playing machine to change the machine's playing of checkers—perhaps assigning 1 for winning and 0 for losing. In this way you teach the human values of what a good translation is to the machine.

You can transfer values from one machine to another in a similar way. This ability is really very important. It makes possible a self-reproducing machine that will make other machines in its own image. There is a definite mathematical theory supporting this possibility. We can use one machine to condition a second to have the same effect that the original does. And there are still other modes of interaction possible between machines. We can have criticism, and this criticism can be used to transfer values. This needs to be worked out in much greater detail, but it is the only promising way that I see for making a translating machine that will be any good.

MORISON. It would be fun to programme the Book of Job on a machine that has made another machine in its own image and see how the relationship between God and man works out.

WIENER. In the machine that makes another machine in its own image you have the Book of Genesis, not the Book of Job. You have essentially the Book of Job in the checker-playing machine where a man plays a game with his own creation.

MORISON. I have lost on my own ground.

MCCARTHY. I am wondering whether the speakers really take as gloōmy a view of matters as they have indicated. In Professor Wiener's parable we have a magic paw that will grant wishes, and we supposedly have no idea just how it does this. But it seems to me that the computer engineer who designs a magic amulet probably does have some notion of how it is going to treat our particular wishes. If you want to insert some values, then you must convince the engineer.

WIENER. The point is that it is extremely difficult to insert the whole value system at the beginning. It generally will develop from continued interaction. You may ask, "Why can't we make the learning machine 'safe'?" The answer is that "safe" is a human value, and the machine cannot very easily state what safe is without reference to man. For example, if you have a machine for programming atomic war, there is no reason why the machine should care whether the human race is completely burnt up or not. "Safe" is a human idea. If you have not put this idea into the machine, it is unreasonable to expect it to get there by itself.

Another point is that since we do not have full control over the learning machine, as illustrated by the checker-playing machine's defeating the man who programmed it, the unsafe act may not show its danger until it is too late to do anything about it. It is possible to turn the machine off, but how are we to know when to turn it off? If there is any possibility of its going wrong, we should turn it off at the very start. Otherwise, by the time that anything becomes manifest about the danger, it may be too late to avoid the consequences that have come from the use of the machine up to that point. You cannot make a perfectly safe learning machine.

CLAPP. I should like to ask the panel a question. There is no doubt that the computer is here to stay. You may be correct in your gloom and your prognostications that we may all blow up because we have computers, but I wonder if there is not some middle ground?

WIENER. Obviously there is a middle ground. We have to make every effort to understand for ourselves what the dangers are, and this points up a fundamental thing about computers : They involve more thought and not less thought. They may save certain parts of our efforts, but they do not eliminate the need for intelligence.

SNOW. Even though we have expressed grave disquiet, not only about machines, but about the whole set of associated phenomena which are characteristic of our times, I do not think any of us feels that these problems are unsolvable. I do not think any of us wishes to give that idea. But it is going to take great intelligence, and in my view, great moral judgment.

GRISOFF. I wonder if the panel feels that man can ultimately build machines which will exhibit an intelligence basically different from human intelligence. I notice that there has been very little distinction made between machine intelligence and human intelligence, and I think that there might be a very basic difference here.

WIENER. As long as the machine has beat the man who programmed it in checkers, it will in some sense compete with human intelligence over a limited scope. My hunch is that for quick action over a limited scope, the machine can be made better than the man. For higher logical-type judgments, for vague ideas, and for a large class of other things, the machine is a long way from competing with the brain. I think that there will always be a shifting boundary between the two, but I don't dare to venture where it will lie.

LOWEN. Would it help us to remember the difference between intelligence and wisdom? The machine might help our intelligence, but as of now it has no bearing on our wisdom.

WIENER. This is connected with the question of logical type. Primitive statements—statements about one or two things—we shall call intelligence. Statements about statements wil be more nearly wisdom. Statements about statements about statements will be even more nearly wisdom. I think the whole issue is closely connected with Russell's theory of types. The brain is at its best on relatively high types, and the machine is at its best on relatively low types.

GYFTOPOULOS. I should like to ask Sir Charles whether he feels that the big outer and small inner-circle phenomenon in decision-making is a sign of our times or whether it has always been in evidence historically. It seems to me that whenever I participate in a big group and a difficult question comes up, there is always a committee of two or three appoined to make the decisions.

SNOW. It is perfectly true that there have been times in the past when very little of what I described as Brownian movement was operating, and a whole set of decisions was taken by a very small oligarchy. The Council of Ten in Venice is one example. But I believe that from the time of the Industrial Revolution a very large number of important decisions typically have bubbled up out of society. It seems to me extremely important that this process should not be interrupted. One of my worries is that the current nature of world tension, the nature of our particular problems, is throwing once again undue weight upon secret decisions by extremely small numbers of people.

MORISON. What troubles Sir Charles in this connection also troubles me. In this country, historically, Presidents and their cabinets have made decisions within a context of what they knew society would let them do. Examples are the prosecutions of trusts in the first ten years of this century, and the Monroe Doctrine. Society had enough general evidence available to gather out of the air, as Sir Charles said, an attitude within which the President had to operate. In the future, it may be increasingly difficult on certain kinds of very important questions to have that information available, so that in a sense men will be acting much more irresponsibly.

WIENER. There is something here that is analogous to a biological problem. A society in which those in control cannot act effectively is suffering from paralysis, a society in which those in control do not get sufficient feedback of the consequences of their actions is suffering from ataxia, which is just about as bad. If a man can move his muscles perfectly well, but cannot get any report from his sensory organs on what his muscles are doing, he is just about as badly off as if he were paralyzed.

References

1. Snow, C.P., *Science and Government* (The 1960 Godkin Lectures of Harvard University), Harvard University Press, Cambridge, 1960.
2. Samuel, A.L., "Some Studies in Machine Learning, Using the Game of Checkers," *IBM Journal of Research and Development*, Vol. 3, 210-229 (July, 1959).
3. Jacobs, W.W., "The Monkey's Paw," in *The Lady of the Barge*, Dodd, Mead, and Company; also in *Modern Short Stories*, Ashmun, Margaret, Ed., The Macmillan Co., New York, 1915.

Index